DEMOGRAPHY AND HEALTH PROFILE OF THE TRIBALS

DEMOGRAPHY AND HEALTH PROFILE OF THE TRIBALS

(A Study of M.P.)

Edited by

Dipak Kumar Adak

Biswanath Bhattacharya, Rohini Ghosh

Manoranjan Pal, Premanand Bharati &

T.S. Vasulu

ANMOL PUBLICATIONS PVT. LTD.

NEW DELHI - 110 002 (INDIA)

ANMOL PUBLICATIONS PVT. LTD.
4374/4B, Ansari Road, Daryaganj
New Delhi - 110 002
Ph.: 23261597, 23278000
Visit us at: www.anmolpublications.com

Demography and Health Profile of the Tribals

First Edition, 2003

ISBN 81-261-1475-4

PRINTED IN INDIA

Published by J.L. Kumar for Anmol Publications Pvt. Ltd., New Delhi - 110 002 and Printed at Mehra Offset Press, Delhi.

Contents

Foreword

Tribals comprise an appreciable component of the autochthonous population in India, constituting about one-tenth of the total population: the country is not, of course, homogenous in regard to the proportion or the composition of the tribal population. In 1991, about one-fifth of the people in the (new) State of Madhya Pradesh were tribals, numbering 10 million, larger than in any other State in India.

The debate of whether tribals in India should be brought into the mainstream of development or left, with their way of life undisturbed, had been raging, particularly after independence in 1947, with Pandit Nehru, the first Prime Minister, and Verrier Elwin, the eminent anthropologist, participating. What have been the demographic and health profiles of tribals half a century later?

This admirably produced collection of studies, entitled "Demography and Health Profile of the Tribals of Madhya Pradesh", edited by Dipak K. Adak, Biswanath Bhattacharya, Rohini Ghosh, Monoranjan Pal, Premananda Bharati, and T.S. Vasulu at the Anthropological Survey of India and Indian Statistical Institute (ISI), Kolkata, attempts to answer some of the questions. The studies are based on large-scale survey data, relating to tribals in the region, and also case study and focus group types of data in some specific parts of the region.

The studies show that while the population in Madhya Pradesh is backward than that of India on every education and demographic indicator considered literacy, age of women at (first) marriage, fertility, nutritional status of women and children, infant mortality, child mortality, knowledge of family planning, and ante- and pre-natal care. The tribals are more backward in these regards.

A number of social and economic correlates have been identified in the studies. These include: dependence of shifting cultivation, uncertainty of food supplies during lean seasons (such as the summer and the rains), lack of proper health and educational facilities, poor housing conditions, faulty feeding habits and some traditional belief systems. Transition in the health and nutritional status of tribals has been very slow. These are important research findings. For action programmes to ensue from these findings, they should be set in a wider perspective. The tribal infants in Madhya Pradesh are known to suffer from high sickle-cell anemia; there is a high prevalence of TB; deforestation has resulted in the depletion of traditional medicines, and the shape and structure of houses are not conductive to healthy living, couple this with inadequate health infrastructure with little access to the services of a trained nurse not to speak of an M.B.B.S. physician, and you have the prescription for the deterioration of the quality of life of people. A commendable study such as this should serve as a wake-up call for action at government and community levels. The overarching concern should be brought to the forefront: social and economic development must have a human face.

I am grateful to Dr. Ganesh Devy, Director, Tribal Training, and Prof. Moni Nag, Department of Anthropology, Columbia University, New York, for discussion. The views expressed are, of course, my own.

—Ranjan K. Som
Former Professor & Head of NSS Population Division, ISI;
United Nations Special Advisor on Population, New York (Retired)

Preface

Madhya Pradesh has been fascinating the social scientists, particularly the anthropologists, for its rich tribal and cultural heritage. Nearly one fourth of the population of Madhya Pradesh and Chhattisgarh is tribal. There are about 46 tribal groups of which 7 are primitive tribes. Distribution of the tribal populations is not uniform across the districts in Madhya Pradesh and Chhattisgarh. In some areas, the tribal population outnumbers the non-tribal population.

The state of Madhya Pradesh, as it existed according to the 1991 population census has since been divided into the states of Chhattisgarh and Madhya Pradesh. The tribal population in the new state of Madhya Pradesh was 15.4 million in 1991, which was almost one fourth of the population of the state. In terms of numbers, the new state of Madhya Pradesh still has the largest tribal population in the country.

The recently conducted (1998-99) National Family Health Survey (NFHS-2) shows that although socio-demographic and health situation in Madhya Pradesh has improved since NFHS-1 (1992-93), still it is far from satisfactory. Compared to the Country as a whole, level of education and age at marriage, particularly among women, are much lower in Madhya Pradesh. Infant and child mortality is higher and so is fertility. The knowledge and use of family planning methods is lower in the state. The nutritional status of women and children is not up to the mark. Within the state socio-demographic status of tribal population is lower than non-tribal population (IIPS and ORC Macro, 2000).

Besides, acute poverty (over 90 per cent below poverty line), high illiteracy (over 90 per cent illiterate), is prevalent in these tribes. The tribes lead a secluded life far removed from modern conveniences. They are vulnerable from nutritional standpoint. Because of their large dependence on primitive agricultural practice, like shifting cultivation, they often face uncertainty of food supply. Lack of proper health and educational facilities, faulty feeding habits and certain irrational belief systems are prevalent among them.

Socio-economic, health and nutritional studies on tribal populations of central India are not many. It is felt that the different studies which have been conducted very recently on these tribes should be put together in order to have a comprehensive picture with regard to health, nutritional and socio-economic status, beliefs, etc. of the tribal population in this region.

This collected work is divided into two parts:

I. The different features of the tribes in this region as such mainly based on large scale sample surveys or based on data which are already available from well known large scale sample surveys such as NFHS and

II. The different features of tribes in some specific parts of this region, which are mainly based on case studies.

Ali's paper, however, falls in neither of these groups. He stresses in the paper "Health Status of Tribals in India — An Overview" that the challenge of poverty, ignorance, lack of health, education etc. of tribal can be met only with the involvement of the tribals themselves. He emphasized that health standards of the tribal population can be improved if location-specific and need-based health planning is done.

Nath and Dey in their paper "The Health Profile of the Madhya Pradesh Population" gave a brief account of the state of Madhya Pradesh, its richness of natural resources. He however indicated that majority of the population in Madhya Pradesh remains in a very disastrous stage in terms of health and development.

A brief introductory note giving a rough idea about the tribes of Central India is given in the paper "The Tribes of Madhya Pradesh: A Brief Ethnographic Note" by Adak et al. This presentation is based mainly on the published materials on "The Scheduled

Tribes" by Singh (1994) and 'Encyclopaedic Profile of Indian Tribes' by Sachchidananda and Prasad (1998).

The studies made in this book mainly centres around Health and Demographic status of the tribals. Different dimensions of health status are discussed. The status of reproductive and child health (RCH) is discussed in two separate papers. The first one is "The Status of Reproductive and Child Health (RCH) Amongh Scheduled Tribe Population in Madhya Pradesh: An Observation from NFHS Survey in 1992-93 and 1998-99" by Dey and the other one is "Reproductive and Child Health Status of the underprivileged in Central India" by Ram et al. Dey found high fertility and mortality and less use of family planning method among the tribals. Also status of antenatal and postnatal cares is alarming and nutritional status of women and children are very poor. Analysis by Ram and others also indicates the need of training of the large number of *Dai* from the same community who are easily accessible to these communities. The trained *Dai* can help in promoting hygienic practices in general and during menstrual period in particular. This may accelerate the utilization of RCH services and reduce the reproductive morbidity.

Another paper on health status of tribal population in Madhya Pradesh can be found in "Health and Nutritional Status of Tribal Population in Jhabua and Dhar Districts of Madhya Pradesh" by Ranjan. The author observed that that the process of transition in the health and nutritional status of tribal population in the two districts was extremely slow despite all investments in the health sector. It appears that focussed efforts to accelerate the process of social and economic development are strongly needed to accelerate health transition in the population surveyed.

Since aspects of health and demography go side-by-side, discussions of demography of tribes invariably entails discussions on health. Studies on fertility and mortality can be found in "Household Factors Affecting Infant Mortality levels in Scheduled Tribes of Madhya Pradesh" by Nanda, "Some Factors Associated With Infant Mortality at District Level in Madhya Pradesh" by Dwivedi, "Infant Mortality Rate as an indicator of Health Status: A Review of

Raipur district" by Nanda and Mitra, "A Comprehensive study of Fertility and Contraceptive Practice Among Scheduled Tribes of Madhya Pradesh" by Dey, "Fertility Differentials in Khairwars of Madhya Pradesh" by Pandey and Roy and "Fertility and Mortality Profile of the Khairwar of Madhya Pradesh" by Sharma and Adak.

Nanda, Dwivedi and Nanda & Mitra have used state of the art statistical tools for finding the causes of high infant mortality among the tribes of Madhya Pradesh. Nanda concludes that majority of infant deaths have occurred within the prevailing situation due to poor household conditions. The article by Dwivedi describes the relationship of infant mortality rate (IMR) with predictor variables crude birth rate (CBR); urban population percentage; percentage literacy etc. considering district level data of Madhya Pradesh in three categories: (i) IMR > 160; (ii) 140 < IMR < 160; and (iii) IMR < 140. For this, regression analysis using best subsets algorithms were carried out. The results of the analysis clearly reveal that subsets of important predictor variables change with the level of infant mortality rate. The analysis of the data made by Nanda & Mitra reveals that M.P. is having fifth highest rank by IMR in all over India and one of the "BIMARU STATES" (very backward poor performing states). They stress the urgent need to promote infant health survival and to reduce disparities between and within developed and developing states and nations as early as possible with particular attention to eliminate the patterns of excess and preventable mortality among infant girls.

Study on fertility is as essential as that of mortality. The analysis using Rapid Household Survey made by Dey provides a comprehensive fertility and contraceptive use status among scheduled tribes of Madhya Pradesh. He found that the proportion of third and higher order births for Madhya Pradesh is as high as 53 per cent and the CBR is as low as 44 per cent. These statistics indicate that a gigantic task is to be undertaken by the Government of Madhya Pradesh to reach its replacement level of fertility target by 2011. The study by Pandey and Roy advocates improvement in literacy level and better understanding of reproductive and child health care practices among the females to improve the prevailing situation of low fertility and high infant mortality in the tribe. The study by

Sharma and Adak however reveals a high level of fertility and mortality among the Khairwar of Madhya Pradesh.

The discussion of fertility, mortality and other health status of the tribals will not be complete if morbidity patterns are not discussed. Sharma in his paper "Trends of Morbidity Among Bharias of Patalkot, Madhya Pradesh" does just the same. He studied the possible aspects of trends of morbidity among the primitive tribe of Bharia of Patalkot of Madhya Pradesh and concludes that malaria, fever, dysentery and diarrhoeas, skin diseases and nutritional disorders of various kind affect maximum of individuals of all age groups and sexes. Bharias of Patalkot suffer from extreme poverty, abundant magico-religious beliefs, taboos and unawareness regarding available medical facilities.

One should also give proper attention to the reproductive health of the tribals such as done in "Reproductive Behaviour of Tribal Women in Madhya Pradesh" by Meera et al., and "A Study of Socio-Cultural Factors Affecting Reproductive Health Among the Primitive Tribes of Madhya Pradesh" by Pandey and Tiwary. According to Meera et al., a large majority of tribal women get married before reaching the legal minimum age at marriage. Most of the tribal women lack knowledge of spacing methods. Use of contraceptive methods is very low in Madhya Pradesh. They say that low use of contraception can be attributed to high illiteracy and low standard of living of tribal population. From the study by Pandey and Tiwary, it is clear that the primitve tribes of Madhya Pradesh have a number of misconceptions, irrational beliefs etc. regarding Birth Related Practices and thus, affecting reproductive health of their women.

There are quite a few papers on Demography of Tribes in Madhya Pradesh. The papers are: "Demography of Tribes: A Case Study of Sidhi District, M.P." by Kumar et al. "Socio-Demographic and Nutritional status of Tribal Population in Three Ecological Zones of Madhya Pradesh" by Rao et al. and "The Raj Gond of Sagar District, Madhya Pradesh: A Demographic Study" by Tiwari et al. The objective of the study by Kumar et al. is to analyse the dynamics of growth of tribal population, emphasizing on the inter-tribal variation and to assess the relative position of tribal population in respect of certain demographic parameters in Sidhi district of M.P. All the tribal communities, as reported by them, showed more or less a similar pattern in demographic behaviour and demographic indices are found slightly lower than the average level of the state. According to Rao et al., the tribals face uncertainty of food especially during lean seasons such as rainy and summer months. Tiwari et al. calculated index of aging, young and old dependency ratio and index of total opportunity for selection among other things. A relatively low index of aging (5.67) is recorded among them. Side by side, the value of young dependency ratio (84.59) is found to be quite high among the study population, whereas the value of old dependency ratio (4.79) is quite low in the same population. However, the index of total opportunity for selection (I: 0.3623) among the Raj Gond is found to be more towards the higher level of Indian populations.

We hope that the contributions to this volume will be of much interest to the researchers and educators in the field of Demography, Medical Science, Social and Physical Anthropology.

—Editors

Chapter 1

Health Status of Tribals in India: An Overview

A. Ali

While there is a broad understanding of the health and nutrition problems of the general population, particularly of the urban and rural communities of India, such information on tribal population is meager. Studies pertaining to health and nutrition status among different tribal groups of India are very few, very patchy and scanty. But there is general agreement that the health and nutrition of tribal people in India is very poor. Inspite of paucity of studies, available ones try to establish this with the help of morbidity and mortality statistics. Though exact estimates on vital indices in tribal population of India are not known, it appears that the infant mortality rate and maternal mortality rate among these people is also comparatively greater than the non-tribal population. Wide spread poverty, illiteracy, malnutrition, a hostile environment, the absence of sanitary living conditions, ignorance of the causes of diseases, lack of health services or inability to seek and use them have been traced, in several studies, as possible factors contributing to the deplorable health conditions among the tribal groups.

The overall health status of the tribal community is the outcome of several interacting factors:

- Effects of environment where the tribals inhabit,

- Behavioral pattern and life styles of the tribals,
- Health care delivery services in tribal areas and
- Hereditary and genetic determinants.

All these above-mentioned sub-systems make up the totality of the health status of the tribals. Therefore, the health and nutrition problems of the vast population of India are as varied as the tribal groups themselves. The health problems and health status of all tribal groups are not of the same type. Different tribal groups of India are characterized by their individual socio-cultural, socio-biological and socio-economic attributes and in a strict sense they are distinct biological isolates. The health of these tribal populations is, as such, a function of the interaction between socio-cultural and socio-biological practices, genetic attributes and the environmental conditions. In this context, proper understanding of the tribal setting of India and a broad idea on tribal development in India become two essential pre-requisites for understanding the health status of tribals in India in a holistic perspective.

Tribal Setting of India

About half of the total population of world's indigenous people referred to as tribal groups or scheduled tribes live in India. "Original" or "Native Inhabitants" of a country are, otherwise, known as Indigenous people. The aborigines in Indian language are known as "Adibasi" -"Adi" and "Basi" standing for "Original" and "Inhabitants" respectively. Constitutionally, these human groups are known as "Scheduled Tribe (ST)" or "Anusuchit Jati". "Vanjati", "Vanabasi", "Pahari", "Adimjati", etc.

The term 'Tribe' is nowhere defined in the constitution and in fact, there is no satisfactory definition anywhere. No standard term has been accepted to denominate the people who are classified as of tribal origin. According to article 342 of the Constitution, the Scheduled Tribes are the tribes or tribal communities, which may be notified by the President. The census enumerates only such tribal population as are scheduled under the relevant constitutional order in force at the time of the Census.

India has the largest tribal population in the World. As per the 1991 census the tribal population of India was over 67.8 million constituting about 8.1 per cent of the country's population. This figure of Schedule Tribes excluded Jammu and Kashmir where the 1991 census enumeration did not take place. The Table-1 shows the distribution of scheduled tribe population in different states/UTs and their percentage with respect to (a) total tribal population in India (b) total population of their respective states/UTs and (c) number of varieties/types of STs recognized in the states/UTs. It may be noticed there from that the population of scheduled tribes varies a great deal from one state to another. Their largest population is found in undivided Madhya Pradesh (15,399,034). The second largest number of tribals is enumerated in Orissa (7,032,214) immediately followed by undivided Bihar (6,616,914). But their largest proportion to total population among all the state is found in Mizoram (94.75%) followed by Nagaland (87.70%), Meghalaya (85.30%) and Arunachal Pradesh (63.66%). Among Union Territory Lakshadweep (93.15%) ranks first followed by Dadra Nagar Haveili (78.99%). The tribals in the 1991 census were enumerated throughout the country except in two states viz., Haryana and Punjab and three UTs. viz., Delhi, Chandigarh and Pondicherry where no Scheduled Tribes have been notified by the President of India.

Table 1: Distribution of Scheduled Tribe Population over States/UTs

State/UT	*Total Population*	*ST Population*	*% share to ST Population*	*% ST to State/UT Population*	*No. of STs*
India	846,302,688	67,758,380	8.01	-	573
A.P	66,508,008	4,199,481	6.47	6.31	33
Arunachal Pradesh	864,558	550,351	0.85	63.66	12
Assam	22,414,322	2,874,441	N.A.	N.A.	14
Bihar	86,374,465	6,616,914	0.20	7.66	30
Goa	1,169,793	376	Neg.	0.03	5
Gujarat	41,309,582	6,161,775	9.50	4.22	29
Haryana	16,463,648	-	-	-	-

(*Contd...*)

Himachal	5,170,877	218,349	0.34	4.22	8
J&K	7,718,700	N.A.	N.A.	N.A.	8
Karnataka	44,977,021	1,915,691	2.95	4.26	49
Kerala	29,098,518	320,967	0.47	1.10	35
M.P	60,181,170	15,399,034	23.73	23.27	46
Maharashtra	78,937,187	7,218,281	11.28	9.27	47
Manipur	1,837,149	362,173	0.97	34.41	29
Meghalaya	1,774,778	1,517,927	3.34	85.53	17
Mizoram	689,756	653,565	1.01	94.75	14
Nagaland	1,209,546	1,060,822	1.64	87.70	5
Orissa	31,659,736	7,032,214	0.84	22.21	62
Punjab	20,281,969	-	-	-	-
Rajasthan	44,005,990	5,474,881	8.44	12.44	12
Sikkim	406,457	90,901	0.14	22.35	2
Tamilnadu	55,858,946	574,194	0.88	1.03	36
Tripura	2,757,205	853,345	1.32	30.95	19
Uttar Pradesh	139,112,287	287,901	0.44	0.21	5
West Bengal	68,077,965	3,808,760	5.87	5.60	38
Andaman & Nicobar	280,661	26,770	0.04	9.54	6
Chandigarh	642,015	-	-	-	-
Dadra & Nagar Haveli	138,477	109,380	0.17	78.99	7
Daman & Diu	101,586	11,724	0.02	11.54	5
Delhi	9,420,744	-	-	-	-
Lakshadwip	51,747	48,163	0.07	93.15	
Pondichery	807,785	-	-	-	-

Source: Census of India, 1991

The estimated/projected tribal population is over 80 million. The tribal communities belong to different ethno-lingual groups, profess diverse faith and are at various levels of socioeconomic development. Spread along the entire spectrum ranging from hunters and gatherers of forest produce to the urbanized skilled or industrial wage earners – tribal communities constitute vary important segment of the Indian population.

The size of the tribal communities varies greatly. There are 9 large tribes each having population over a million and Bhill is the largest tribe with a population of over 7.5 million. On the other extreme, there are numerically small tribes like Jarwas and Onges of Andaman and Nicobar Islands, barely a hundred strong.

The tribal population of India belongs to three racial groups-Negritoes, Austroloids and Mongoloids. Linguistically, the tribes are classified into four major language families-Austro-Asiatic, Tibeto-Chinese, Indo-European and Dravidian. The tribals in India speak over 105 different languages with 225 subsidiary ones.

The Spatial distribution of the tribal communities is characterized by the striking tendencies to cluster in a few pockets of diverse degree of isolation. Ecologically, the tribal homelands are far from homogenous and as such display a diversity of high order. The areas of tribal concentration have been generally described as the forest and hilly areas of the country. No systematic classification of the tribal areas had been attempted until the beginning of 5th plan period when a new strategy for tribal development was evolved and the areas of tribal concentration were systematically identified and demarcated on some objective criteria. A clear picture of the areas of the tribal concentration in the national scene has emerged only thereafter. Now the tribal areas of India can be broadly divided into 7 regions Viz., South Central, North Central, North Western, North Eastern, Southern and Oceanic groups. Each region has some distinguishing characteristics of its own. They differ considerably amongst themselves in terms of geo-climatic condition, resource potential and demographic characteristics.

Tribal Development in India

In the recent years there has been increased emphasis on tribal development. It is well known that the strategy for integrated development led to the launching of the tribal sub-plan concept in the Fifth Plan period. Three basic parameters of the tribal situation in the country were recognized in the formulation of the concept. First, there is variation in the social, political, economic and cultural milieu among different scheduled tribe communities in the country. Second that their demographic distribution reveals their concentration in parts of some states and dispersal in others. Further that the primitive tribal community lives in secluded regions. So the broad approach to tribal development has to be related to their level of development and pattern of distribution. In predominant tribal regions, area approach with focus on development of tribal communities has been favored while for primitive groups community oriented program have been preferred. The sub-plan has been conceived to be a smaller plan for the tribal areas within the state plan.

Development blocks more than 50 per cent tribal population were identified and aggregated to form Integrated Tribal Development, Projects (ITDPs) and in two states viz. A.P. and Orissa these were termed as Integrated Tribal Development Agencies (ITDAs). During 6th five-year plan Modified Area Development Approach (MADA) was included in order to cover smaller areas of tribal concentration having a population of 10,000, of which more than 50 per cent were tribals. During 7th plan period the norm got even further relaxed to 5,000 and the Cluster concept was introduced. There are in all 194 ITDPs, 259 MADA pockets, 82 Cluster projects and 75 Micro projects for Primitive Tribal Groups (PTGs) operating in the country.

Broad Classification of the Tribals

Though there are about 250-300 types of different tribal communities in the country, considering some of the common/general features of their (i) eco-system (ii) economy and (iii) recent "impacts of the so-called modernization/civilization", the tribes of India can be classified broadly into three types/categories. This classification has relevance from the point of view of planing and implementation of health programmes. The three broad categories are as follows:

i. **Remote forest dwellers (self contained in forest-base):** The tribes which are in a sense isolated, untouched by the so-called "civilization" living in remote forest areas and are more or less unaffected by the developmental process going on in the rest of the country. The tribes which fall under this category and depend mostly/exclusively on forest resources for their livelihood by practicing hunting, gathering and collecting.

ii. **Forest dwelling, secluded but forest resource eroded (living under deforested conditions/denied access to land/forest-based resources):** The tribes which have maintained their own identity and seclusion, even in the face of extensive deforestation, displaced from their original habitat and erosion of their resource base (due to exploitation of forest resources, irrigation and other development projects, mineral exploitation etc.)

iii. **The so-called "acculturised" tribes (tribal identity retained but mixing and influenced by civilization):** The tribes, which have come in contact with external civilization, mingling with non-tribals, utilized for labour. In the process, the combination of their own native and social customs together with the exploitations by the urban and rural people, has resulted in altogether different pattern of health problems. Sizable agglomeration of tribal population in some parts of the country has moved to mining, industrial urban areas for earning a secured living through wage-labor. During the last few decades the process of industrial urbanization in the tribal has been accelerated through the operation of mines and establishment of industries.

The relevance of the above classification for planning and implementation of health and related programmes is shown by the following characteristics of these three different situations/settings.

The isolated remote tribes living in thick impenetrable forests show the following characteristics and need appropriate actions. Owing to their extreme remoteness, health infrastructure is very poor. People have to travel 10-20 kms. to reach a health center. The closed tribal culture and tradition total unawareness of availability of health/ medical services, the remoteness of their habitation for health workers to reach out, deficient transportation/travel budgets for PHCs, lack of proper roads etc. have resulted in almost no or very little contact of these tribals with the personnel of the existing health care delivery services. On the positive side are, their access to more or less good/ satisfactory nutrition from forest-based resources (though of late even the rich forest resources of these remote areas have also began to deplete), access to medicinal herbs and plants for practicing their own medicine. The major health problems faced by the tribals of this group include mostly, the communicable diseases – malaria, diarrhea, scabies and leprosy – and in some pockets tetanus and lack of medical care during child-birth and childhood illness, are observed among them. These high death rates are by and large balanced by the high birth rates. Thus, most of these tribes are either static in population growth or even dwindling in number. The severe problem of malnutrition (particularly PEM), which is common among the other categories, is not very prominent in this group.

The tribes exposed to the adverse effects of civilization in the form of erosion of their forest resource base and adverse effects of mining and some developmental projects like irrigation etc., but still retaining their cultural identity, show different pattern of problems. Owing to lack of access to forest produce like honey, wild roots and tubers, ban on shifting cultivation enforced by forest and law and other officials, deforestation by the government forest corporation as well as other private vested interests, disappearance of medicinal herbs/ plants/trees on which relied for their remedies, lack of formal ownership documents of land, ignorance of the law, prohibition of hunting even small game (it is another matter whether wild games are available or not in the process of ever depleting forest resources) have led to very high incidence of malnutrition among all age groups. The women and children, high incidence of communicable disease, because of lack of adequate coverage by health care services, in spite of some degree of availability of health infrastructure and lack of adequate staff in these health centers (PHCs and Sub-centers) due to unwillingness of staff to be posted there. Other aspects such as high infant mortality and maternal mortality afflict the group and in some of the tribes belonging to this category in some specific pockets, the infant mortality (particularly the neonatal mortality) and even adult mortality is high enough to outstrip tribes which are actually dwindling.

Health Status

Based on the findings reported by various research workers (both published and unpublished) and also on my own earlier field work experience in the area of Tribal Health (in different tribal pockets of India) spanning over last two and half decades, the following observations on the health status of tribals in India have been made. The health status and the nature of health problems of the tribes of India are largely determined by two sets of factors.

1. 1st Set: Health problems common to all categories (3 categories) of tribes:
2. 2nd Set: Health Profiles/problems typical of each tribal category (situation/setting-wise) Specifically:
   - Health problems of remote tribal forest dwellers (self-contained in forest base);
   - Health problems of forest dwelling secluded but forest resources eroded (living under deforested conditions/ denied access to land/forest based resource); and
   - Health problems of the so called "acculturised" tribals coming in close social contact with non-tribals living on the substratum of the developing civilization around them, tribal identity, but mixing.

1. Health Problems Common to All Categories of Tribes

The first set of factors include those which are common to most of the tribal population irrespective of the influence of isolation from the developmental process going on around them. These factors include:

- **Marked Lack of Health and Medical Services:** In spite of provisions for greatly expanded health infrastructure in tribal areas (one sub-center for every 3000 population and one PHC for every 20,000 population), the actual establishment of health infrastructure has been very inadequate and even wherever those are established, staff are not in position, or they do not travel to interior forest areas to spread awareness of health or provide them. There is a conspicuous lack of maternal and child health services and consequently the tribal demographic scenario is one of high fertility, high maternal mortality and high infant mortality rate. Mortality and morbidity from other preventable and easily treatable diseases is also very high.

- **Genetic Diseases/Disorders:** Some of the tribals of India have a gene pool that is relatively unmixed with other non-tribal population. High degree of inbreeding among some of the tribal groups results in relatively high prevalence of genetically inherited diseases. It can be postulated that different genetic background may have some effect on the body constitution and responses to various disease agents. At least two genetic diseases/disorders are known to be common among the tribals. They are Sickle Cell Disease (Sickle Cell Trait and Sickle Cell Anaemia) and Glucose-6-Phosphate Dehydrogenase (G-6-PD) deficiency.

- **Maternal and Childcare:** Most of the tribes studied by many other Anthropologists/Medical Scientists and me appear to have observed a few common practices regarding maternal and childcare. Expectant mothers are expected to restrict their diet in quantity, as there is a common fear that if the baby is too large, delivery would be difficult and might lead to death of the mother. Even in terms of quality, many of the nutritious, particularly protein rich foods are not permitted, with the result that cultural taboos result in greater maternal malnutrition and anemia than what is necessitated by the circumstances.

Among most of the tribes, gastrointestinal disorders particularly dysentery and parasitic infestations are very common leading to marked morbidity and malnutrition. Malnutrition among women and children due to this problem is common even among tribes with adequate nutrient intake.

- **Accidents and Trauma:** Tribals live in a physical environment, which is full of accidents and traumas. Fall from tree or hills, violent fights, encounters with wild animals, burns while sleeping near the fire in a cold night are common causes, Traumatic illness are far more common in the tribal areas than urban/rural areas.

- **Infections/Communicable diseases:** The most important parameters affecting transmission of infections from one human being to another are:

— The closeness of contact; and

— The size of human settlement

As we know the general character of tribal societies are:

- Lower population density
- Small settlements (even small hamlets)
- Comparatively/relatively, short range of individual movements
- Comparatively/relatively greater settlement
- Isolation from the outside world
- More contact with fewer people

Most of the tribal communities still live in settlements of less than 500 population (generally 200-300). The inter-human contact within the community is intense so that all the community shares the microbial flora and infections. But as the contacts between the settlements and with outsiders is much less, the import of epidemics from outside is common. In such situations whether an infection will be common in the tribal community or not depends on two characteristics of the infecting organism.

Whether it has an extra-human host or not?

Whether its infectious period is short or long?

Infections like measles which survive only in human beings which have a short infectious period during which the virus is emitted out of the body, need a large human settlement size to survive in that community throughout the year. The population size is between two lakh to ten lakh. In a small settlement, the virus, after infecting everybody, dies down because the susceptible host is no more available. As against this, an infection like Varicella which causes chickenpox but which lingers in human body for years, can survive and continue to infect new individuals as they are born in a settlement size as small as 400.

Thus, it is obvious that the acute infections without an extra human host cannot survive in the tribal areas, where the size of settlement is small. They may appear occasionally if the infection is imported from outside but persistence within the settlement is not possible. On the other hand chronic infections (tuberculosis, leprosy, yaws, helminthes, STD/Syphilis) or infections which have extra-human hosts (Malaria, Kalazar etc.) shall continue to plague the tribal community.

2. Health Profiles Typical of Each Tribal Category (Situation/ Setting-Wise)

The second set of factors influencing health and nutrition of the tribal people relates to the local situations which can be broadly categorized into three categories as indicated earlier. Thus, the tribals living in remote forest settings with their own self contained economy, living on the forest resources and experienced little or no change, through the centuries till date, have different type of health profile and problems, the tribals still retaining their own independent identity and culture, not mixing with the non-tribals, but themselves severely affected by the developmental and deforestation processes going on around them, have a distinct type of health and nutrition profile and problems and the tribals, who mingle with the non-tribals, living on the substratum of the developing non-tribal society and influenced by them tend to have different type of health profile and needs.

In the following paragraphs the major health characteristics of these three categories of tribals, together with illustrative example are outlined. This categorization could provide some initial guideline for administrators and voluntary organizations to plan health programmes with appropriate stress on particular programmes for a particular area.

Group-I: Health Problems of Remote Tribal Forest Dwellers

This category of tribes living in remote forests largely unaffected by the developmental process going on in the country, unaffected by the forest laws, is mostly found in the dense inaccessible areas of the country. In most of these areas, the major health problems are diarrhoea, dysentery, skin diseases, respiratory diseases and malaria.

As mentioned earlier, these forest dwelling, remote tribes are relatively better off when it comes to nutrition, as compared with the other two categories. Adult nutrition is fairly good owing to access to the forest resources and animal, and also owing to their dependence on millets rather than refined cereals for their staple food. The cause of minor malnutrition among this group is worm infestation, dysentery, diarrhoea, and not, deficient intake. Thus among these groups, the strategy for combating malnutrition should be one of health education and mass deworming, and not so much of supplementary nutrition and such other welfare programmes. In most of these tribes, however, seasonal malnutrition is often found.

Next to infectious and parasitic diseases, come respiratory diseases particularly pneumonia followed by the next category accidents, poisoning and violence including falls from trees, poisonous bites etc. The risk of respiratory diseases among the forest dwelling tribes is due to the practice of lighting fires at night for warmth in ill-ventilated huts. Burns – trivial, serious, or even fatal – are another hazards due to their practice of sleeping close to open fires.

Thus in this group the major nutritional problems could be summarized as:- mild caloric under-nourishment of adult males from time to time, no protein malnutrition among adult males, almost nil or low prevalence of Vitamin-A, C or B Complex deficiencies, undernourishment of mothers with anaemia due to food taboos, protein energy under-nutrition and few cases of Vitamin deficiencies of children due to general lack of awareness of child care and infant feeding practices.

Group-II: Forest Dwelling Either Living Under Deforested Living Conditions or Denied Access to Land/Forest based Resources

These tribals are under acute distress because of their strong tribal identity and livelihood skills purely rooted in food gathering, hunting, shifting cultivation, collection and barter of minor forest produce and traditional healing with forest herbs.

These tribal groups have been displaced overnight (by dams, mines, and similar national developmental activities) or they have been deprived of their traditional rights over the forest resources, overnight by forest laws and regulations, resulting in a vacuum, as far as livelihood, cultivable land and nutrition are concerned. The health profile shows a major shift from the first group. For the first time isolated nutrient deficiencies can be observed. Protein calorie malnutrition is markedly present due to lack of food, sometimes for days together. In some areas where tribals are totally denied access even for gathering of berries and leaves, Vitamin-A and Vitamin-C deficiency has come up. Otherwise, isolated Vitamin-A and C deficiencies are not common. Since these tribals retain their millet-eating habits, B-complex deficiencies are uncommon, as also problems such as appendicitis. The major causes of morbidity are Malaria, Gastro-intestinal disorders, Acute Respiratory Infections, Tuberculosis, Leprosy, and Accidents in that order.

Group-III: Tribals Coming in Close Social Contact with Non-tribal Living on the Substratum of the Developing Civilization Around Them

The health problem of these tribals include not only the conventional problems of gastrointestinal diseases, skin diseases and maternal and child health problems, but added to these are the adverse influences of coming in contact with civilization.

The health problems common to most of the tribes belonging to this category (arising as a result of their situation) is as follows:

Change of dietary habits from a composite balanced diet to rice based diet. In this, group B-Complex deficiencies such as peripheral neuritis, glottises and angular stomatitis is very common. Protein deficiency, Vitamin-A and Vitamin-C deficiency is also frequent. Other two major problems of this category are is Sexually Transmitted Diseases (STDs) and alcoholism.

Major Tribal Health Problems of India - at a Glance

*Communicable diseases/Infectious diseases – Malaria, TB etc.

*Gastrointestinal disorders – diarrhoeal diseases, dysentery

*Parasitic Infections

*Acute Respiratory Infections

*Inbreeding resulting in genetic disorders

Remote, self contained in Forest Base *(First Category)*	*Forest Dwelling Secluded but Forest Resource eroded* *(Second Category)*	*Tribal Identity, but mixing and influenced by Civilization* *(Third Category)*
(1)	(2)	(3)
Vitamin A deficiency uncommon due to intake of green leafy and other Products	Vitamin A deficiency frequent due to lack of forest resources of leafy vegetables	Major malnutrition Vitamin A and B-Complex
B-Complex deficiency uncommon	Food still millet based so Vitamin B deficiency less marked	Habits of rice eating without an otherwise balanced diet. Millet habit disappeared. No concept of vegetables or fruits, only to fill the stomach with rice
Protein malnutrtion uncomon. Caloric under nutrition sometimes only. Seasonal but still better than other groups	Caloric and Protein under nutrition is marked	Protein calorie malnutrition. (Calorie malnutrition may or may not be present but protein undernutrition more marked)
Poor hygiene-scabies diarrhoeal diseases, leprosy in some pockets	Other communicable disease are found as in all tribes	Alcoholism with disruption of social structure, liver diseases, Vitamin B deficiency, poor maternal and child health
Major cause of morbidity & death, respiratory diseases due to indoor fires; infectious diseases including malaria & T.B.	Morbidity and causes of death tends to be more due to diseases rather than accidents, poisoning, violence group	STDs viz., Syphilis-high incidence
Accidents, poisoning and violence, burns Genetic disorders-Sickle cell Disease	TB more common pneumonia due to smoke of indoor fires. Genetic disorders, Sickle cell anaemia and G-6-PD deficiency	Peptic ulcers, gasrointestinal malignancy, hypertension, oral cancers.

It would not be out of place to mention that my own studies on tribal health behaviour have revealed that though there are innumerable types of beliefs and practices, the one thing that is common and certain among all health seeking behaviour is the faith on empiricism. It is the empirical result that is valued most, irrespective of the system of medicine and the healer. A hospital, CHC, PHC or a Government health worker is very much open alternatives to the tribal as his traditional healer and offerings to god.

It is also observed that the allopathic/western medicine, when available was accepted and the magico-religious system never came in conflict with western medicine. Wherever facilities are available their health seeking behaviour has gone in favour of modern medicine. For example from my own experience during my field work with the Langia Saoras - one of the primitive tribes of Orissa, have found that there was no cultural resistance to acceptance of modern medicine as long as they are efficacious, are available and accessible to them. Again, some of our own studies, no doubt, have indicated a very strong faith in traditional methods of treatment (for treating a particular type of disease) but again, I have also observed that the two methods of treatment (both traditional and modern) operate side by side in the same situation. In fact, the inadequate nature of modern facilities available in most of the remote areas of the, country are often responsible for the lack of faith in modern treatment.

It is therefore, pertinent to know, understand ana appreciate about the tribal's preference of various systems of medicine. Quite often it is said that the tribals are so traditional oriented that they do not use the modern facilities and the commonly held dream of many intellectuals is that everything "traditional" and "herbal" is beautiful and works, if only the polluting effects of the modern medicine are not there! These views are definitely not borne out by facts. These are myths and perhaps the time has come to examine and evaluate these views properly and criticaliy.

Our health care programmes are more or less uniform throughout the country and virtually the same package of service delivery is being offered both in tribal and non-tribal areas. Unfortunately enough, not only the utilization of health services is reported to be very poor but also there seems to be significant changes in so far as important indices of health like IMR, MMR and incidence of communicable disease and malnutrition is concerned. Therefore, it is becoming undoubtedly clear that optimal level of health among tribal communities cannot be achieved only through linear expansion of the existing system of health services. As mentioned earlier, the present approach of health care delivery for tribal areas is the same as in the general population, except the ratio of population to PHC, Sub-center and multipurpose worker has been reduced by 66 per cent to compensate for the low population density (e.g. according to the existing norms there is a provision of 1 PHC for 30,000 population for general areas as compared to 20,000 population for tribal areas, in case of Sub-center the norms for tribal areas are relaxed to 3,000 population as compared to 5,000 in case of general areas). All said and done, it is only more of the same health care on the paper. In reality, many PHCs and Sub-centers in remote tribal areas are chronically without doctors or health workers. The distances between the villages are vast and roads non-existent. There are some areas in remote parts in the country, where the nearest health centre is as far away as 20-25 kms. There is no in-built provision in such a situation to provide health care. There is also no provision for care of diseases like STDs, Sickle-cell disease or G-6-PD deficiency, which are highly prevalent in some tribal pockets of the country. Victims of accidents and traumas are left to take care of themselves. Falciparum malaria is highly prevalent in some remote pockets. The TB control programme does not provide any care to tribal patients in these areas. In short, the health care services as it is existing today in the tribal areas of India, is not suitable/appropriate at the level of planning, non-operative at the level of implementation and whatsoever rudiments of health care exist in these areas, serve our national goal-targets of, family planning/immunization, rather than those of the poor tribal. Against this backdrop, the health care planning for tribal areas must be conceived and planned anew. The priority problems must be decided based on the local disease pattern of the concerned tribal group/tribal area, problems like accidents, burns, sickle-cell disease, malaria, TB, leprosy, STD, may need special attention. Autonomous, decentralized decision-making is the hallmark of tribal social organization. Due to the above two reasons, the most important features of Primary Health Care for tribal areas must be decentralized planning and decision making. Trained workers from outside perhaps will not become stable in tribal areas. So can we think of workers being selected from among the local tribes and trained. Education level among some groups being quite low, the personnel policy/pattern may have to be different from standard one.

Till such time, proper location-specific and need based health plans are evolved, some of the recommendations relating to strengthen specific health programmes for improving health status of the tribals could be dovetailed in the existing health care programmes. Some specific recommendations in this regard are the following:

- Maternal and Child-health: The maternal and child mortality rates are high amongst, most of the tribal groups. In a research study conducted on "Infant Mortality in relation to fertility" by the Family Planning Foundation (now Population Foundation of India-PFI) in 5 tribal districts of Orissa (where I was involved as the principal Investigator for the state) has identified ten most important risk factors as determinants of Infant Mortality and they are:

  -Inadequate dietary intake of mothers

  -Poor health of mother

  -low-birth weight of baby

  -labour complications

  -Poor health of the child

  -Inadequate supplementary feeding

  -lack of immunization

  -Unsafe drinking water

  -Poor housing and

  -low income

- Most of the factors identified were of maternal origin. Therefore, there is a need to strengthen our efforts on health education regarding antenatal care, nutritional care, safe delivery practices, immunization, infant and childcare. Training inputs and delivery kits to tribal birth attendants for hygienic cord cutting can make a major dent especially since most of the tribes have a culture and skills of childbirth practices, most conducive for normal childbirth. The anaemia prophylaxis programmes need to be given special emphasis. So should be the case with mass deworming in pockets reported endemic to parasitic infections.

- Control of water borne and sanitation related disease: The very high prevalence of water and sanitation related disease particularly fatal dysenteries and diarrhoea, points to an urgent need for action in this direction in all tribal areas.
- Health education regarding personal hygiene and environmental sanitation also needs strong emphasis in tribal areas to cut the transmission of diarrhoeal disease and parasitic infestations. Health education on personal hygiene and implementation of Oral Rehydration Solution with the use of locally available material should also be launched on a priority basis.
- Nutrition programmes: It is observed that the tribal cannot (in most cases) go back to his traditional, variegated, forest-based diet, and is facing a crisis of resources: Among the third category of tribals, the tribals have adopted certain harmful dietary practices of non-tribals without the other correcting dietary aspects of the non-tribals. Keeping in view the high incidence of malnutrition due to inadequate dietary intake among the second and third categories, nutrition education, supplemented with income generation programmes, would greatly enhance the status of tribals.
- Control of mortality due to respiratory diseases since tribals are particularly prone to pneumonia (mortality rate is relatively high), and other respiratory tract disease, the health staff in the tribal areas should be alerted to this. Adequate stock of penicillin and other substitute antibiotics should be maintained at all PHCs in tribal sub-plan areas.
- Control of malaria: The malaria situation in some of the tribal areas of country has puzzled the most imaginative health administrators. The remote habitations in heavy rainfall areas are difficult to reach for spraying or other

vector control operation. This situation is further complicated by possible prevalence for radical treatment can be fatal. All health staff need to be particularly sensitized to the contra indications of Primaquine for tribes known to have G-6-PD deficiencies.

- Scabies control: Scabies and skin diseases are reported by most of the tribal health researchers/doctors as a major health problem. The PHCs and Sub-centres in tribal areas should be adequately provided with anti-scabies drugs for local use as well as antibiotics. Numbers of tribes that have been scheduled in each/UT do not serve the purpose and the Health staff should be asked to periodically undertake mass treatment on family basis or even hamlet basis along with health education regarding bathing and personal cleanliness to prevent recurrence.

- Control of Leprosy: As there are tribal areas where leprosy is highly prevalent, therefore, a vigorous anti-leprosy program is needed among the tribals. Keeping in view the remote habitations and difficulty to keep up continuity of treatment due to distance factor, awareness factor and sheer lack of motivation of the average tribal to keep up efforts at any activity over a long period, the leprosy control programme needs to be implemented with the close cooperation and participation of the tribal communities. It may be necessary to think of such situations as stocking the drugs with a local health volunteer and training him to provide the drugs since he is easily accessible. The community volunteers have to ensure early detection of cases and regularity of treatment.

- Control of Tuberculosis: TB has been identified as a significant problem due to high level of malnutrition. The TB control activity in tribal areas also needs to be planned in a similar basis as the leprosy programme.

- Detection of Genetic Diseases and Genetic Counseling: The problem of genetic diseases like Sickle-cell anaemia, G-6-PD deficiency are being aggravated by high levels of inbreeding particularly in some tribes due to customary consanguinity. To counter this problem, it is recommended that researchers should undertake studies to establish the prevalence rates of these diseases. In the area of high prevalence, simple kits should be provided at PHC level and the staff trained to screen the population for these traits. Genetic counseling to avoid risk should be a part and parcel of services of these PHCs. Medical officers and paramedic should be sensitized to these aspects.

Epilogue: The magnitude and gravity of the health problems of the tribals in India compounded as they are by widespread poverty, ignorance, lack of health education are daunting. Nevertheless, much can be done to improve health standards of the tribal people, if location-specific and need-based health planning is done. This of course is a big challenge. To meet this challenge in the field of tribal health without the involvement of the tribal themselves, we cannot succeed. With their involvement, we cannot fail.

Annexure- 1

Tribes of India: At a Glance

• Scheduled Tribe (ST) Population	67.8 million(1991 census) Estimated: 80.0 million (Current)
• Percentage of ST Population to Total Population	8.08
• Sex-ratio among ST (Females/1000 Males)	972
• ST literacy rate %	
Combined	21.7
Male	31.1
Female	11.9
• Number of ST Communities (Types/Varieties)	573,562,518,437,427(Their is a confusion on the exact number*) However there are about 250-300 tribal communities
• Number of Numerically large tribes (Population over 1 million)	9
• Numerically largest tribe	Bhill (Over 7.5 million)

(Contd...)

• Number of Primitive Tribal Groups (PTGs)	75
• Total population of PTGs	Over 1.32 million
• Number of ITDPs/ITDAs	194
• Number of MADA pockets	249
• Number of Cluster projects	82
• Number of Micro projects (for PTGs)	75

*There is confusion on exact number about the varieties/types of tribes in the country, the reason being there is no single list at the central level and each state/UT has its own list. Just adding the numbers of tribes that have been scheduled in each/UT does not serve the purpose and the total number thus arrived should not be taken as total number of tribes in the country. For example Santhals have been notified in Orissa, Bihar, West Bengal, so is the case with the Bhills which has been notified in Gujrat, Rajasthan, Maharastra, Madhya Pradesh etc. Like wise Gonds and many other tribes have been notified in more than one state. Therefore there is lot of multiple counting. There are even states/UTs like Haryana, Punjab, Chandigarh, Delhi and Pondicherry, where, no tribe has been scheduled. However, there are about 250-300 tribal groups in the country.

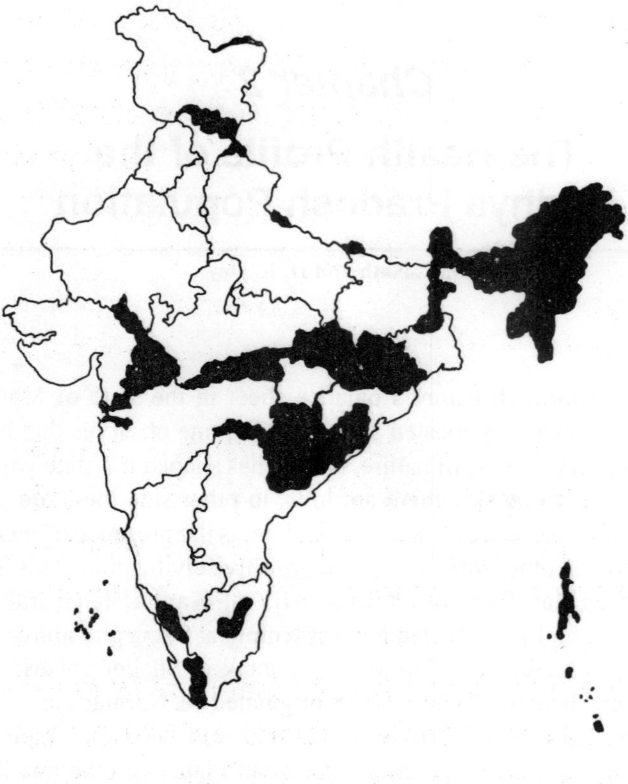

Region of Tribal concentration in India

Chapter 2

The Health Profile of the Madhya Pradesh Population

D. C. Nath and D. K. Dey

If one goes through nature's balance sheet in the state of Madhya Pradesh, the centrally located state of India, one observes that it has each and every aspects of nature. Nature has shaped the state with all its beauties. In one side there are hills, in other side there are plain lands with green beauties. In one side there is the presence of modern civilization, in other side there is old primitive civilization. This is the state which has famous national park at Kanha, Khajuraho at Chhatarpur, highly respected Maiyar temple at Satna and above all a place of spiritual meditation at Amarkantak in Shahdol district, the place from where two famous rivers originated i.e. Narmada and Sone. Distinguished scholar Banbhatt also achieved "nirvana" (spiritual infinity) by sitting in meditation on a small Plateau on the middle of the river "Bonas" at Gopad Bonas tehsil in Sidhi district of Madhya Pradesh. This is the largest state in India before division of Chattisgarh and after division it is the third. It is one of the most backward states in India in many respects. We shall however see only the health status in the light of National Population policy 2000 (NPP 2000).

In view of National Population Policy 2000 wherein it has been envisaged to improve the quality of lives that people lead, to enhance their well-being and to provide them with opportunities and choices to become productive assets in the society, it has become pertinent to see the existing position of the people and to examine the chance of achieving the goal with the objectives laid down in the policy. The immediate objective of the NPP 2000 is to get available the unmet needs of contraceptives, health care infrastructure, and health personnel, and to provide integrated service delivery for basic reproductive and child health care. The medium term objective is to bring the TFR to replacement level of 2.1 by 2010, through vigorous implementation of intersectoral operational strategies and the long term objective is to achieve a stable population by 2045, at a level consistent with the requirements of sustainable economic growths, social development, and environmental protection. To improve the quality of lives so that the people become productive assets in the society, it is important that other than contraceptives availability there should have a well-established health care infrastructure and health personnel to provide service delivery for basic reproductive and child health care. If one sees the infrastructure in health which is the immediate objective of the NPP 2001, it is seen that for estimated population of 7.42 crores in 1996 in Madhya Pradesh, the state has only 363 hospitals out of which 245 in rural areas as per record as on 1.1.1996. It means one hospital covers approximately 2,04,440 population including private hospitals, which are mostly in urban areas, whereas for most advance state like Kerala one hospital covers only 15,000 population and for the country as a whole it is 62,000. The number of Primary Health Centres in Madhya Pradesh as on 1.4.1996 is 1376 only. With the infrastructure availability in the state the IMR has come down from 135 in 1971 to 98 in 1998 whereas the same for Kerala it has come down from 58 in 1971 to just 16 in 1998 and for India from 129 in 1971 to 72 in 1998. So it is very clear that Madhya Pradesh has to go a long way to be at par with the ideal state like Kerala.

After the division of the state, Madhya Pradesh is not far better than Chattisgarh as the latest available IMR of Chattisgarh (78) for the year 1999 is lower than that of Madhya Pradesh (90). The provisional population at 00.00 hours of 1.3.2001 of Madhya Pradesh is 60.4 million whereas that of Chhatisgarh is 20.8 million, that is about one fourth of old Madhya Pradesh. It is interesting to note that the number of districts also maintain the same proportion as Madhya Pradesh has 45 districts and Chhatisgarh has 16 districts. So far as health and social status are concerned the new Madhya Pradesh does not seem to be in a better position. Madhya Pradesh has 920 female per 1000 male. The sex ratio for Chhatisgarh is 990 female per 1000 male (Census 2001). Of course both the states have improved marginally in removing disparities between male and female as in case of Madhya Pradesh the sex ratio has come up from 912 in 1991 to 920 in 2001 and the same for Chhatisgarh has increased from 985 in 1991 to 990 in 2001. It is also interesting to note that one is below the national average (933 female per 1000 male) and the other is above. Even as per 2001 census the literacy in Chhatisgarh (65.18%) is more than that of Madhya Pradesh (64.11%). Female literacy in Chhatisgarh (52.40%) is slightly higher than Madhya Pradesh (50.28%). Both the states are below the national literacy rate 2001.

Three broad areas truly reflect the health condition of a state. These are mainly population of age group less than one, female of reproductive age 15 to 49 and population of age more than 60. Childcare is an important component of any Government health policy and the same has been taken as the immediate objective in NPP 2000. With the infrastructure availability in the state it is difficult to fulfill minimum requirement when one hospital is available for more than two-lakh population, not to talk what facilities that exist in the hospitals. The data available in SRS (Sample Registration System, the largest demographic survey conducted by the Office of the Registrar General, India) for IMR fully supplement the doubt as the same for 1996, 1997 and 1998 are 97, 94 and 98 respectively which are more or less close to the highest in the country. The 1999 IMR of course has come down to 90 for Madhya Pradesh and 78 for Chhatisgarh. Even if they have to go a long way to achieve the objective if they want to come at par with the rest of the country not to talk of Kerala whose latest (1999) IMR is just 14. Now let us look at the causes responsible for these high rates of infant deaths. As per data available under the Survey of Causes of Deaths (Rural) a scheme of ORGI it is seen that in 1997 maximum deaths in rural area occur due to "Prematurity" (27.6%) followed by "Pneumonia"(21.7%) and "Respiratory infection of new born babies" (7.1). In 1996 the percentage of deaths are respectively 35.6, 22.2 and 12.0 due these causes. Though other causes are also there, the main causes are supposed to be these three.

Another important sector of health indicator is death of married women in the age group 15-49 during pregnancy and childbirth. The situation in this sector is quite unfortunate in Madhya Pradesh as the maternal mortality rate in the state in 1997 was 498 per 100,000 life births and the same figure was also seen in 1998 showing no sign of improvement in this important sphere of health services. This is much above the national average of 407 in 1998. The significant improvement has been achieved in the reproductive health care by Gujarat whose MMR for 1998 is only 28. The major cause of female deaths in the reproductive age groups in the rural areas in Madhya Pradesh for 1997 is due to "Burns" (15.2%) followed by "T.B of lungs" (9.0%), "Cancer" (7.0%) and "Suicide" (5.7%). The figures for 1996 were 15.3, 8.8, 7.1 and 6.9 per cent respectively. Figures are more or less close to those of 1997 showing no sign of improvement.

Table 1: Expectation of Life at Birth by Sex and Residence, India and bigger States1992-93

India/States	*Total*			*Rural*			*Urban*		
	Total	*Males*	*Females*	*Total*	*Males*	*Females*	*Total*	*Males*	*Females*
India#	60.7	60.1	61.4	59.4	58.9	59.8	66.3	64.9	67.7
Andhra Pradesh	62.0	60.8	63.0	61.0	60.0	61.9	65.5	63.5	67.0
Assam	56.2	56.1	56.6	55.6	55.6	55.9	64.6	64.4	65.5
Bihar	59.4	60.2	58.2	58.7	59.7	57.5	66.0	64.8	67.5
Gujarat	61.4	60.5	62.5	60.5	59.8	61.1	63.7	62.0	65.7
Haryana	63.8	63.4	64.3	62.9	62.8	63.1	67.6	65.8	69.5
Himachal Pradesh	64.9	64.4	65.0	64.9	64.3	64.8	66.8	65.0	68.4
Karnataka	62.9	61.1	64.5	61.3	59.5	63.0	67.1	66.1	67.9
Kerala	73.1	70.2	75.8	72.8	70.3	74.9	73.6	69.5	75.9
Madhya Pradesh	55.2	55.1	54.7	53.7	53.9	53.4	63.0	61.6	63.4
Maharashtra	65.2	63.8	66.2	62.8	61.7	63.9	69.5	67.7	71.2
Orissa	56.9	56.9	56.6	56.1	56.4	55.8	64.7	62.1	66.0
Punjab	64.7	66.4	68.6	66.7	65.9	67.5	70.4	67.6	71.5
Rajasthan	59.5	58.6	59.6	57.5	57.6	57.5	64.5	64.4	64.8
Tamil Nadu	63.7	62.8	64.8	62.2	61.4	62.8	67.5	65.6	69.5
Uttar Pradesh	57.2	57.7	56.4	56.3	57.1	55.4	61.6	60.8	62.3
West Bengal	62.4	61.8	63.1	60.8	60.2	61.5	67.9	67.1	69.2

Another age group responsible for maximum death with 52.5 per 1000 persons is 60+. This figure seems to be stationary as it remains to at fifty around for quite some years implying not much improvement in this field so far as medical facilities are concerned. However, the figures of death rates for the years 1996, 1997 and 1998 for the country as a whole are 50.3, 49.9 and 52.5 respectively. In Madhya Pradesh this rates are higher. In 1997, it was 55.3 and in 1998 it was recorded as 59.9. The maximum deaths occurred due to major cause responsible for this group of people at the national level for the year 1997 is "Symptoms, signs, and abnormal clinical findings not elsewhere mentioned" (34.9%) followed by "Diseases of the respiratory system" (20.3%), "Diseases of circulatory system" (14.1%), "Inflammatory diseases of central nervous systems" (7.7%) and "Infectious and parasitic diseases" (6.0%). The corresponding figures for 1996 are 37.2, 21.6, 12.5, 6.9 and 5.9 respectively. Figures for Madhya Pradesh are not available.

Table 2: Expectation of Life at Birth by Sex and Residence, India and Bigger States 1993-1997

India/States	*Total*			*Rural*			*Urban*		
	Total	*Males*	*Females*	*Total*	*Males*	*Females*	*Total*	*Males*	*Females*
India#	61.1	60.4	61.8	59.9	59.3	60.2	66.6	65.1	68.1
Andhra Pradesh	62.4	61.2	63.5	61.4	60.3	62.2	65.9	63.8	67.2
Assam	56.7	56.6	57.1	56.1	56.1	56.3	65.1	64.5	65.7
Bihar	59.6	60.4	58.4	58.9	59.9	57.7	66.1	65.1	65.7
Gujarat	61.9	60.9	62.9	61.0	60.3	61.6	64.1	62.5	66.1
Haryana	64.1	63.7	64.6	63.1	63.3	63.3	67.8	66.0	69.6
Himachal Pradesh	65.1	64.6	65.2	65.1	64.4	65.0	67.0	65.3	68.8
Karnataka	63.3	61.6	64.9	61.6	59.9	63.4	67.5	66.6	68.3
Kerala	73.3	70.4	75.9	73.2	70.6	75.2	73.8	69.7	76.0
Madhya Pradesh	55.5	55.6	55.2	54.1	54.4	53.9	63.4	62.0	63.8
Maharashtra	65.5	64.1	66.6	63.2	62.0	64.2	69.6	67.9	71.4
Orissa	57.2	57.1	57.0	56.5	56.6	56.3	64.9	62.3	66.2
Punjab	67.7	66.7	68.8	67.0	66.3	67.8	70.6	67.9	71.5
Rajasthan	60.0	59.1	60.1	58.0	58.1	58.0	65.0	64.8	65.2
Tamil Nadu	64.1	63.2	65.1	56.7	61.8	63.3	67.8	65.9	69.9
Uttar Pradesh	57.6	58.1	56.9	56.7	57.6	55.9	61.8	61.1	62.6
West Bengal	62.8	62.2	63.6	61.2	60.6	62.0	68.2	67.3	69.4

Health scenario in Madhya Pradesh seems to be in a better condition so far as life expectancy at birth is concerned. It has increased from 47.2 years in 1970-75 to 55.2 years in 1992-96. But once we compare with Kerala it is discouraging, as the same has come up from 62.0 in 1970-75 to 73.1 in 1992-96. Even national life expectancy at birth is more than Madhya Pradesh as it has come up from 49.7 in 1970-75 to 60.7 in 1992-96. Rural scenario is rather worse than the total as for 1992-96 it is 53.7 against 55.2 and for 1970-75 it was 45.7 against 47.2. The latest available life expectancy at birth for the period 1993-97 for the state of Madhya Pradesh is 55.5 with rural 54.1 and urban 63.4. Normally expectation of life of female is more than male. But in case of Madhya Pradesh it is reverse as expectation of life of male is 55.6 for the period 1993-97 but of female it is 55.2. This is due to rural area as expectancy in rural area for female (53.9) is lower than the male (54.4) whereas in urban the same for female (63.8) is more than that of male (62.0).

With so many natural gifts, the status of health in the state stands at rank 1st or 2nd or 3rd from the bottom of the list of the states of India. It needs vigorous efforts to implement the National policies for health care to improve the condition of the people. It is imperative note that at present very few people have access to health care services.

Data Source: SRS, Office of the Registrar General of India, New Delhi.

Chapter 3

The Tribes of Madhya Pradesh: A Brief Ethnographic Note

D.K. Adak , B.N. Bhattacharya , R. Ghosh, M. Pal , P. Bharati and T.S. Vasulu

The tribes of India are the indigenous and autochthonous people of the land who had settled in different parts of the country before the Aryan-speaking people penetrated Indian subcontinent. Historical reference suggests that the word tribe can be traced to the word "Jana" which was used in the ancient society. Linguistic and archaeological evidence suggests that, the pre-Aryan indigenous "Janas" were settled originally on the plains and river valleys of the lane. However, the definition and reference "Scheduled Tribes" was made after the Constitution of Republic of India came into force. The criteria for listing the Scheduled Tribes prepared in the year 1950 were the primitiveness and backwardness (Sachchidananda and Prasad, 1998). Since this volume is planned Madhya Pradesh and Chattisgarh, it is appropriate to have some brief description of the Scheduled Tribes living in the region.

Table 1: Some Facts of Madhya Pradesh

Madhya Pradesh	*Total*	*Schedule tribe*
Population	66.2 million	15.4 million
Infant mortality	92.5	101.0
Child mortality	57.6	87.4
Use of family planning	44.3	32.9

Source NFHS, 1998-2000.

Madhya Pradesh has an area of 443 sq. kms. At the time of 1991 census population in this region was 66.2 million. Madhya Pradesh is inhabited by the largest concentration of tribal population. Central India also has one of the fastest growing populations than other parts of the country. During the decade 1981-91, the population of this region increased at an average annual growth rate of 2.4 per cent per year. Primary reason behind this rapid population growth is persistent high fertility. There is also high level of disparity (as evident from Table 1) in population growth among different tribal groups in this region over four census years 1961, 1971, 1981 and 1991. However, this high level of disparity might be due to the under enumeration in Census data. This part of India is known for its poor demographic and health situation. Reasons behind this may be traced to high levels of mortality that had persisted over time along with low levels of social, economic and infrastructure development in the rural areas. According to the annual survey of causes of death, deaths due to complications of pregnancy and delivery, commonly known as maternal deaths, in 1993, accounted for more than 2 per cent of total deaths in the childbearing period in the rural areas of this region (Government of Madhya Pradesh, 1996).

There are about 46 tribal groups of which 7 are primitive tribes. These are: Korwa, Baiga, Avujhmaria, Bhariya, Kamar, Sahariya and Birhor. Distribution of the tribal populations is not uniform across the districts in Madhya Pradesh and Chhattisgarh. Fig.1 shows the percentage of tribal population to total population in different districts of erstwhile Madhya Pradesh.

Madhya Pradesh has been fascinating the social scientists, particularly the anthropologists, for its rich tribal and cultural heritage. Nearly one fourth of the population of this region is tribal. In some areas, the tribal population outnumbers the non-tribal population. The life style patterns, social values, social structures and other community level institutions of tribal people are significantly different from non-tribals. The tribes inhabit in this region mostly belong to proto-Australoid racial stock, who speak a variety of languages and show diverse physical features. The religion of these tribes is of animistic character, which comprised beliefs and practices, described as 'primitive religion' by anthropologists. During the decades of contact with other castes and communities, many of them have blended their beliefs and rituals with others like Hinduism, Christianity etc. Majority of them has a sub-human standard of living and depends mainly on food-gathering type of subsistence economy. Only a small proportion of them is settled cultivator with small land holding. Bulk of the tribe in this region is facing acute poverty and large section of their work force is engaged in labor category.

In the following paragraphs a brief introductory note on each of these tribes of Madhya Pradesh is given. This presentation is based mainly on the published materials on 'The Scheduled Tribes' by Singh (1994) and 'Encyclopedic Profile of Indian Tribes' by Sachchidananda and Prasad (1998). It is needless to state that many noteworthy changes have taken place among these tribes in the present century. This has happened mainly due to the result of developmental activities by the government.[1] However, a brief ethnographic note of the tribes will give a rough idea about the people. The general profile of various tribes is shown in Table 2.

Abujhmaria

The Abujhmaria a Gond group who live in undulating terrain and thick dense forest of Abujhmarh region in Bastar district of Chhattisgarh. They are considered as primitive tribe. There are about 20 clans among the Abujhmaria. All these clans are exogamous. They practice child marriage. Cross-cousin marriages, junior levirate and junior sororate are allowed. Marriages are arranged through negotiation, trial, purchase and elopement. Monogamy is the common form of marriage among them but polygyny is also noticed. They have primitive economy and still practice slash-and-burn cultivation.

[1] It is interesting to note that as per 1981 Census there is a sudden increase in population figures among many tribes of Madhya Pradesh, India. Probable reason behind this may be due to the fact that while in 1961 and 1971 Census the total number of tribes of MP were 58 and 60 respectively, it came down to 46 in 1981 Census. The tribes like Nat, Nihal and Mogia are not mentioned in the Census. Moreover many of the tribes are clubbed together on the basis of some ethnic stock. The names of Gond, Khairwar, Kol, Saharia are noteworthy in this connection (Table 2). However the reasons for the drastic increase in some tribes during 1981-1991should be investigated further.

They also make bamboo baskets and collect forest produce to sell at the weekly markets. Religion of the Abujhmaria is animistic in character.

Agaria

The Agaria are chiefly concentrated in the Sarguja, Bilaspur, Raigarh and Rajnandgaon districts of Chhattisgarh and in the Shahdol and Mandla districts of Madhya Pradesh. The name Agaria is derived from 'aag' (fire), appropriately associated with the furnace used for smelting iron. They also call themselves Lohar (loha meaning iron). The Agaria are considered to be an offshoot of the Gond tribe. They have mainly two endogamous groups namely, Patharia and Khuntia. Other smaller divisions are Kalha, Asur and Mahali. The Agaria like most of the tribes of Madhya Pradesh are divided into a number of 'Gots' (clan). The Gots are exogamous. Commonest form of marriage among them is monogamy. Main occupation of the Agaria is iron smelting. Though some of them are engaged in cultivation and forest produce collection. Religion of the Agaria is considered to be animistic in character.

Andh

The Andh is a small tribal group in Chhattisgarh. The Andh are mainly found in the state of Maharashtra. They have a number of clans, which are associated with plant and animal totems. These are Bansala, Dukre, Deokar, Fafre, Gohade, Khairkar, Khadke, Magre, Mitkari, Natkor, Nagmoti, Pardhi, Sakharkar, Tadche, Thote, Umare and Waghmare. Marriage with one's mother's brother's daughter or sister's daughter is preferred. Monogamy is the common form of marriage among them, however, polygyny was also found. Both nuclear and joint type of family is seen in the Andh society. Traditional occupation of the Andh is cultivation. They also practice food gathering, hunting and fishing. Now-a-days many of them are seen working as agricultural and daily labourers. They worship a number of deities such as Mahadeva, Kandoba, Massai, Munja and Krishna. Their major festivals are Akhadi, Gudipadva, Nagapanchami, Pola, Sivaratri, Dussehra and Holi.

Baiga

The Baiga are primitive tribe of Central India who reside both in the states of Madhya Pradesh and Chhattisgarh. They also live in Bihar, Maharastra, Orissa and West Bengal. The Baiga speak in 'Baigani' language. The Baiga are divided into ten endogamous groups, which are Binjhwar, Bharotia, Narotia or Nahar, Raibhaina, Kathbhaina, Kondwan or Kundi, Gondwaina, Kurka-Baiga, Sawat-Baiga and Dudh-Bhaina. All these groups are divided into a number of clans and the clans are exogamous. Monogamy is the common form of marriage among the Baiga. Marriage between cross cousins is allowed. However, the system of marriage by service (ghar-jowai) and marriage by elopement still exists. The payment of bride price is obligatory. Many Baigas are landless. They often collect forest produce like fuel wood and medicinal herbs to sell at the markets where they buy their daily needs.

Bhaina

The Bhaina are known to be an offshoot of the Baiga. They are mainly concentrated in Bilaspur districts of Chhattisgarh. They are divided into four endogamous sub-divisions. These are Laria or Chhattisgariya, Uriya, Jhalyara and Ghantyara. Adult marriage is the norm. They practice junior levirate and junior sororate marriages. Marriage through negotiation, by elopement and with mutual consent is also prevalent. Monogamous marriages are recognized. They speak in Chattisgarhi and Indo-Aryan language at home and use the Devnagri script. The Bhaina are non-vegetarian, but don't eat beef or pork. Rice is their staple food. The economic life of the Bhaina depends on cultivation, which they control individually. They also depend on forest produce collection and daily wage labour. Their religion is animistic in character.

Bharia

The Bharia are a primitive tribe of Madhya Pradesh, who live in the forest of Chindwara and Seoni districts of the state. The Bharia are divided into various clans like Bhardia, Bijaris, Amolia, Bapothia, Pachalia, Thakuria, Mehamia, Angaria, Nahal, Chalthia, Raotia and

Gadaria which regulate marriage alliances. They are monogamous and observe clan exogamy. Arranged marriage and marriage through service is commonly found among them. Nuclear and joint family are common among them. The Bharia mainly depend on land and forest produce for their subsistence economy. Since most of them are landless they now live by wage-earning. They believe in 'mana' and observe 'taboos'.

Bhatra

The Bhatra are mainly concentrated in Bastar district of Chhattisgarh. They claim to have come to Basra from North India. Their own dialect is 'Bhatri'. They are divided into three groups viz. Amnit Bhatra or Bade Bhatra, Sargimundi or Majhli Bhatra and Batamundi Masnimara or Pit Bhatra or Shan Bhatra. They have both nuclear and extended type of families. Property of a man is inherited equally by his sons. The Bhatra are monogamous, however, polygyny is also permitted. They are mainly cultivators. Most of them have cultivable land where they can produce crops. The Bhatra also depend on basketry, hunting and gathering of forest produce. The Bhatra are divided into two religious groups on the basis of their religious practices. These are 'Jagatlok' and 'Bhagatlok'. The Jagatlok Bhatra practice their traditional religion, whereas the Bhagatlok worship only one formless supreme authority called 'Alekh Mahaprabhu'.

Bhil

The Bhil, second largest scheduled tribe of India is found in four states namely, Maharashtra, Rajasthan, Gujarat and Madhya Pradesh. The Bhil are organized into a number of patrilineal exogamous clans. They include the sub-tribal groups of Bhil-Garais, Dholi-Bhil, Dungri-Bhil, Dungri-garasia, Mowari-Bhil, Rewal-Bhil, Tadvi-Bhil, Bhagalia, Pawra, Vasava and Vasave. Traditionally the Bhil practice polygyny. They are cultivators but also depend on forest produce. The rituals and religion of the Bhil have been influenced by the Hindu contact but despite this they continue to recognize most of their religious traits. However, the population of Hindus among them is declining due to the influence of Christianity, Buddhism and other religions.

Bhilala

The Bhilala are a Hindu tribe of western Madhya Pradesh. They are commonly considered as a mixed tribal group who sprang from the alliances of the Rajput men and Bhil women. They are also found in Maharashtra, Rajasthan and Gujarat. They speak a 'Bhilli' dialect, which is mixed with Malwi Hindi. The Bhilala are divided into four sub-groups, e.g., Rathia, Bhagor, Urappa and Darbar Bhilala. They are regarded as Hindu tribe who profess some of the Hindu deities and observe the festivals of the Hindu. This happened under the influence of the local Rajputs. A good number of them own land and are engaged in cultivation. Wage labour is the other source of income among them.

Bhunjia

The Bhunjia are concentrated in Raipur district of Chhattisgarh. It has been established by some that the Bhunjia are a section of Halba who migrated from Bastar. Socially, the tribe has been derived into two main sections namely, the Chukutia Bhunjia and Chinda Bhunjia, the former represents the traditional and conservative section and the latter, the acculturated and progressive section. The common form of marriage is monogamy among them but the practice of polygyny is also observed. They subsist on agriculture. These days they also work as agricultural labourers. The Bhunjia are polytheists and worship a number of gods and goddesses.

Biar

The Biar are found in the states of Madhya Pradesh and Chhattisgarh. They recall their migration from the Dudhi tehsil of Mirzapur in Uttar Pradesh. The Biar speak Bagheli Hindi language in Sidhi district of Madhya Pradesh while in Sarguja district of Chhattisgarh they speak Chhattisgarhi dialect. The Biar have two endogamous sub-divisions. The Barhariya, who take their name from pargana Barhar, north of the river Son, and the Dakkhinaha or Southerners, who live south of the river. The most popular form of marriage among them is monogamy. Polygyny is rarely practiced. Bride price is paid during marriage. The Biar Mainly depend on cultivation, daily wage earning and forest produce collection for their subsistence economy. Their religion is entirely of animistic character. They also worship Hindu gods and goddesses.

Binjhwar

The Binjhwar are chiefly concentrated in Raipur, Bilaspur and Raigarh districts of Chhattisgarh and Balaghat district of Madhya Pradesh. The Binjhwar are divided into exogamous clans (goitar) like Savcur, Katmohi, Dehd, Juwadi, Chandrama, Singhi, Bhaisa, Kisaru, Bokra, Deharia and so on. They strictly follow monogamy but marrying one's deceased wife's younger sister is permissible. The Binjhwar are a landowning community and their primary occupation is agriculture. They also work as agricultural labourers. The main deity of worship for the Binjhwar is Panigosain who is also called Sarat. They worship clan and village deities like Thakurdev, Mahadev, Makin Dai and Mathin Dai.

Birhor

The Birhor are one of the primitive tribes of Bihar. They are also found in the district of Raigarh in Chhattisgarh. Linguistically they belong to the Austro-Asiatic Mundari group. In Birhor society lineages are as a rule exogamous but remarriage may occur within the same lineage. They are usually monogamous, though polygyny is permitted. The chief vocation of the Birhor is rope making with wild bark fiber, supplemented by hunting, gathering and fishing. Their religion is entirely of animistic character. They are the followers of Hindu gods and goddesses too.

Damor

The Damor are a small tribe, who claim to be of Rajput origin and recall their migration from Gujrat. They have two moieties, one upper Damor and other lower Damor. Both groups treat themselves superior. They prefer nuclear family. There is no preference of cross cousin and parallel cousin marriage. Polygyny does not exist in this tribal group but exceptions can be seen. Economy of the Damor is mainly based on agriculture. They have accepted many Hindu gods and goddesses with the passage of time.

Dhanwar

The Dhanwar are mainly found in the hilly region of Bilaspur, Raigarh and Sarguja districts of Chhattisgarh. The Dhanwar are probably an offshoot of the Gond or Kawar tribe or a mixture of both. They have exogamous totemic clans (gotis) like Vika, Sonvani, etc. The Sonvani clan assumes a higher status than the others. The Dhanwar are either agriculturists or agricultural labourers. Some of them subsist by collecting forest produce like tendu leaves and Mahua flowers. They worship Dulha Deo, clan deities like Desgosain and Dhurpatala and village deities like Markidevi and Kaira Rani.

Gadaba

The Gadaba are an aboriginal tribe of Southern Orissa. They are also found in Bastar, Raigarh and Bilaspur district of Chhattisgarh in lesser number. The Gadaba family is mostly nuclear. Classificatory cross-cousin marriage, junior levirate, sororate and remarriage of widows, widowers and divorces are permitted. The tribe is composed of several sub-sections such as, Bada Gadaba, Ollar Gadaba, Kapu Gadaba and Kalanji Gadaba. Among them the Bada Gadaba occupy the highest rank and the Kalanji Gadaba the lowest. Agriculture is the mainstay of the life of the Gadaba. They follow both Hinduism and traditional tribal religion.

Gond

The Gond are found in the states of Madhya Pradesh, Chhattisgarh, Maharashtra, Andhra Pradesh, Bihar, Gujarat, Karnataka, Orissa and West Bengal. Numerically they are the most dominant tribe of India. The Gond speaks the 'Gondi' dialect, which belongs to the Dravidian family of languages. The Gond includes 51 other names, some of which are distinct ethnic groups, such as Dhobas, Nagwanshis etc. Other sub-tribes of the Gond are Dhulia, Gaiki, Kalanga, Khatola, Monghya, Nagarchi, Ojha etc. Though the traditional marriage i.e. marriage by capture is not prevalent among them cross-cousin marriage, marriage by exchange and marriage by service is seen. They mainly depend on agro-forest economy. The member of each clan worship its own deity described as 'persa pen'.

Halba

The Halba are mainly found in the districts of Bastar and Raipur of Chhattisgarh. Their total populations came to 236,375 according to the 1981 census. They are also found in the state of Maharashtra and Orissa. The Halba have local subdivisions known as Chhattisgarhia, Bastariha and Marethia. Like most of the tribes of Central India they are also divided into a number of Got (clan). The commonest form of marriage among them is monogamy. The primary occupation of the Halba is agriculture and agricultural labour. The Halba are Hindu and their principal deity is Danteswari. They worship clan deities like Mawli, Maha Mai and also village deities.

Kamar

The Kamar is a primitive tribe of Chhattisgarh who are found in Raipur district of the state. This tribe is characterized with their pre-agricultural level of economy, low literacy level and declining population growth rate. They speak 'kamari' a dialect close to Halbi and Marathi. They have two territorial sub-divisions, the Paharpatiya or hill dwellers and Bundhrijiya or plain dwellers. These groups are however, not endogamous. They practice child marriage, and cross-cousin marriages. Junicr levirate and junior sororate are permissible. The economic life of this tribe mainly depends on shifting cultivation and basketry though now-a-days it is in transition. The Kamar profess Hinduism and worship some household, clan and village deities like Burharaja, Mata etc.

Kanwar

The Kanwar are mainly found in the districts of Raigarh, Sarguja and Bilaspur in Chhattisgarh. They trace their origin from the 'Kauravas' of the Mahabharata. The Kanwar are divided into several endogamous sub-tribes. All of these are divided into several exogamous clans. Marriage is generally monogamous. Polygyny is allowed only if the first wife is barren. The Kanwar speak Chhattisgarhi dialect of Hindi. Economic life of this tribe mainly depends on cultivation. As a subsidiary occupation, they work as labourers. They worship their principal deity, Dulhadeo, village deities like Mahamai, Thakurdeo, Gaongosai etc., their clan gods and other Hindu gods.

Karku

The Karku belong to the ethnic group known as Kolarian tribe and their dialect is from the Munda group of languages. The Karku are divided into a number of totemic clans. They practice polygyny but it is on decline. Their economic activities include agriculture, picking up of minor forest produce and working as labour on farms in the forest. They also practice settled traditional agriculture. The Karku are animistic. They also worship Hindu gods and goddesses.

Khairwar

The Khair are mainly found in the districts of Bilaspur and Sarguja in the state of Chhattisgarh and in the districts of Satna, Sidhi, Chatarpur and Rewa of Madhya Pradesh. There are two endogamous divisions among them, the Muda Khairwar and Surya Vanshi Khairwar. At present none of the Khairwar pursue the traditional occupation of catechu making. Settled cultivation and agricultural labour are their primary occupation. Their principal deity is Dulha Deo. In addition they worship clan and village deities and some Hindu deities of the wider pantheon.

Kharia

The Kharia are found in Bilaspur, Raipur and Sarguja districts of Chhattisgarh. They are also found in Bihar, Orissa and West Bengal. They are divided into a number of clans. The common form of marriage among them is monogamy. Cultivation is the primary occupation of the Kharia and most of them own cultivable land. The landless work as labourers in agricultural and non-agricultural sectors. Their traditional religious practices include ancestor worship and worship of the earth, sun, moon, hills, jungle and other such natural objects.

Kir

The Kir is one of the small tribes of Madhya Pradesh. They are mostly found in Hosangabad, Raisen and Sehore of Madhya Pradesh.

They are said to have migrated from Gujarat and Rajasthan long ago. The Kir are divided into a number of exogamous clans namely Banya, Nayar, Dayma, Namehuria , Jat, War, Muchi, Kirka, Gadri and Wal. Monogamy is the common forms of marriage among them though a few cases of polygyny have been reported. They derive their livelihood largely from the cultivation of fruits and vegetables along the riverbeds. The Kir is mainly animistic.

Kol

The Kol tribe is found in the states of Madhya Pradesh, Maharashtra and Orissa. However, they are principally found in Madhya Pradesh. The Kol are divided into several endogamous groups and each of these groups contains exogamous lineage groups or 'kur'. Monogamy is the most common form of marriage among them though few polygyny can also be noticed. Their religion is of animistic character but now-a-days many of them profess Hinduism. A large section of the Kol depends on agriculture labour for their subsistence economy.

Kolam

The Kolam are Dravidian-speaking people. They are mainly found in the state of Maharashtra. They are concentrated in Sagar and Betul districts of the state. Marriage by negotiation, intrusion and capture is very common among them. Monogamy is the most common form of marriage. The Kolam are mostly cultivators or wage labourers. They profess Hinduism and worship Bhimdeo, Pochimai and Narimoi as household deities. Trees and animals are also worshipped.

Kondh

Chief concentration of the Kondh is in the state of Orissa. In Central India they are principally found in the district of Raigarh in Chhattisgarh. Families among the Kondh are mostly nuclear, patrilineal and patrilocal. Succession of property is always through males. Marriages are generally monogamous but their tradition allows polygyny. Kondh practice shifting cultivation settled agriculture and animal husbandry. Besides, there are wage earners, hunters and food gatherers. Their religion is a mixture of the traditional tribal faith and Hinduism.

Korku

The Korku are mainly found in the states of Maharashtra and Madhya Pradesh. They belong to the Kolarian group and their dialect is from the Munda group of languages. The Korku are divided into several totemic clans. Each clan name indicates some natural objects like a tree, creeper, animal, bird, soil etc. The most common ways of acquiring spouses among the Korku are by negotiation and mutual consent. They are primarily cultivators. Some of them work as farm labourers on daily wages or on an annual contact basis, and some work in various government and non-government agencies. The Korku are influenced by Hinduism, but have not given up their traditional religious belief altogether.

Korwa

The Korwa are mainly concentrated in the districts of Sarguja, Raigarh and Bilaspur in Chhattisgarh. They are also found in the states of Bihar, Orissa and West Bengal. The Korwa are a branch of great Kolarian tribal group. Their dialect belongs to the Mundari branch of the Austric family of language. The tribe has two sub-tribes: i) Pahari Korwa- hill dwellers and ii) Dihari Korwa- plain dwellers. The Pahari Korwa i.e. the Hill Korwa is categorized as one of the primitive tribe of Chhattisgarh State. Marriage alliances are usually negotiated and monogamy as wall as polygyny is practiced. Economic life of the Korwa mainly depends on food gathering, hunting and shifting cultivation. Many of them have taken to settled agriculture and some work as wage labourers or do other menial jobs. The community worship deities like Dulha Deo, Andhari Mata, Dargia Thakur, Thakur Deo and Murki Mata.

Manjhi

The Manjhi means boatman. This tribe is divided into sub-divisions such as Kisan (Kanwar) Manjhi, Kol (Mundari) Manjhi, Dhanwar Manjhi, Binjhwar Manjhi and Gondh Manjhi etc. Marriage alliances are usually negotiated. Monogamy is the norm, but polygyny is permitted. Traditional occupation of the Manjhi was fishing; some worked as boatman. Today their primary occupation is agriculture and agricultural labour. They now profess Hinduism instead of their traditional religion.

Manjhwar

The Manjhwar are a mixed tribal group who is believed to be originated from the Gond, Munda and Kanwar tribe. They are mainly concentrated in Bilaspur districts in Chhattisgarh.The Manjhwar have two divisions, namely Manjhwar and Bode Manjhwar. Marriages are generally arranged through negotiation. Cases of elopement have been reported. They prefer cross-cousin marriage and allow junior levirate and junior sororate. The Manjhwar depend mainly on agriculture and agricultural labour for subsistence. They profess Hinduism.

Mawasi

The Mawasi are considered to be a branch of the Korku tribe. Since they hail from Mawas region of Maharashtra, they are called Mawasi. In Madhya Pradesh they are sporadically distributed in the hill tracts of the Hoshangabad, Panna and Satna districts. The Mawasi are an endogamous group and divided into a number of clans. The clans are generally totemic. Marriage by service and through negotiation is in practice. They are monogamous. They depend on agriculture and agricultural labour. Hunting is their secondary occupation. Mawasi religious faith and practices comprise a blend of their traditional form of religion and the worshipping of some Hindu deities.

Meena

The Meena are the largest tribal group of Rajasthan. In Madhya Pradesh they are found in Sironj sub-division of Vidisha district. Agriculture is the mainstay of the Meena tribe. Though during the last three decades, they made great progress in other fields like defense service, technical service and administrative service.

Munda

They are also known as Horo-hon or Mura, which means headman of a village. They are dispersed over Bihar, Orissa, West

Bengal, Madhya Pradesh and Tripura. The Munda are divided into a number of clans, known as 'kili' which are exogamous. The dominant form of family among them is nuclear. Monogamy is the usual practice of marriage. The Munda are settled agriculturists. They are mainly nature worshippers. They also worship their ancestors.

Nagesia

The nomenclature of Nagesia has been derived from the word 'nag' meaning snake. They are found in the districts of Raigarh and Sarguja in Chhattisgarh. They are also found in Bihar. Monogamy is the most common form of marriage among them. Negotiation is the usual mode of acquiring spouses. Previously those people practiced shifting cultivation, which has now been totally abandoned. In addition to their settled cultivation, some of them are agricultural wage laborers. The Nagesia are Hindus, who observe Phagun, Diwali and Magh Parab festivals.

Oraon

The Oraon are mainly found in Bihar. In Chhattisgarh they are found in the districts of Raigarh, Jashpur and Sarguja. They are divided into a number of totemic clans. Marriage among them is mainly monogamous. The Oraon are mostly settled agriculturists and also depend on hunting, fishing, cattle-rearing etc. They worship local village deities like Andheri Pat.

Panika

This community from Madhya Pradesh had a tradition of weaving. They have two endogamous sub-tribes, Saktha and Kabiraha. The Saktaha are those who belong to Sakta sect, which means they eat flesh and drink liquor. The Kabiraha are follower of Kabirpanth and they do not eat flesh, fish and do not drink. Each of the sub-tribes is divided into a number of clans. The Panika practiced adult marriage and spouses are acquired through negotiation and by elopement. Monogamy is common practice, but polygyny is permissible. They now cultivate land and work as agricultural laborers. These people are Hindu by religion.

Pao

The Pao are mainly found in the Rewa division of Madhya Pradesh. These people have several clans such as Umanisha, Musgudia, Kisan, Kannujia and Khandiha. Monogamy is the most common form of marriage among them. Mates are acquired through negotiation and they pay bride price during the marriage. The Pao are primarily agriculturists. They also depend on wage earning. Most of the Pao follow the Hindu religion and celebrates various Hindu festivals.

Pardhan

The Pardhan are ethnically a part of the great Gond tribe. There were instances when the Pardhan served the Gond rulers as ministers. The Gond regards the Pardhan as inferior to them. The Pardhan being a sect of the Gond speak the 'Gondi' language. Their clan organization closely resembles that of the Gond. Spouses are acquired through negotiation. Cross-cousin marriage is allowed. They mainly depend on agriculture for their subsistence economy. Some of them are engaged in wage earning. Religion of the Pardhan is animistic in character.

Pardhi

The Pardhi are found in the districts of Bastar , Raigarh, Raipur, Sarguja and Bilaspur in Chhattisgarh. The Pardhi have large number of endogamous sub-divisions. The main sub-divisions are the Shikari or Bhil Pardhi, Pahnse Pardhi, Langotia Pardhi and Tukankar Pardhi. They have five totemic clans. Basket making is their primary occupation, while agriculture and agricultural labour are their secondary occupation. They worship family and village deities like Mata, as well as clan and they propitiate regional deities like Dateswari.

Parja

The Parja are an offshoot of the Gond tribe. They are divided into four sub-divisions: Bada Parja or Sadia Parja, Bada Jodia or Pengh Parja, Burung Jodia Parja and Kondh Parja or Salia (Chhelic) Parja. Among the Parja clan, village exogamy is followed during marriage.

Agriculture is the main source of livelihood. They also collect forest produce and work as daily labour. The Parja worship gods and spirits. These deities are appeased regularly to protect village from epidemics, wild animals etc.

Saharia

The Saharia are a primitive tribe of Madhya Pradesh. They are distributed in the districts of Bhopal, Bidisha, Shivpuri, Guna, Datia and Gwalior in the state. The Saharia society is endogamous and divided into a number of exogamous clans. Commonest form of marriage among them is monogamy. Agriculture is their main occupation. Collecting firewood from the jungle and selling is their subsidiary occupation. They are followers of Hinduism.

Saunta

The Saunta are a small tribal group of Central India. They are distributed in Katghora tehsil of Bilaspur district of Chhattisgarh. The Saunta are divided into a number of exogamous clans. Negotiation is the prevalent mode of acquiring mates among them. They prefer cross-cousin marriage. Payment of bride price is compulsory. Traditionally, the occupation of the Saunta was basket making and collection of forest produce. But in recent times agricultural labour and cultivation are their primary occupations. They worship their clan, village and regional deities like Dulhadeo, Thakurdeo and others.

Saur

The Saur are concentrated in the rural areas of Tikamgarh, Panna, Satna and Chhatarpur districts of Madhya Pradesh. The Saur have five exogamous clans. They are Bela, Bararjoia,Rajoria, Sunaria and Lathbadhia. They practice junior sororate but avoid levirate. The parents through negotiations fix marriage alliances. The traditional occupation of the Saur is the collection of firewood from the nearby forest. They sell this at the market. Nowadays thay have taken up cultivation and agricultural wage labour in a big way. The Saur are Hindus by faith. They pay homage to their family deities such as Deviji and Gour.

Savara

Besides Madhya Pradesh the Savara are also found in the states of Orissa and Andhra Pradesh. They are divided into a number of totemic clans. Majority of the Savara families is nuclear and patrilocal. The Savara depend on agriculture, forest produce collection, fishing, hunting and wage-earning for their subsistence economy. Their religion is mainly animistic in character.

REFERENCES

Census of India, 1995 and 1994. Series-1, Part-II-B (III), Primary Census Abstract for Schedule Tribe Population. Office of the Registrar General of India, New Delhi.

Chaurasia, A.R. 2000. The Institutional Context of Fertility and Reproductive Health in Madhya Pradesh, India. University of Washington, Seattle.

Government of India, 1994. Annual Report of Survey of Causes of Death (Rural). Registrar General of India, New Delhi.

Government of Madhya Pradesh,1996. Report on the survey of Causes of Deaths in Madhya Pradesh (Rural). Directorate of Economics and Statistics, Bhopal.

Sachchidananda and Prasad, R.R. 1998. Encyclopedic Profile of Indian Tribes. Discovery Publishing House, New Delhi.

Singh, K.S. 1994. The Scheduled Tribes. People of India, National Series, Volume III. Oxford University Press, Delhi.

Table 2: Decadal Variation in Scheduled Tribe Populations in Central India

Name of Tribes	*Total Population 1961*	*Total Population 1971*	*Total Population 1981*	*Total Population 1991*	*% Decade Variation 1961-'71*	*% Decade Variation 1971-'81*	*% Decade Variation 1981-'91*
Agaria	11761	17548	55757	71721	49.20	217.74	28.63
Andh	2	8	153	2044	300.00	1812.50	1235.95
Baiga	14132	176934	248949	317549	25.21	40.70	27.56
Bhaina	19748	24740	39136	47833	25.28	58.19	22.22
Bharia	92639	117795	195490	223284	27.15	65.96	14.22
Bhatra	72103	71145	117297	153258	-1.33	64.87	30.66
Bhil	2950	13883	2500530	3436743	370.61	17911.45	37.44
Bhilala	5038	9395	5358	7077	86.48	-42.76	32.08
Bhunjia	5205	6605	9524	9141	26.90	44.19	-4.02
Biar	2385	3859	7369	10105	1.80	90.96	37.13
Binjhwar	48343	57013	92079	105125	17.93	61.51	14.17
Birhor	513	738	561	2206	43.86	-23.98	293.23
Damor	-	-	1112	2883	-	-	159.26
Dhanwar	20987	24161	34386	37223	15.12	42.32	8.25
Gadaba	1118	3728	3254	7134	233.45	12.71	119.24
Gond	2647883	3221937	5349883	6727838	21.68	66.05	25.76
Halba	126794	173374	236375	274628	36.74	36.34	16.18
Kamar	11781	19750	17517	20565	67.64	-11.31	17.40
Kanwar	327715	410743	562200	667244	25.33	36.87	18.68
Karku	6423	10065	469	4328	56.70	-95.34	822.81
Khairwar	24466	31770	14374	103459	29.85	-54.76	619.76
Kharia	18896	23228	6692	34694	22.92	-71.19	403.40
Kir	4346	6099	9894	15333	40.34	2.22	54.97
Kol	80363	114515	123811	781032	42.50	8.12	530.83
Kolam	-	351	299	4937	-	-14.81	1551.17
Kondh	4514	6899	1670	9790	52.84	-75.79	486.23

(Contd...)

Korku	21910	27019	66781	452149	23.32	147.16	577.06
Korwa	41902	67303	15340	85585	60.62	-77.21	457.92
Manjhi	471	4138	11074	86346	778.56	167.62	679.72
Manjhwar	27420	33489	6509	43910	22.13	-80.56	574.60
Mawasi	8601	8808	11012	69861	2.41	25.02	534.41
Mina	293	1182	383	2005	303.41	-67.60	423.50
Munda	3657	14007	1579	12639	283.02	-88.73	700.44
Nagesia	46682	60513	14471	82461	29.63	-76.09	469.84
Oraon	280013	370652	88819	544959	32.37	-76.04	513.56
Panika	35988	43988	52979	64169	22.23	20.44	21.12
Pao	23496	23074	7223	47416	-1.80	-68.70	556.46
Pardhan	50226	69633	18234	101339	38.64	-73.81	455.77
Pardhi	885	1522	1831	3291	71.98	20.30	79.74
Pardhi (incl. Bahelia)	4778	10835	8066	9754	126.77	-25.56	20.93
Parja	518	8350	1408	2410	1511.97	-83.14	71.16
Saharia	4911	6311	261816	332748	28.51	4048.56	27.09
Saunta	6101	9709	3174	3411	59.14	-67.31	7.47
Saur	16576	27798	68034	122914	67.70	144.74	80.67
Sawar	48132	59535	63773	69949	23.69	7.12	9.68
Sonr	17334	1149	48657	51907	-93.37	4134.72	6.68
Total	4317179	5395298	11987031	15399034	24.97	122.17	28.46

Chapter 4

Reproductive Behaviour of Tribal Women in Madhya Pradesh

A. Meera, P. Nangia and T. K. Roy

The recently conducted (1998-99) National Family Health Survey (NFHS-2) shows that although socio-demographic and health situation in Madhya Pradesh has improved since NFHS-1 (1992-93), still it is far from satisfactory. Compared to the country as a whole, level of education and age at marriage, particularly among women, are much lower in Madhya Pradesh. Infant and child mortality is higher and so is fertility. The knowledge and use of family planning methods is lower in the state. The nutritional status of women and children is also poorer. Within the state socio-demographic status of tribal population is lower than non-tribal population (IIPS and ORC Macro, 2000).

Concentration of tribal population is quite high in Madhya Pradesh. Forty-six different tribes in the state are recognized as scheduled tribes. According to 1991 census, one-fourth of the population in the state is considered as scheduled tribe, whereas in the country as a whole 8 per cent of the population is designated as scheduled tribe (Census of India, 1991). Most of the population in Madhya Pradesh belonging to scheduled tribes (95%) lives in rural areas. The districts, which have highest concentration of scheduled tribe population, are Shahdol, Sidhi, Jhabua, Dhar, Mandla, Sarguja, Raigarh and Bastar. The highest proportion of scheduled tribes to the total population is found in Jhabua district (86%), followed by Bastar

(67%). However, one-tenth of the total scheduled tribe population in the state is located in Bastar district alone. Generally, the districts with dense forest cover have relatively larger concentration of tribal population (Census of India, Madhya Pradesh, 1991).

The tribal areas in the state are divided into four zones, the Central, Eastern, Western and Southern. The Gonds, which constitute the largest group among the tribes in this state, are concentrated in the Central zone along with Korkus, Kols and Baigas. The Eastern zone is inhabited by Oroans and Pandos; Southern zone by Muria, Hill Maria, Halbas, Dorlos; and Western zone by Bhils (Ali, 1973).

Profile of tribes in Madhya Pradesh

The 1991 Census has revealed a literacy rate of 21.5 per cent among the scheduled tribe population in the state. Among the scheduled tribe males the literacy rate was 32.2 per cent and among females it was 10.7 per cent. In terms of literacy rate females are far behind their male counterparts both in rural and urban areas. In Madhya Pradesh, the work participation rate among scheduled tribes in 1991 was 52.7 per cent- 44.4 per cent were main workers and 8.3 per cent were marginal workers. Cultivation is the main occupation of scheduled tribes with 63.2 per cent workers engaged in it, followed by agricultural labourers with 29.5 per cent. Thus agricultural activities (cultivators and agricultural labours taken together) engage 92.7 per cent to the total working population.

Bhil is the largest tribe in western India, mainly concentrated in Rajasthan, Madhya Pradesh, Gujarat and Maharastra. This is an important primitive tribe in India, which has references even in Ramayana and Mahabharata. Agriculture is the base of their economy. The Gond is the most widespread tribe in Madhya Pradesh. Earlier their main occupation was hunting and fishing. But now they have switched over to cultivation and service sector. Muria and Hill Maria widely practice shifting cultivation known as Jhum. Hill Maria also subsists on food gathering and hunting. Munda and Mina are settled agriculturists. Pradhans of Madhya Pradesh survive by performing acrobatic feats and entertaining people. Women are of great economic help in tribal way of life, since they help in agriculture, collecting forest produce, looking after their children and household affairs (Shukla, 1986).

Reproductive Behaviour

Muria tribes have youth dormitories, known as Gothuls, where bachelors and maidens stay together whole night. In Gothuls singing and dancing is very common along with drinking. In some dormitories unmarried couples also indulge in sexual activities. When Murias indulge in sexual relations they keep in view post menarche sterility period and use rhythm method of birth control. Sometimes they also offer prayers to prevent pregnancy. Studies on usage of family planning methods reveal that some tribal communities use indigenous concoctions to avoid pregnancy (Ali, 1973).

Sharma and Sharma (1999) reported that contraceptive acceptance among Gonds is very low and they attributed factors like religious attitudes of the people, agricultural system of economy, illiteracy and high death rate as reasons for low acceptance of contraception.

Choudhury and Kumar (1976) found estimated birth rate of Bhils as 43.5 per 1000 population in Jhabua district of Madhya Pradesh. Sharma and Khan (1990) observed the average fertility rate among Kharwar of Sarguja district as 4.85 (quoted by Basu, 1994). Basu and Kshatriya (1989) reported fertility estimates based on genealogical data collected from 792 households of Muria, Mariya, Bhattra and Halba of Bastar district. Their findings show that the mean number of children ever born to the women of these tribes is 5.64, 6.00, 5.95 and 5.89 and these values are higher than the usual rural non-tribal groups (Basu and Kshatriya, 1989).

With this background in mind, the present study is focused on the knowledge and usage of family planning methods among scheduled tribe women in Madhya Pradesh. It also attempts to throw light on their fertility and fertility preferences. The aim of the study is to compare scheduled tribe women with other women. It is also geared to find out the determinants of contraceptive use and fertility among tribal women.

The data used for this study are obtained from National Family Health Survey (NFHS-2), which was conducted in Madhya Pradesh during 1998-99. During this survey 6,749 households and 6,941 ever-married women age 15-49 belonging to these households were interviewed. Among them 1,602 households and 1,571 ever-married women belonged to the scheduled tribe category. The households were selected through stratified random sampling to provide regional level estimates of demographic and health parameters in the state. Since NFHS provides data only for scheduled tribes and not all the tribes, the analysis pertains only to scheduled tribe population. However, the terms scheduled tribe and tribe are used interchangeably in this paper.

Living in Madhya Pradesh

According to 2001 census, a large majority of population in Madhya Pradesh (73%) lives in rural areas. The quality of life in the state is comparatively poor. The NFHS-2 shows that only one-fifth of the households in the state stay in pucca houses, three-fourths in semi-pucca houses and the rest in kutcha houses.

In the state as a whole, one-third of the households (32%) do not have electrical connection. Four out of every five households do not have any toilet facility. Twenty-seven per cent households get piped drinking water, 39 per cent use hand pumps and the rest get drinking water from the wells. Wood is the major type of fuel used by three-fourths of all the households. The NFHS-2 has used a summary measure called the standard of living index (SLI)[1], which is based on housing condition, amenities in home, ownership of land and livestock

[1] SLI summary measure is calculated by adding the following scores for each household:

- House type: 4 for pucca, 2 for semi-pucca, 0 for kachha;
- Toilet facility: 4 for own flush, 2 for public or shared flush toilet or own pit toilet, 1 for shared or public pit toilet, 0 for no facility;
- Source of lighting: 2 for electricity, 1 for kerosene, gas, or oil, 0 for other source of lighting;
- Main fuel for cooking: 2 for electricity, liquid petroleum gas, or biogas, 1 for coal, charcoal, or kerosene, 0 for other fuel;

and possession of durable goods. This index reflects upon the economic status of the household. According to this index, 37 per cent of households in the state have low standard of living, 47 per cent have medium standard of living and 16 per cent have high standard of living (IIPS and ORC Macro, 2001).

Table 1 is based on the information collected from households in NFHS-2. It emerges very clearly from the table that scheduled tribe population in the state is more deprived than other population in an already socio-economically backward state of the country. Most of the tribal households are concentrated in rural areas. Only 6 per cent tribal households reside in urban areas, whereas 31 per cent of the non-tribal households live in urban areas.

Less than half of the tribal households (47%) have electrical connection compared to three-fourths (75%) of the non-tribal households. Most of the tribal households (96%) do not have any toilet facility. Among the non-tribal households less than three-fourths (72%) do not have any toilet facility. Flush toilet within the household is available to only 4 per cent of the tribal and 25 per cent of the non-tribal households.

- Source of drinking water: 2 for pipe, hand pump, or well in residence/yard/plot, 1 for public tap, hand pump, or well, 0 for other water source;
- Separate room for cooking: 1 for yes, 0 for no;
- Ownership of house: 2 for yes, 0 for no;
- Ownership of agricultural land: 4 for 5.0 acres or more, 3 for 2.0-4.9 acres, 2 for less than 2.0 acres or acreage not known, 0 for no agricultural land;
- Ownership of irrigated land: 2 if household owns at least some irrigated land, 0 for no irrigated land;
- Ownership of live stock: 2 if owns live stock, 0 if does not own live stock;
- Ownership of durable goods: 4 each for a car or tractor, 3 each for a moped/scooter/motorcycle, telephone, refrigerator, or colour television, 2 each for a bicycle, electric fan, radio/transistor, sewing machine, black and white television, water pump, bullock cart, or thresher, 1 each for a mattress, pressure cooker, chair, cot/bed, table, or clock/watch.

Table 1: Per cent Distribution of Households by Residence, Availability of Amenities and Standard of Living Index, Madhya Pradesh, 1998-99

Background	*Scheduled tribe*	*Non-tribe*
Type of place of residence		
Urban	6.1	31.4
Rural	93.9	68.6
Electricity	47.2	74.6
Availablity of toilet facility		
Flush	4.0	25.4
Pit	0.5	2.3
No facility	95.5	72.3
Standard of living		
Low	51.8	32.2
Medium	44.9	48.1
High	3.3	19.7
Source of drinking water		
Piped	9.0	32.0
Hand pump	42.2	34.3
Well	42.3	30.7
Other	6.5	3.0
Number of households	1602.0	5149.0

Only 9 per cent of the tribal households get piped drinking water, 42 per cent use hand pumps and another 42 per cent get drinking water from the wells. Among non-tribal population each of these sources is used by about one-thirds of the households.

In Madhya Pradesh, tribal population has a relatively low standard of living. More than half of the households (52%) have low standard of living and only 3 per cent enjoy a high standard of living. On the other hand, 32 per cent of the non-tribal households have a low and 20 per cent a high standard of living.

Socioeconomic Characteristics of Women

This section and subsequent sections of this study are based upon

---

Index score ranges from 0-14 for a low SLI to 15-24 for a medium SLI and 25-66 for a high SLI.

the information collected by NFHS from ever-married women age 15-49. Table 2 shows the educational level of women and their husbands, work status of women and their exposure to mass media.

Illiteracy is widespread among women in Madhya Pradesh. Educational status of tribal women is much lower than the non-tribal women. Eighty-seven per cent of the tribal women are illiterate compared to 63 per cent of the non-tribal women. Only 2 per cent of scheduled tribe women have completed at least high school education, a level of education, which has been achieved by 12 per cent of non-scheduled tribe women.

Table 2: Per cent Distribution of Ever-married Women by their Background Characteristics, Madhya Pradesh, 1998-99

Characteristics	*Scheduled tribe*	*Non-tribe*
Education of the respondent		
Illiterate	86.5	63.2
Literate < middle school	9.2	18.4
Middle school complete	2.5	6.7
High school complete and above	1.7	11.7
Work status		
Working in family farm/business	42.7	21.3
Working for others	31.8	26.1
Self-employed	2.5	3.9
Not worked in the past 12 months	23.0	48.6
Earns cash for work	44.3	60.1
Exposure to mass media		
Newspaper	5.3	19.6
Radio	23.8	19.6
Television	21.1	51.3
Not regularly exposed	65.1	40.2
Education of husband		
Illiterate	51.7	26.5
Literate < middle school	28.6	29.6
Middle school complete	8.3	14.7
High school complete and above	10.7	29.0
Number of women	1571	5369

Although work participation rate among tribal women is much higher than among non-tribal women, a lower proportion of them earn cash for their labour. Nearly three-fourths of the tribal women are engaged in some form of work apart from their usual household work, whereas only half of non-tribal women fall in this category. Forty-three per cent of the tribal women work in family farm or business and 32 per cent work for others. The corresponding figures for non-tribal women are 21 and 26 per cent, respectively. Among tribal women, who worked during one year prior to the survey, 44 per cent earned cash for their work, which is much lower than 60 per cent for non-tribal women who earned cash for their work.

In a society where most of the women are illiterate or have very little formal education, mass media can play an important role in bringing about modernization. In Madhya Pradesh, 2 out of every 3 tribal women and 2 out of every 5 non-tribal women are not exposed to any mass media. Only 5 per cent of the tribal women read newspaper, 24 per cent listen to radio and 21 per cent watch television at least once a week. The corresponding figures for non-tribal women are 20 per cent, 30 per cent and 51 per cent, respectively. Lower exposure to mass media and high illiteracy among tribal women may affect their reproductive behaviour and contraceptive acceptance.

Husband's education may work as a catalyst in modernizing reproductive behaviour of women. Educational level of tribal males is also lower than non-tribal males. More than half of the tribal women (52%) have husbands who are illiterate and only 11 per cent have husbands who have completed at least high school education. On the other hand, the husbands of 27 per cent non-tribal women are illiterate and 29 per cent have completed at least high school education.

Women's Autonomy

To have some idea of women's autonomy, in NFHS-2 women were asked about their participation in household decision-making, freedom of movement, and access to money that they could spend as they wish. Women's autonomy is important as it is likely to have a significant impact on the demographic and health seeking behaviour of the couples. Table 3 reflects upon women's autonomy through their decision making power. Only 22 per cent tribal women themselves can take a decision about their own health care and 16 per cent have to take this decision jointly with other family members. Sixty-two per cent of tribal women reported that they are not involved in decision regarding their own health care. The pattern regarding decision about their own health care is quite similar for non-tribal women.

Table 3: Per cent of Ever-married Women Who are Involved in Making Different Types of Decisions, Madhya Pradesh, 1998-99

Type of decision	*Scheduled tribe*	*Non-tribe*
Decision regarding spending money		
Respondent alone	30.1	33.9
Respondent with others	31.8	30.1
Only others	38.1	36.0
Number of women	535	1658
Decision regarding health care		
Respondent alone	21.8	21.4
Respondent with others	16.3	14.7
Only others	61.7	63.9
With access to money	42.5	51.3
Permission needed to visit friends or relatives		
No	17.6	20.0
Yes	81.5	78.7
Not allowed to go	0.8	1.3
Permission needed to go to market		
No	19.0	21.5
Yes	72.7	68.5
Not allowed to go	8.3	10.0
Number of women	1571	5369

With respect to decision regarding spending money, autonomy is more or less same for both tribal and non-tribal women, as 62 per cent of tribal and 64 per cent of non-tribal women reported their partial involvement in the money matters. Forty-three per cent of tribal women have access to money, which is kept aside for use as per their wishes. In comparison 51 per cent of the non-tribal women have access to money.

A large majority of tribal women (82%) need permission to visit friends or relatives and 73 per cent need permission to go to the market. A slightly lower proportion of non-tribal women need such permission. All these indicators show that tribal women have high dependence upon others and enjoy very limited autonomy. In this regard, the condition of non-tribal women is significantly better (in statistical sense), except in the case of decision regarding spending money.

Age at Marriage

Age at marriage is a very important factor that determines fertility and age at onset of child bearing. The overall age at marriage is very low in Madhya Pradesh. Three-fourths of the women age 20-49 in the state are already married by 18 years of age, including half of the women who get married by 15 years. The problem is more acute in rural areas where 58 per cent of women get married by 15 years and 84 per cent by 18 years of age. Similarly, tribal women also get married earlier than non-tribal women. Even among the young women age (20-24) that got married more recently, 42 per cent tribal and 29 per cent non-tribal women got married by 15 years of age. Another 42 per cent tribal and 40 per cent non-tribal women got married at age 15-17 years. Only 17 per cent of the tribal women, got married after completing 18 years of age, the minimum legal age at marriage as set by the Child Marriage Restraint Act, 1978. In comparison, the proportion of other women getting married above age 18 is 31 per cent (Table 4).

Table 4: Per cent Distribution of Ever-married Women Age 20-24 by Age at Marriage, Madhya Pradesh , 1998-99

Age at marriage	*Scheduled tribe*	*Non-tribe*
< 15	41.5	29.3
15-17	41.8	39.9
18 and above	16.8	30.8
Number of women	328	969

Family Planning

The following section discusses the knowledge and use of

different contraceptive methods by standard of living of the household, husband's education and region where women live. NFHS-2 provides information on women's knowledge and use of seven contraceptive methods, namely the pill, condom, IUD, female sterilization, male sterilization, rhythm method and the withdrawal.

Knowledge of Family Planning Methods

Knowledge of any contraceptive method is almost universal in Madhya Pradesh (Table 5). Ninety-eight per cent of non-tribal and 96 per cent of tribal women have knowledge of at least one modern contraceptive method.

Table 5: Percentage of Ever-married Women Knowing Contraceptive Methods by Standard of Living, Madhya Pradesh, 1998-99

Knowledge	*Scheduled tribe*			*Non-tribe*		
	Lower SLI	*Higher SLI*	*Total*	*Lower SLI*	*Higher SLI*	Total
Knowledge of any method	95.9	95.0	95.5	96.7	98.6	98.1
Knowledge of any modern method	95.9	95.2	95.5	96.7	98.6	98.1
Pill	44.5	55.8	50.7	54.8	77.0	71.1
IUD	22.4	29.8	26.5	37.7	63.6	56.7
Condom	31.0	41.5	37.1	41.4	67.5	60.5
Female sterilization	95.2	93.7	94.4	95.3	97.5	96.9
Male sterilization	75.0	74.5	74.8	76.1	84.1	82.0
Knowledge of all modern methods	15.0	22.8	19.2	27.1	52.6	45.8
Knowledge of all modern spacing methods	16.4	25.1	21.1	30.2	56.6	49.6
Knowledge of at least one modern spacing methods	49.6	60.7	55.6	60.6	81.1	75.6
Number of women	708	860	1572	1441	3914	5369

The knowledge of female sterilization is most widespread. Ninety-four per cent of tribal and 97 per cent of non-tribal women know about female sterilization. The other well-known method is male sterilization, which is known to 75 per cent tribal and 82 per cent non-tribal women. The difference in the knowledge of other methods among tribal and non-tribal women is quite significant. Pill is known to only 51 per cent of tribal and 71 per cent of non-tribal women, whereas 27 per cent of tribal and 57 per cent of non-tribal women have the knowledge of IUD. Similarly, the knowledge of condoms also varies greatly. Compared to 37 per cent tribal women 61 per cent non-tribal women know about condoms.

However, the knowledge of all modern methods is very limited, particularly among tribal women. Less than one-fifth of the tribal women (19%) know of all modern methods, whereas 46 per cent of non-tribal women have the knowledge of all modern methods of contraception. Similarly, there are wide differences in the knowledge of all modern spacing methods between tribal (21%) and non-tribal (50%) women. In the absence of knowledge about alternative methods of contraception women have limited choice to plan their families. More than half of the scheduled tribe women (56%) know of at least one modern spacing method. For a greater success of the family planning programme and reduction in fertility it is essential to increase the knowledge and encourage the usage of spacing methods.

Table 5 also shows the knowledge of contraceptive methods among tribal and non-tribal women by the standard of living of the household[2]. As expected, women belonging to households with higher SLI have a better knowledge of each modern spacing method for both tribal and non-tribal groups. For example, among tribal women pill is known to 56 per cent women belonging to higher SLI households compared to 45 per cent women belonging to lower SLI households. Similarly, among the non-tribal women 77 per cent and 55 per cent of women belonging to the two categories of SLI, respectively, know about the pill. However, the knowledge of female sterilization among

[2] Since only 4 per cent of the tribal population belongs to the households that have a high standard of living, the medium and high categories of SLI have been clubbed together to make one category called higher SLI, which has been compared with low or lower SLI.

the tribal women is marginally higher for women belonging to lower SLI households.

Husband's education improves women's knowledge about contraceptive methods. The findings show that with improvement in husband's education women's knowledge of each family planning method goes up. Compared to 48 per cent tribal women whose husbands are illiterate, 86 per cent of tribal women whose husbands have completed at least high school education know at least one modern spacing method. The knowledge of all modern contraceptive methods for the two groups is 14 and 40 per cent, respectively (data not shown). Similar pattern regarding knowledge of family planning methods by husband's education is observed in non-tribal women as well.

Table 6: Per cent of Ever-married Women Knowing Contraceptive Methods by Region, Madhya Pradesh, 1998-99

Knowledge	*Scheduled tribe*			*Non-tribe*		
	Chhatisgarh	*Central*	*Western*	*Chhatisgarh*	*Central*	*Western*
Knowledge of any modern method	95.1	94.9	96.6	97.9	98.2	98.1
Pill	54.7	43.0	53.5	73.0	64.7	76.1
IUD	26.3	24.6	28.6	46.5	53.4	65.1
Condom	45.9	29.2	33.3	59.6	54.7	66.4
Female sterilization	94.8	92.9	95.5	96.8	97.1	96.8
Male sterilization	81.6	69.2	71.0	87.1	84.1	77.2
Knowledge of all modern methods	21.5	16.1	19.4	40.3	44.0	50.4
Knowledge of all modern spacing methods	23.6	18.1	20.9	41.6	45.4	57.8
Knowledge of any modern spacing methods	59.6	48.9	57.5	76.8	70.5	79.9
Number of women	636	491	445	1143	2048	2178

Table 6 shows women's knowledge about contraceptive methods by region[3]. Tribal women in Chhatisgarh have much better knowledge of different contraceptive methods and the women in Central region (Vindhya, Central and South Central) have the poorest knowledge. For example, 22 per cent women in Chhatisgarh as against 16 per cent in Central region know all the modern methods of contraception. The knowledge of any one spacing method for the two regions is 60 and 49 per cent, respectively. Among the non-tribal women knowledge of contraceptive methods (except sterilization) is better in the Western region (Malwa Plateau, South Western and Northern) than in Chhatisgarh or Central region.

Ever Use of Family Planning Methods

Although nearly all currently married women know of at least one method of contraception only half of them have ever used a method. Table 7 shows the ever use of different contraceptive methods. By far female sterilization is the most common method ever used. Twenty-eight per cent of tribal and 38 per cent of non-tribal women have under-gone sterilization. Another 3 per cent of the tribal women and 2 per cent of the non-tribal women have husbands who have undergone sterilization. Six per cent of tribal women and 7 per cent of non-tribal women have ever used pills. A much larger difference is observed in the ever-use of IUD and condoms between tribal and non-tribal women. Only 1 per cent of tribal and 5 per cent of non-tribal women have ever used IUD. Nearly 3 per cent of tribal and 8 per cent of non-tribal women have ever used condoms. Overall, 37 per cent of tribal and 51 per cent of non-tribal women have ever used a modern contraceptive method. Additional 3 per cent tribal and 2

---

[3] There are seven regions in Madhya Pradesh, namely Chhatisgarh, Vindhya, Central, Malwa Platerau, South Central, South Western, and Northern. Keeping in view their geographical congruence and concentration of tribal population they have been regrouped into three regions. The composition of these regions is given below:

New region	Component regions
1. Chhatisgarh	Chhatisgarh
2. Central	Vindhya, Central, and South Central.
3. Western	Malwa Plateau, South Western, and Northern

per cent non-tribal women have ever used a traditional method. Six per cent tribal and 4 per cent non-tribal women have ever used rhythm or safe period method. Less than two per cent of both tribal and non-tribal women have ever-used withdrawal method. A very large proportion of women (61% tribal and 47% non-tribal) have never used any method.

Table 7: Per cent of Currently Married Women by Ever Use of Family Planning Methods, Madhya Pradesh, 1998-99

Ever use	*Scheduled tribe*	*Non-tribe*
Modern spacing methods		
Pill	6.3	7.0
IUD	1.0	4.6
Condom	2.9	8.2
Modern permanent methods		
Female sterilization	27.9	38.0
Male sterilization	2.9	2.4
Traditional method		
Rhythm method	5.6	4.0
Withdrawal	1.8	1.7
Women who ever used		
Traditional	3.0	1.7
Modern	36.5	51.0
No method	60.5	47.3
Number of women	1471	5101

Current Use of Family Planning Methods

Table 8 shows the current use of contraception by standard of living of the household. Only one-third of the scheduled tribe women (33%) are currently using any contraceptive method, including 2 per cent who are using traditional methods. Overall, 30 per cent of the tribal women are using sterilization, out of which 28 per cent are using female sterilization. Among the sterilized women more than two-fifths (43%) do not know any other method of contraception. Use of modern contraceptive methods among tribal women is marginally higher for women who belong to households with higher SLI (32%) than the households with lower SLI (30%). The most widely used method is female sterilization (28%), irrespective of standard of living of the household. Husbands of 2 per cent women belonging to both, higher SLI and lower SLI households are sterilized. IUD is the most unpopular method and the use of other spacing methods is less than 1 per cent. The patterns of current contraceptive use are quite similar for non-tribal women. Among non-tribal women two-fifths have adopted terminal methods. However, the use of female sterilization and condoms is much higher for women from higher SLI households than women from lower SLI households. More than three-fourths (77%) of the sterilized non-tribal women know at least one other modern contraceptive method. This reflects upon the continuous emphasis in the programme on the sterilization method.

Table 8: Percentage of Currently Married Women by Current Use of Contraceptives According to Standard of Living, Madhya Pradesh, 1998-99

Contraceptive method	*Scheduled tribe*			*Non-tribe*		
	Lower SLI	*Higher SLI*	*Total*	*Lower SLI*	*Higher SLI*	*Total*
Modern method						
Pill	0.6	0.7	0.6	0.7	1.2	1.1
IUD	0.0	0.0	0.0	0.1	1.3	1.0
Condom	0.3	0.5	0.4	0.7	4.7	3.6
Female sterilization	27.9	28.0	27.9	33.2	39.7	38.0
Male sterilization	1.7	2.6	2.2	2.5	2.2	2.3
Women currently using						
Any modern method	30.4	31.8	31.1	37.1	49.2	46.0
Any traditional method	2.0	1.6	1.8	0.5	2.0	1.6
Not using any method	67.6	66.6	67.1	62.4	48.8	52.4
Number of women	659.0	811.0	1471.0	1360.0	3727.0	5102.0

Among tribal women husband's education increases acceptance of family planning. Among women with illiterate husbands 28 per cent are using modern contraceptive methods as compared to 37 per cent women whose husbands have completed at least high school education. Among the non-tribal group use of spacing methods, particularly condoms, goes up considerably with increase in the level of husband's education (data not shown).

Table 9 shows the current use of contraceptive methods by region. Contraceptive use is comparatively higher in Chhatisgarh than the other two regions both for tribal and non-tribal women. The use among non-tribal women is at a much higher level than among tribal women in all the regions and for almost all the methods.

One-third of the tribal women (32-33%) in Chhatisgarh and Western region, and 28 per cent in Central region are currently using modern contraceptive methods (mostly sterilization). Use of modern contraceptive methods among the non-tribal women varies from 44 to 48 per cent in the three regions. In all three regions a much higher proportion of non-tribal women rely on spacing methods compared to the tribal women.

Table 9: Per cent of Currently Married Women by Current Use of Contraceptives According to Region, Madhya Pradesh, 1998-99

Contraceptive method	*Scheduled tribe*			*Non-tribe*		
	Chhatis-garh	*Central*	*Western*	*Chhatis-garh*	*Central*	*Western*
Modern method						
Pill	1.0	0.0	0.9	0.7	1.0	1.3
IUD	0.0	0.0	0.0	1.6	0.7	1.1
Condom	0.3	0.4	0.7	3.2	3.5	3.9
Female sterilization	29.0	25.3	29.0	38.3	36.3	39.4
Male sterilization	1.9	2.6	1.9	4.0	2.3	1.4
Women currently using						
Any modern method	32.3	28.2	32.6	47.7	43.8	47.0
Any traditional method	2.9	1.3	0.7	2.6	1.7	1.2
Not using any method	64.8	70.5	66.7	49.7	54.5	51.8
Number of women	582.0	462.0	427.0	1076.0	1965.0	2063.0

Determinants of Contraceptive Use

It is pertinent to know the socio-economic characteristics that determine the use of contraceptive methods among tribal population. To find out the role of different parameters in contraceptive use, a logistic regression analysis is done taking current contraceptive use as a dependent variable. The independent variables included in the analysis are age of women, square of age (to take into account the non-linear relationship between age and contraceptive use), woman's education, husband's education, experience of child mortality for the first two children, number of surviving children, whether a woman has surviving sons or not, region, and standard of living index. The results of logistic regression are presented in Table 10.

Table 10: Effect of Socio-economic and Demographic Variables on Current Contraceptive Use among Tribal Women- Results of Logistic Regression, Madhya Pradesh, 1998-99

Independent variables	*B*	*Odds ratio*
Age	0.542*	1.720
Age square	-0.007*	0.993
Women's education		
Illiterate (R)		
Literate	0.359*	1.432
Husband's education		
Illiterate(R)		
Literate up to middle school	0.308*	1.361
Middle school complete and above	0.469*	1.598
Child Mortality experience for the first two children		
No (R)		
Yes	-0.283*	0.753
Whether has at least one surviving son		
No(R)		
Yes		
Total number of surviving children	2.188*	8.918
Standard of living		
Lower(R)		
Higher	-0.002	0.998
Region		
Chhatisgarh(R)	0.290*	1.337
Central	-0.053	0.948
Western	0.022	1.023

* Significant at 0.1 per cent level.

The findings suggest that the use of contraception among tribal women increases significantly with age of women and educational level of their husbands. Literate women are more likely to use contraception than illiterate women. Women who have surviving sons are more likely to use contraceptives than women who do not have any surviving son. The odds ratios of contraceptive use are nine times higher among women who have surviving sons than among women who do not have any surviving son. However, the total number of surviving children does not make any significant difference on the use of contraception, although son preference is high in tribal community. Women who have experienced child mortality are less likely to use contraceptives than women who have not experienced child mortality.

Women belonging to households with higher SLI are more likely to use contraceptives. There is no significant effect of region on the use of contraceptive methods. In other words, in all the regions women are equally likely to use a contraceptive method while controlling for the other socio-economic and demographic variables used in the analysis.

Fertility and Fertility Preferences

This section discusses fertility level and its determinants among tribal women. It also throws light on fertility preferences, particularly son preference. Both fertility levels and preferences are compared for tribal and non-tribal women. In this study, the level of fertility is expressed by the number of children ever born to a woman, which is a cohort measure of fertility and reflects upon fertility in the past. In Madhya Pradesh, the mean number of children ever born (CEB) to women age 15-49 is 2.8 for all women. Table 11 shows the mean CEB for tribal and non-tribal women by the standard of living, husband's education and age of women. Tribal women have marginally higher CEB (3.4) than non-tribal women (3.3). Standard of living makes a marginal difference in the mean number of children ever born to tribal women. However, among non-tribal women CEB is comparatively higher for women from low SLI households. Among women belonging to households with lower standard of living there is hardly any difference in CEB between tribal (3.5) and non-tribal (3.6) groups. These differences increase for women belonging to higher SLI households, where CEB for the two groups is 3.4 and 3.1 respectively.

Table 11: Mean Number of Children Ever Born to Ever-married Women by Background Characteristics, Madhya Pradesh, 1998-99

Characteristic	*Scheduled tribe*	*Non-tribe*
SLI		
Lower	3.5	3.6
Higher	3.4	3.1
Husbands education		
Illiterate	3.8	3.8
Literate < middle school	3.4	3.6
Middle school complete	2.8	2.9
High school complete and above	2.5	2.5
Age		
< 30	2.3	2.0
30 and above	4.7	4.5
Total	3.4	3.3
Number of women	1571.0	5379.0

Husband's education plays an important role in determining the fertility. In both tribal and non-tribal groups mean CEB declines with increase in education of husband. In both the groups CEB declines from 3.8 for women with illiterate husband to 2.5 for women whose husbands have completed at least high school education.

Table 11 also shows that fertility among tribal women starts earlier as CEB for younger tribal women less than 30 years is higher (2.3) compared to non-tribal women (2.0). The CEB for older women (30 years or more) is more than double the CEB for younger women in both the groups. The differences in the CEB for younger and older women suggest that while fertility of tribal women is equally distributed among younger and older women, fertility of non-tribal women is concentrated more in the older ages.

Another way of understanding fertility is by looking at the proportion of births of different order. Table 12 shows the proportion of births of order 3 and above during the past three years to currently married tribal and non-tribal women. In both the groups fertility is low among women belonging to higher SLI households. For example, among tribal population belonging to higher SLI category, the proportion of births of order 3 or above is 51 per cent as against 69 per cent for births to women from low SLI households. The respective proportion of births in the non-tribal group by SLI is 45 per cent and 61 per cent, respectively. However, the number of children of higher birth order (3+) is lower among non-tribal women than tribal women.

Table 12: Per cent of Births of Order 3 and Above during the Past Three Years to Currently Married Women by Background Characteristics, Madhya Pradesh, 1998-99

Birth order	*Scheduled tribe*		*Non-tribe*	
	3+	*Number of women*	*3+*	*Number of women*
Standard of living				
Lower	68.7	339	61.2	690
Higher	51.4	356	45.1	1443
Education of husband				
Illiterate	68.4	380	62.9	582
Literate < middle school	54.2	190	57.4	606
Middle school complete	59.2	49	44.9	350
High school complete and above	31.4	70	34.3	600
Region				
Chhatisgarh	46.5	213	49.1	428
Central	64.8	230	51.8	853
Western	67.2	253	49.7	858

The effect of husband's education on fertility is also clearly visible. For example, among births tribal women whose husbands are illiterate, 14 per cent births were of order 1 and 52 per cent of births were of order 4+. On the contrary, among births to women whose husbands have completed at least high school education, 47 per cent births were of order 1 and 14 per cent were of order 4+. Similarly pattern is observed for non-tribal women also. Fertility of tribal population is highest in the Western region. The proportion of women with four or more children is 20, which is highest among the three regions. However, for non-tribal women the pattern is somewhat different, as their fertility is highest in the Central region.

Socio-economic Determinants of Fertility

To find out the effect of different socio-economic variables on fertility of tribal women regression analysis is performed by taking the number of children ever born as dependent variable. The independent variables considered in the analysis are age of woman, square of age, her literacy status, educational level of her husband, experience of child mortality, standard of living of the household, and the region where her household is located.

Table 13: Effect of Socio-economic and Demographic Variables on Children Ever Born to Tribal Women-Results of Regression Analysis, Madhya Pradesh, 1998-99.

	Regression coefficient
Age	0.453**
Age square	-0.005**
Respondents education	
Illiterate	
Literate	-0.692**
Husbands education	
Illiterate	
Literate up to middle school	-0.142*
Middle school complete and above	-0.489**
Standard of living	
Lower	
Higher	-0.110*
Region	
Chhatisgarh	
Central	0.320**
Western	0.291**
Child Mortality for the first two children born	
No	
Yes	0.616**

*p<0.05 **p< 0.01

The results of the analysis show that, as expected, fertility goes up as the age increases. Increase in education of husband helps in reducing the number of children ever born. Literate women have lower CEB than illiterate women. Similarly, women who belong to households with higher SLI have lower fertility. Child mortality increases fertility significantly. Tribal fertility in Western and Central MP is significantly higher than fertility in Chhatisgarh.

Son Preference

A strong preference for sons is found in Indian society, effecting both behaviour and attitude towards children. (Arnold,et al: 1998; Basu, 1989: Das Gupta, 1987; Kishor, 1995). In NFHS women were asked to state their ideal number of children and the sex composition of children. Table 14 shows the mean ideal number of children according to their standard of living and husband's education. On an average a scheduled tribe woman in Madhya Pradesh wants to have 3.4 children. Tribal women desire to have more boys than girls (1.8 boys and 1.3 girls on an average). The desired number of children among other women (2.8) is lower by half a child. Nevertheless, these women also wish to have more boys than girls, which reflect upon a strong son preference prevailing in both tribal and non-tribal groups.

Standard of living does not seem to make any difference in the ideal number of children among scheduled tribe women, but women from lower SLI category have a greater desire for boys than women from households with higher SLI indicating, thereby, that son preference is higher among tribal women from lower SLI households. Among the non-tribal women, mean number of ideal children is slightly higher for women from lower SLI households (3.0) than higher SLI households (2.7). Son preference is also strong in both the groups.

Husband's education is directly related to the desired fertility. Among tribal women, as the educational level of the husband goes up the desired number of children goes down (from 3.5 for women with illiterate husbands to 2.8 for women with husbands who have completed at least high school). It is important to note that with the increase in educational level of husband, the gap between desired number of boys and girls goes down from 0.5 children for women whose husbands are illiterate to 0.2 children for women whose husbands have completed at least high school education. A similar pattern of desired number of children and their sex composition is observed for non-tribal women, of course, at a lower level. The gap between desired number of boys and girls declines from 0.6 children for women with illiterate husband to 0.4 children for women with husbands who have completed at least high school education. In other words, son preference reduces as the level of education of husband improves.

Table 14: Mean Ideal Number of Children among Currently Married Women by Background Characteristics, Madhya Pradesh, 1998-99

Characteristics	*Scheduled tribe (1511)*				*Non-tribe (5142)*			
	Mean Ideal number of				*Mean ideal number of*			
	Children	*Boys*	*Girls*	*Either sex*	*Children*	*Boys*	*Girls*	*Either sex*
Standard of living								
Lower	3.3	1.9	1.3	0.2	3.0	1.6	1.1	0.3
Higher	3.4	1.7	1.3	0.4	2.7	1.4	1.0	0.3
Husbands education								
Illiterate	3.5	1.9	1.4	0.2	3.1	1.7	1.1	0.3
Literate < middle school	3.4	1.8	1.2	0.4	2.9	1.5	1.0	0.3
Middle school complete	3.0	1.6	1.2	0.2	2.7	1.4	1.0	0.3
High school complete and above	2.8	1.3	1.1	0.3	2.4	1.2	0.8	0.4
Number of women	3.4	1.8	1.3	0.3	2.8	1.5	1.0	0.3

Another way of looking at the son preference is to see the sex composition of children when women opted to go in for sterilization. Table 15 shows the percentage of sterilized women by number and sex of surviving children.

Son preference is reflected by the fact that a higher proportion of women going for sterilization after having sons rather than daughters. For example, 31 per cent of tribal women with two children (both sons) went in for sterilization compared to 13 per cent women with two children (both daughters). Among the non-tribal population son preference is even higher, as the respective figures are 47 and 3 per cent. Among tribal women with three children (all sons) 55 per cent opted for sterilization. But if there was one girl out of three children proportion of sterilized women went up to 57 per cent. It declined to

31 per cent if there were two girls and to only 19 per cent if all the three children were girls. Similar trend is true for non-tribal population as well. This high son preference is rooted in social norms that attach greater importance to sons because they are required for the growth of family lineage, old age security, strength of family and performing rituals of the dead.

Table 15: Percentage Distribution of Currently Married Women Who ave Undergone Female Sterilization According to Number of Living Sons, Madhya Pɪadesh, 1998-99

Number and sex of living children	*Scheduled tribe*	*Non-tribe*
1 child	1.5	2.6
1 son	2.9	2.9
No sons	0.0	2.3
Number of women	206	725
2 children	24.4	30.4
2 sons	30.5	47.4
1 son	25.5	27.2
No sons	12.5	2.6
Number of women	283	1005
3 children	45.4	60.6
3 sons	54.8	70.0
2 sons	57.1	72.1
1 son	31.4	45.5
No sons	19.0	10.3
Number of women	306	1164
4+ children	24.6	58.3
2+ sons	45.6	62.8
1 son	29.8	45.8
No sons	17.4	7.7
Number of women	483	1563

Overall, for each category of number of children the proportion of women who are sterilized is much higher for non-tribal than for tribal women. The gap increases with the number of children. For example, 24 per cent of the tribal women with two children are sterilized as compared to 30 per cent of non-tribal women. On the other hand, compared to 25 per cent of tribal women with four or more children 58 per cent of non-tribal women with that many children are sterilized.

Summary and Conclusion

The socio-economic status of tribal population in Madhya Pradesh is lower than non-tribal population. Tribal women and men have a lower level of education than others in the state, which is considered as educationally backward state in the country. Compared to non-tribal women, contribution of tribal women is more in economic activities but a higher proportion of them are not paid for the work they do.

The age at marriage for tribal women is lower than non-tribal women. A large majority of tribal women get married before reaching the legal minimum age at marriage. The use of family planning methods is low, although almost all the women know at least one method of contraception. The knowledge of spacing methods is much lower than the knowledge of sterilization, particularly female sterilization. For each method of contraception, knowledge of non-tribal women is higher than tribal women. This could be attributed to high illiteracy and low level of media exposure among tribal women.

The use of contraceptive methods is very low in Madhya Pradesh. Less than half of the non-tribal and one-third of the tribal women are using any method of contraception. The most popular method is female sterilization, used by 28 per cent tribal and 38 per cent non-tribal women. The use of spacing methods is also very low.

The mean number of children ever born is slightly higher among tribal women and so is the desire to have children. The mean desired and actual family size of tribal women is same, but the desired family size of non-tribal women is lower by half a child than their actual family size. Like tribal population non-tribal population also shows son preference, which is rather of a higher magnitude. Women desire to have more sons than daughters. Tribal fertility is lowest in Chattisgarh and highest in the Western region of the state. Better education of women and their husbands, improvement in the standard of living and prevention of child mortality can increase family planning acceptance and subsequent reduction in fertility among tribal population in the state.

REFERENCES

Ali, S.A. 1973. Tribal Demography in Madhya Pradesh: A socio-economic study 1901-1973. Jai Bharat Publishing House, Bhopal.

Arnold, F., Choe, K.M. and Roy, T.K. 1998. Son preference, the family-building process and child mortality in India. Population Studies, 52: 301-315.

Basu, A. 1989. Is discrimination in food really necessary for explaining sex differentials in child mortality? Population Studies, 43: 193-210.

Basu, S.K. 1994. Tribal Health in India. Manak Publications Pvt. Ltd., New Delhi.

Basu, S.K. and Kshatriya, G.K. 1989. Fertility and Mortality in Tribal Population of Bastar District, Madhya Pradesh, India. Biology and Society, 6: 100-112.

Census of India 1991, Paper-1 of 1992. Final Population Totals. Registrar General and Census Commissioner of India, New Delhi.

Census of India 1991, Madhya Pradesh. Primary Census Abstract for Scheduled Castes and Scheduled Tribes. Series-13. Part-II B (ii). Directorate of Census Operations, Madhya Pradesh, Bhopal.

Choudhury, N.R. and Kumar, R. 1976. Demographic Profiles of Bhils. Eastern Anthropologist, 29: 273-280.

Das Gupta, M. 1987. Selective discrimination against female children in rural Punjab, India. Population and Development Review, 13: 77-100.

International Institute for Population Sciences (IIPS) and ORC Macro, 2000. National Family Health Survey (NFHS-2), 1998-99: India. IIPS, Mumbai.

International Institute for Population Sciences (IIPS) and ORC Macro, 2001. National Family Health Survey (NFHS-2), 1998-99: Madhya Pradesh. IIPS, Mumbai.

Kishor, S. 1995. Gender Differences in Child Mortality: A Review of Evidence. In: Das Gupta, M., Chen, L.C. and Krishnan, T.N. (eds.): Women's Health in India: Risk and Vulnerability. Oxford University Press, Bombay.

Sharma, S.P. and Sharma, J.B. 1999. Tribal Demography. Radha Publications, New Delhi.

Shukla, H.L. 1986. Tribal Heritage of Madhya Pradesh: An Annotated Bibliography. B.R. Publishing Corporation, New Delhi.

Sharma, K.K.N. and Khan, A.S. 1990. Fertility and Mortality Trends of the Khairwar Tribal Women of Madhya Pradesh. Man In India, 70: 446: 446-453.

Chapter 5

A Comprehensive Study of Fertility and Contraceptive Practice among Scheduled Tribes of Madhya Pradesh

A.S. Dey

The National Population Policy, 2000 (NPP 2000) aims to bring fertility level to replacement level by 2010 providing reproductive and child health needs of the people of India: The operational strategies of NPP 2000 puts an emphasis on under-served population groups like urban slums or tribal communities who do not have adequate access to affordable health care services and little or no access to potable water, sanitation facility, or adequate nutrition. The state of Madhya Pradesh, marked by a complex social structure, a predominantly agrarian economy, a difficult and inaccessible terrain, and scattered settlements over vast area, which poses several formidable problems to family planning and reproduction health delivery systems. The state has highest number and percentage of tribal popuiation in the country with 45 scheduled tribes (ST) that account for 23 per cent of the state population. The present paper provides a comprehensive fertility and contraceptive use status among scheduled tribes of Madhya Pradesh. Besides this, an attempt is also made to study factors responsible for high or low fertility and contraceptive use. Also, to know how far scheduled tribes differ from non-tribes, a comparative analysis between them is carried out. The analysis is based on Rapid Household Survey-RCH data covering all the 45 districts of Madhya Pradesh (present Madhya Pradesh and Chattishgarh states together) during 1998-99.

It can be seen from Table-1 that in absolute terms scheduled tribe population of Madhya Pradesh increased from 6.7 million in 1961 to 8.4 million in 1971, 12.0 million in 1981, and 15.4 million in 1991. The proportion of scheduled tribe population in the state increased from 20 to 23 per cent during 1961-1991 as compared to 7 to 8 per cent for the whole country.

The decade variation of scheduled tribe population in Madhya Pradesh is 26, 43, and 28 per cent during 1961-71,1971-81, and 1981-91. The exponential growth rate is 23,36, and 25 per cent during the corresponding period. It can be mentioned that a sudden rise in scheduled tribe population in Madhya Pradesh during 1971-81 is due to the modification of the scheduled caste and scheduled tribe schedule in 1976. Before modification a few scheduled tribes were recognized as tribes only in certain districts, but not in the other districts of the state. For example, the Bhils-Bhilalas was recognized as scheduled tribe only in Jhabua, Dhar, Ratlam, and in Khargone districts but not in the other districts. The anomaly was removed after modification of the schedule.

Fertility

Consummation of Marriage: Fertility of a woman is highly influenced by the age at which she begins to cohabit with her husband. The data show that average age of cohabitation among currently married women age 15-44 among scheduled tribes is 16. From Table-2 it can be seen that there is hardly any change in the age at cohabitation during the last two decades. The average age at cohabitation for women age 20-24 is seen as 16.1 as compared to 15.8 for women age 40-44. Even the NFHS-2 survey in 1998-99 shows the median age at first cohabitation for women age 20-49 in scheduled tribe population of Madhya Pradesh as 15.7 (age 20-24, 15.7 and age 40-49, 15.8). It can be seen from the table that three-fourth of all women started cohabitation even before the legal age at marriage of 18. Seventy-three per cent of women age 20-24 as compared to 79 per cent women age 40-44 started cohabitation before age 18. It seems teenage marriage among scheduled tribe population is widespread. Looking into norms and customs of scheduled tribe population social interventions are needed to change nuptiality pattern of this group for reduction of fertility.

Children Ever Born (CEB) and Surviving: In Madhya Pradesh among scheduled tribe women age 15-44, the average number of children ever born and surviving are seen as 3.4 and 2.8 respectively. The corresponding figures among non-tribes of Madhya Pradesh are 3.19 and 2.74 respectively. The average number of children ever born and surviving for the scheduled tribe women age 40-44, who have virtually completed their childbearing are 5.1 and 4.1 respectively. The corresponding figures for non-tribe women are 4.8 and 4.0 respectively. As expected children ever born increases steadily with age. In the six quinquennial age-groups the average number of children born to a scheduled tribe women can be seen as 0.61, 1.88, 3.32, 4.20, 4.69, and 5.09 as can be seen from Table-3. The corresponding figures for surviving children are 0.53, 1.55, 2.79, 3.53, 3.87, and 4.11. It can be mentioned that average number of children died to scheduled tribe woman as 0.58 (boys 0.31, girls 0.27) as compared to 0.45 (boys 0.23 and girls 0.22) to non-tribes. Thirty-four per cent of scheduled tribe women as compared to 27 per cent for non-tribe women have lost at least one child.

Table-4 shows that, 45 per cent of the scheduled tribe women age 15-19 have entered into motherhood during their teenage. The modal family size is three children. The distribution is skewed towards higher family sizes. Among women in the age group 40-44, who are about to complete their reproduction, 2 per cent of women have never given a birth suggesting that, primary infertility among scheduled tribe is low. Further, 4 per cent of them have stopped at one child, 8 per cent at two children, 14 per cent at three children, and 72 per cent at four or more children.

Fertility Differential

Average number of children ever born (CEB) among scheduled tribes and non-tribes according to different socio-economic and demographic characteristics are shown in Table 5. Among 11 characteristics considered here, two are at district level, and of the rest four are socio-economic, and five are demographic characteristics of women. The two district level characteristics considered here are district human development index (HDI) and concentration of scheduled tribe population in the district. For the first district level variable, district wise HDIs as computed by Govt. of Madhya Pradesh (Human Development Report, 1998) are taken into consideration. HDIs were computed based on district wise indicators of health, education, and income following UNDP pattern. Based on value of HDI, all districts are grouped into three categories, 9 districts having High (HDI > 0.55), 16 districts having Medium (HDI 0.50 to 0.55), and 20 districts having Poor level of human development index (HDI < 0.50). For the second district level variable, all the 45 districts are divided into three groups, high, medium, and low based on proportion of scheduled tribe population in the district. The first group (high) comprised of three districts namely, Jhabua, Bastar, and Mandla where proportion of scheduled tribe population are 87, 67, and 61 per cent respectively. The second group (medium) consists of 11 districts having proportion of scheduled tribe population between 25 to 60 per cent of population of the district. The remaining 31 districts which have scheduled tribe population less than one-fourth of their population are considered as third group (Less).

The four socio-economic characteristics of women chosen here are place of residence, type of house, religion, and education of women. The five demographic characteristics of the women considered here are as age at consummation of marriage, marriage duration, death of any child, and current use of family planning.

It is seen that scheduled tribe women from high HDI districts have about 1 child less than women from poor Hill districts (CEB: high Hill districts 2.96, poor Hill districts 3.76). The corresponding difference among non-tribes is seen as 0.4 children. Also, scheduled tribe women from scheduled tribe dominated districts have slightly higher fertility (CEB 3.6) as compared to the other districts having less concentration of scheduled tribes (CEB 3.4).

Among scheduled tribes, a difference of 1.6 children is pronounced between illiterates (CEB 3.6) and high-school level educated women (CEB 1.9),0.3 children between rural (CEB 3.4) and urban (CEB 3.1) women, 0.1 children between Hindus (CEB

3.4) and Non-Hindus (CEB 3.5). The corresponding difference among non-tribes is seen to vary between 0.3 to 1.5 children.

Among demographic characteristics, as expected, marriage duration played a major difference. A difference of 3.4 children among scheduled tribes as compared to 3.3 children among non-tribes is seen between the recent (women having marriage duration less than 10 years) and the old (marriage duration 20 or more years) marriage cohort. Among scheduled tribes and non-tribes a difference of 2.5 children is noticed between mothers who have lost at least one child (average CEB as 5.05) and mothers who have had no such loss. (average CEB as 2.56). Surprisingly, among family planning users (CEB 4.14) on average 1.1 more children are noticed than non-users (CEB 3.06). Similar fertility differentials can be seen from the 2nd column of Table 5.

For women age 40-44 who have virtually completed their childbearing are of particular interest. The 2nd and 4th column of Table 5 provide CEB among scheduled tribes and non- tribe women age 40-44. It is seen average number of children born is very high (CEB more than 5) among women who have lost a child (CEB: ST 6.4, Non-tribes 6.3) or from tribal dominated districts (CEB: ST 5.4, Non-tribes 4.1). Relatively a less fertility is noticed for women who have not lost any child (CEB: ST 4.0, Non-tribes 3.9), those with late consummation of marriage (CEB: ST 3.1, Non-tribes 2.5), and those with high-school or more level education (CEB: ST 3.2, Non-tribes 3.3).

Correlates of Fertility

In the earlier section the level of fertility of scheduled tribes is compared with that of non-tribes. Also, the linkage of fertility of women with socio-economic and demographic variables is presented. But, in reality the relationship is more complex. Under similar conditions why some women go for more or less children depend on simultaneous reaction of several factors. To understand these factors multiple classification analysis (MCA) was attempted here. The MCA provides a profile of dependent variable over the categories of predictors. Besides, adjusted and unadjusted mean, MCA also gives other summary statistics like Eta and Beta coefficients. The coefficients show relative importance of the predictor to explain variation in the dependent variable. The dependent variable considered for the analysis is CEB. Eight variables are included in the list of independent or predictor variables. It included, district human development index (HDI), scheduled tribe dominated districts, place of residence (rural or urban), religion, type of house, education of women, age at consummation of marriage, death of any child. The two variables, age and marriage duration are controlled and considered as co-variates. The result of analysis is presented in Table-6. According to the analysis, while there is no control, as seen earlier, death of any child to a woman, education of woman, age at consummation of marriage, and HDI are important variables in explaining fertility differentials. The unadjusted Eta coefficient for the four variables is seen to be 0.51, 0.19,0.18, and 0.11 respectively.

After adjustment the variable 'death of any child' turned to be most important variable. Before controlling the effects of other variables, women who have experienced death of any child is seen to have on average have two and a half children more as compared to those who have not experienced such loss. After controlling all factors and the two covariates (age and duration of marriage), the corresponding gap persisted but got reduced to 1.8 children. Adjusted mean number of children among women who had lost a child is seen as 4.6 as compared to the other group having adjusted mean as 2.8. The adjusted Beta coefficient for the variable is seen as 0.36.

Among illiterate women the unadjusted average number of children is 3.56, which is 88 per cent higher as compared to that from high school and above level educated women having average number of children as 1.89. After adjustment the corresponding gap got reduced by 6 per cent from 3.43 for illiterate women to 3.25 for women with high school or above level of education. Similarly, unadjusted difference of one and a half children between early and late consummation of marriage got reduced to 0.4 children after adjustment. The unadjusted difference of 0.6 children between women from high and poor development areas got reduced to 0.2 children after adjustment. With respect to other factor no much difference is pronounced. The adjusted Beta coefficients for the variables can be seen from the last column of Table 6. The value of R^2 is limited to 0.25.

Contraceptive Use

Family Planning Practice: The study shows that about 35 per cent of scheduled tribe women are ever users, 34 per cent current users and 1 per cent past users. Among non-tribes half of the couples are ever users, 48 per cent current users and 2 per cent past users. From Table- 7 it can be seen that 65 per cent couples among scheduled tribes as compared to 50 per cent among non-tribes are never users.

Gap between Knowledge and Practice: A wide gap between knowledge and practice of family planning is noticed both among scheduled tribes and non-tribes. It can be seen from Table-8 that although 94 per cent of women have knowledge about female sterilization but only 27 per cent women have undergone the operation. Knowledge about male sterilization is found to 76 per cent women, but only 2 per cent of their spouse have opted for it. Knowledge about different spacing method varied from one-fourth to one-third of the scheduled tribe women, but their practice was restricted to even less than 1 per cent. Similar gap in knowledge and practice is noticed also among non-tribes as can be seen from the table.

Choice of Method

It is noticed that family planning method was mainly used to limit the family size and spacing of children is quite neglected. Sterilization among scheduled tribe couples accounts 88 per cent of current users as compared to 82 per cent among non-tribes. Female sterilization alone accounts 81 per cent of current contraceptive prevalence. Spacing method (IUD, OP, or CC) is limited to only 5 per cent among scheduled tribes as compared to 13 per cent among non-tribes. Traditional methods (rhythm, withdrawal etc.) accounts for 6 per cent of current users among scheduled tribes while it is 4 per cent among non-tribes, (Table 9).

Motivational Strategy

Table 10 shows the source of motivation to use family planning among scheduled tribes and non-tribes. It indicates that in case of more than three-fourth current users of family planning among scheduled tribes, the decision of acceptance of family planning was made by either of the spouse (wife 45%, husband 32%). The motivational role-played by ANM/Doctor/ Health worker is noticed to be 16 per cent while that of relatives or friends is 4 per cent. Role of media in the motivation of family planning is found limited to less than 1 per cent of the women. The roles played by different sources in motivational work among tribes and non-tribes do not differ much.

Source of Supply: It is seen that 95 per cent of the current users among scheduled tribes obtained supply or services from public sector sources like Govt./Municipal hospitals, PHC/Sub-centres or FP Camps. Only twelve per cent received the supply/service from private doctor or hospital. Only 4 per cent of users received the supply/service from other sources like chemist, mobile clinic etc. Among non-tribes, the public sector accounted 84 per cent, private doctor/hospital 5 per cent and other sources 10 per cent (Table II).

Reasons for Discontinuation among Past Users: Among the scheduled tribe couples, who had discontinued contraceptive practice, the main reason for discontinuation is that the couple wanted to have a child. Table 12 shows that desire for a child is reported by about half of the women among scheduled tribes while that by 52 per cent among non-tribes. Fourteen per cent women among scheduled tribes reported that 'failure of the method' as a reason for discontinuation, while among non-tribes 9 per cent quoted the same reason. It is seen that method related problems like side effects of family planning (bodyache, backache, cramps, weight gain, dizziness etc.), disliking of the existing method etc. are most frequently reported by scheduled tribes (22%) as compared to non-tribes (3%). Supply related problems (difficulties to get method, supply not available etc.) are mentioned by few women among scheduled tribes (3%) as compared to non-tribes (26%).

Need of Family Planning

Table 13 shows that 34 per cent of the currently married women among scheduled tribes have an unmet need for family planning, that is, they are not using contraception even though they do not want more children or want to wait at least for 2 years before the next child. The total need, that is, demand of family planning is the sum of met need and unmet need for family planning. Current users of family planning are said to have met need of family planning. It is seen that 51 per cent of the demand of family planning was unmet among scheduled tribes as compared to 36 per cent among non-tribes.

Non-Users of Family-Planning

Method suggested: It is seen that motivational work for family planning at grassroots level is neglected. Among women who are fecundable and currently not using any family planning method, hardly 9 per cent of them were ever visited by an ANM or health worker for adoption of family planning. Among women who were advised, 82 per cent of them were suggested for female sterilization and 5 per cent for vasectomy operation. Any spacing method (oral pill, condom, or IUD) was suggested by health worker to only 11 per cent of the women. Among non-tribes also similar preference by health worker was noticed. In short, method mix was totally neglected both among schedules tribes and non-tribes.

Future Intention

Women who are not currently using any method of family planning were asked about their future intention to use of family planning. Table 14 shows that both among scheduled tribes and non-tribes a little above half of the women intended to use in future (ST 53%, Non-tribes 56%). Among scheduled tribes, 89 per cent reported their intention for female sterilization, 2 per cent for male sterilization. Oral Pill was reported by 5 per cent, and condom and IUD each was reported by less than 1 per cent. Similar preference of female sterilization and neglect of spacing method is noticed among non-tribes (Table 16).

Reasons for currently not using a method

Among currently not-users and non-pregnant women, 60 per cent of the scheduled tribe women wanted more children, 30 per cent did not want more children, and 10 per cent were undecided. Among the non-users who wanted no more children or did not want at least for 1 year were further asked to mention main reasons for currently not using any method. Their answers were provided in Table-17.

A substantial proportion of women (ST 43% and Non-tribe 41%) referred one or other reason for non-use and is mentioned under 'other'. Among other reasons, method related problems (don't like existing method, afraid of sterilization, worry about side effects etc.) was mentioned by 18 per cent of the scheduled tribe women followed by opposition to family planning 13 per cent, health related problems (health does not permit, difficult to get pregnancy etc.) 12 per cent, and service related problems (inconvenient to get method, costs too much etc.) 3 per cent. The main reasons for non-use among non-tribes are cited as opposition to family planning (20%), method-related problem (13%) and health related problem (14%).

Contraceptive use Differential

Apart from the ten factors considered earlier, one more variable, number of living children with sex is included here. For this variable, all women are grouped into six categories. The first three categories are women having no living children, only one living girl, and only one living son. The remaining three categories belonged to women having two or more living children but having no living son, one living son, and two or more living sons. This variable is considered to see influence of sex preference on contraceptive use.

Table 18 provides proportion of women currently uses any method among scheduled tribes and non-tribes by different characteristics of women. The table also presents current use of any permanent, temporary, and traditional method. The CPR is found low among couples having no living son. It increased marginally from 2 per cent among women having no children, to 6 per cent having only 1 living girl to 13 per cent having only 1 living boy. Among couples having two or more living children, the CPR increases monotonically from 13 per cent having no living son to 36 per cent having 1 living son to 53 per cent having 2 or more living sons. It shows influence of sex preference on use of contraception.

CPR is seen high among scheduled tribe women from high human development districts (42%) or staying in a pucca house (48%) or belonging to the advanced age-group, 40- 44 (58%) or having 20 or more years of marriage duration (57%). The poor CPR is noticed among teenagers, 15-19 (2%) or having married within last 10 years (10%) or women belonging to poor human development districts or from scheduled tribe dominated districts (30 to 31%). It is observed that in all the categories of the factors considered here scheduled tribe women have lower CPR as compared to that from non-tribal women as can be seen from Table 18.

From the table it can be seen that sterilization is high (55%) in the age 40-44 or women having more than 20 years of marriage duration. Spacing method is found neglected in all the categories of women. However, relatively a more use of spacing method (17%) is found among high-school or more level educated women or women staying in a pucca house (11%) or from urban area (8%). Use of any traditional method is found minimum in all the categories of the tribal women.

Factors Influencing Contraceptive Use

After controlling all the variables and the two covariates, age and marriage duration of women the most important variable for contraceptive use is found to be 'sex preference of couples' .This is followed by education of woman, death of any child, and district human development index (Table 19). The adjusted Beta coefficients for these variables are .273, .075, .073, and .065 respectively.

Adjusted CPR varied between 14 to 47 per cent among couples having different number of living sons. Among couples having two or more living children the adjusted CPR increased from 16 per cent for those having no living son to 3.5 per cent from those having one living son to 47 per cent for those having two or more living sons. As regards the influence of child loss on contraceptive use, the unadjusted proportion of contraceptive use among women who have lost a child is seen as 36 per cent which is slightly higher than the proportion for the women who have not lost a child. But, after adjustment the direction is changed, and the adjusted CPR is seen as 37 per cent among couples who have not lost a child as against 29 per cent among couples who have lost a child. The adjusted CPR is found high for women having high-school or more level of education (46%), for women residing in pucca house (43%), for women belonging to district with high human development index (40%), for women with an early age at consummation of marriage (35%). The adjusted CPR is found poor among illiterate women, staying in a kachcha house (33%), belonging to areas with poor human development index (31%) or having late consummation of marriage (22%).

The Government. of Madhya Pradesh has initiated own Population Policy and set up its target to reach replacement level fertility by 2011. The states of Kerala, Tamil Nadu, Andhra Pradesh, and Maharashtra, which have already reached or are in the process of reaching replacement level fertility, have TFR 2.0 to 2.5 as against that of Madhya Pradesh with 3.3. The proportion of third and higher order births for the former group of states are in the range of 21 to 39 per cent whereas for Madhya Pradesh it is as high as 53 per cent. The CPR for the former group of states varies from 52 to 64 per cent whereas for Madhya Pradesh it is 44 per cent. These statistics indicate that a gigantic task is to be undertaken by the Government of Madhya Pradesh to reach its replacement level of fertility target by 2011. In this context, it can be stressed here that in Madhya Pradesh with a significant proportion of its population being tribe that are characterized by early age at marriage, high fertility, less use of contraception and staying in difficult and inaccessible terrain, the tribal group as a whole in the state deserves special attention in its fertility regulation programme.

Table 1: Scheduled Tribe and Non-Tribe Population, Decade Variation and Growth Rate during 1961-91 in Madhya Pradesh

Year	*Scheduled Tribe Population (in million)*	*Decade Variation*		*Exponential Growth Rate*		*Proportion of Scheduled.Tribe Population*	
		Scheduled Tribe Population	*Non-Tribe Population*	*Scheduled Tribe Population*	*Non-Tribe Population*	*Madhya Pradesh*	*India*
1961	6.68	-	-	-	-	20.6	6.9
1971	8.39	25.6	29.5	22.8	25.8	20.1	6.8
1981	11.99	42.9	28.8	35.7	18.9	23.0	7.8
1991	15.40	28.5	26.3	25.0	23.4	23.3	8.0

Table 2: Percentage Distribution of Currently Married Scheduled Tribe Women by Age at Effective Marriage According to Current Age in Madhya Pradesh

Current Age of Women	*Age at Effective Age of Marriage*				*Mean Age at Effective Marriage*	*Number of Women*
	< 15	*15 – 17*	*18 – 21*	*21 +*		
15 – 19	24.8	65.4	09.8	-	15.5	0654
20 – 24	21.0	51.9	25.4	1.7	16.1	1487
25 – 29	22.1	52.8	21.6	3.5	16.0	1681
30 – 34	22.5	55.1	19.4	3.0	16.0	1420
35 – 39	21.4	57.5	18.4	2.7	15.9	1239
40 – 44	26.4	52.7	18.9	2.0	15.8	0904
All	22.6	54.9	20.0	2.5	16.0	7385

Table 3: Average Number of Children Ever Born and Surviving among Currently Married Scheduled Tribe Women in Madhya Pradesh

Current Age of Women	*Children Ever born*	*Children Surviving*
15-19	0.61	0.53
20-24	1.88	1.55
25-29	3.32	2.79
30-34	4.20	3.53
35-39	4.69	3.87
40-44	5.09	4.11
All	3.41	2.83
N	7385	7385

Table 4: Percentage Distribution of Currently Married Scheduled Tribe Women by Number of Children Ever Born in Madhya Pradesh

Age of Women	Children Ever Born									N
	0	1	2	3	4	5	6	7	8+	
15-19	54.9	31.8	11.6	1.2	0.5	-	-	-	-	654
20-24	14.9	27.3	29.5	16.7	7.8	2.7	0.8	0.4	-	1487
25-29	3.7	7.6	20.8	26.6	19.6	11.6	5.6	3.0	1.5	1681
30-34	2.7	3.9	11.3	21.1	20.9	15.9	11.9	6.0	6.3	1420
35-39	2.5	2.7	8.3	16.9	20.9	17.2	13.0	8.2	10.4	1239
40-44	2.3	3.5	8.4	13.5	17.3	14.8	13.4	9.3	17.4	904
All	9.9	11.7	16.3	18.1	15.7	11.0	7.6	4.4	5.4	7385

Table 5: Average Number of Children Ever Born among Currently Married Scheduled Tribe and Non-Tribe Women in the Age-group 15-44 and 40-44 by their Different Characteristics

Characteristics		Scheduled Tribes		Non-Tribes	
		Women, 15-44	Women, 40-44	Women, 15-44	Women, 40-44
District Human Development Index					
	High	3.13	4.72	3.01	4.39
	Medium	3.16	4.63	3.10	4.61
	Poor	3.71	5.60	3.36	5.26
Tribal Dominated Districts					
	High	3.58	5.40	2.87	4.12
	Medium	3.37	4.81	3.09	4.55
	Less	3.34	5.25	3.23	4.94
Place of Residence					
	Rural	3.42	5.13	3.27	5.07
	Urban	3.14	4.49	2.97	4.28

(Contd...)

Type of House				
Pucca	2.84	4.61	2.88	4.19
Semi-Pucca	3.36	4.64	3.11	4.70
Kachcha	3.43	5.15	3.33	5.19
Religion				
Hindu	3.41	5.09	3.17	4.82
Other	3.46	5.00	3.45	5.12
Education				
Illiterate	3.56	5.13	3.58	5.13
Primary	2.77	5.10	3.03	4.59
Secondary	2.05	4.46	2.40	4.21
High School+	1.89	3.08	2.04	3.28
Age of Women				
15-19	0.61	-	0.44	-
20-29	2.65	-	2.28	-
30-39	4.43	-	4.04	-
40-44	5.09	5.09	4.85	4.85
Age at Consummation of Marriage				
<18	3.63	5.27	3.5	5.09
18-21	2.64	4.47	2.4	4.09
21+	2.11	3.11	1.69	2.54
Marriage Duration				
0-9	1.60	-	1.44	-
10-19	3.99	3.15	3.61	2.74
20+	5.01	5.12	4.77	4.91
Death of any Child				
Yes	5.05	6.37	4.99	6.30
No	2.56	3.99	2.54	3.88
Current Use of FP				
Yes	4.14	4.82	3.80	4.63
No	3.06	5.41	2.69	5.28
All Currently Married women	3.41	5.09	3.19	4.85

Table 6: Unadjusted and Adjusted Mean Number of Children Ever Born and Beta and Eta Coefficients as Obtained from MCA Analysis for Currently Married Scheduled Tribe Women of Madhya Pradesh.

		Unadjusted		*Adjusted*	
Characteristics		*Mean*	*Eta*	*Mean*	*Beta*
District Human Development Index		.119		.054	
	High	3.13		3.33	
	Medium	3.16		3.29	
	Poor	3.71		3.54	
Tribal Dominated Districts			.041		.043
	High	3.58		3.59	
	Medium	3.37		3.36	
	Less	3.34		3.34	
Place of Residence			.028		.003
	Rural	3.42		3.41	
	Urban	3.14		3.37	
Type of House			.048		.004
	Pucca	2.84		3.38	
	Semi-Pucca	3.36		3.44	
	Kachcha	3.43		3.40	
Religion			.004		.017
	Hindu	3.41		3.40	
	Other	3.46		3.65	
Education			.185		.026
	Illiterate	3.56		3.43	
	Primary	2.77		3.27	
	Secondary	2.05		3.24	
	High School+	1.89		3.24	
Age at Consummation of Marriage		.182		.043	
	<18	3.63		3.46	
	18-21	2.64		3.23	
	21+	2.11		3.08	
Death of any Child		.508		.363	
	Yes	5.05		4.58	
	No	2.56		2.80	

Table 7: Proportion of Currently Married Scheduled Tribe Women Who are Currently Using Any Method of Family Planning in Madhya Pradesh

	Scheduled Tribes	*Non-Tribes*
Current Users	34.1	47.6
Past Users	1.2	2.4
Never Users	64.7	50.0
N	7385	33868

Table 8: Knowledge and Practice of Different Methods of Family Planning among Scheduled Tribe and Non-Tribe Population in Madhya Pradesh

Method	*Scheduled Tribes*		*Non-Tribes*	
	Knowledge	*Practice*	*Knowledge*	*Practice*
Tubectomy	93.8	27.5	96.5	38.2
Vasectomy	75.6	2.5	78.7	1.2
IUD	27.3	0.3	53.7	1.1
Oral Pill	37.1	0.8	61.1	1.5
Condom	23.8	0.9	45.9	3.5
Rhythm	10.6	0.7	17.9	1.0
Withdrawal	5.5	0.3	9.5	0.7
Other	4.5	1.1	5.4	0.4

Table 9: Choice of Family Planning Method among Currently Married Scheduled Tribe and Non-Tribe Women in Madhya Pradesh

Method	*Scheduled Tribes*	*Non-Tribes*
Tubectomy	80.5	80.2
Vasectomy	7.2	2.4
IUD	0.8	2.4

(Contd...)

Oral Pill	2.5	3.2
Condom	2.6	7.3
Rhythm	2.1	2.1
Withdrawal	1.1	1.5
Other	3.2	0.9
Total	100.0	100.0

Table 10: Source of Motivation to Use Family Planning Method among Current Users of Scheduled Tribe and Non Tribe Women of Madhya Pradesh

Source of Motivation	*Scheduled Tribes*	*Non-Tribes*
Self	45.4	51.2
Husband	31.9	33.5
ANM/Doctor/Health Worker	15.6	8.9
Relative/Friend	4.2	4.6
Media	0.2	0.2
Other	2.7	1.6
N	2519	16140

Table 11: Source of Supply/Service of Method of Family Planning

Source of Supply/Service	*Scheduled Tribes*	*Non-Tribes*
Govt./Municipal Hospital	58.3	62.9
FP Camp	23.6	15.0
PHC/Sub-Centre	12.5	6.9
Private Doctor/Hospital	1.1	5.2
Chemist	1.4	4.2
Mobile Clinic	0.5	0.6
Other	2.6	5.2
N	2359	15419

Table 12: Main Reasons for Discontinuing the FP Method among Past Users

Reasons for Discontinuing	*Scheduled Tribes*	*Non-Tribes*
Wanted a Child	49.5	52.3
Method Failed	14.3	9.5
Method Related Problem	21.9	2.6
Supply Related Problem	3.3	25.6
Other	11.0	10.0
N	91	798

Table13: D emand of Family Planning among Currently Married of Scheduled Tribe and Non Tribe Women of Madhya Pradesh

Need of Family Planning	*Scheduled Tribes*	*Non-Tribes*
Unmet Need	18.02	14.86
Met Need	22.16	16.83
Total Demand (Unmet Need+Met Need)	40.18	31.69
Percentage of Demand Unmet	51.4	36.4

Table 14: Method Suggested to the Non-users Who were Ever Visited by ANM/Health Worker

Method	*Scheduled Tribes*	*Non-Tribes*
Tubectomy	82.2	73.8
Vasectomy	5.2	5.7
Oral Pill	6.5	7.9
IUD	1.8	6.6
Condom	3.3	5.1
Other	0.9	0.9
N	707	2379

Table 15: Future Intention among Currently Non-users of Family Planning

Intend to Use	*Scheduled Tribes*	*Non-Tribes*
Yes	53.2	56.2
No	46.8	43.8
N	4714	17140

Table 16: Preferred Method by Prospective Clients

Method Prefer	*Scheduled Tribes*	*Non-Tribes*
Tubectomy	89.3	92.3
Vasectomy	1.8	1.2
Oral Pill	5.0	3.0
Condom	0.6	1.3
IUD	0.6	0.9
Other	2.7	1.4
N	2506	9625

Table 17: Main Reasons for Currently not Using Any Method of Family Planning among Non-Users Who Want no More Children or don't Want at Least for One Year

	Scheduled Tribes	*Non-Tribes*
Lack of Knowledge	10.3	8.9
Method Related Problem	18.2	13.4
Opposition to FP	13.2	19.8
Health Related Problem	12.4	13.6
Service Related Problem	2.8	1.8
Against Religion	0.6	1.7
Other	42.5	40.8
N	2773	10033

Table 18: Proportion of Currently Married Women Using Any Method, Any Permanent Method, Any Temporary Method, and Any Traditional Method among Scheduled Tribes and Non-Tribes of Madhya Pradesh

Characteristics	*Scheduled Tribes*				*Non-Tribes*			
	Any Method	*Any Permanent Method*	*Any Temporary Method*	*Any Traditional Method*	*Any Method*	*Any Permanent Method*	*Any Temporary Method*	*Any Traditional Method*
Dist. Human Development Index								
High	41.6	37.6	3.7	0.2	55.8	45.8	8.7	1.1
Medium	36.3	31.7	2.1	1.1	49.8	40.2	6.4	2.3
Poor	30.6	26.8	1.6	1.2	41.9	35.5	4.6	1.6
Tribal Dominated Districts								
High	30.0	26.0	1.4	1.3	53.6	46.9	3.9	1.8
Medium	35.9	32.7	1.9	0.4	48.6	42.7	4.9	0.7
Less	34.5	28.9	2.6	1.8	47.2	38.3	6.5	1.9
Place of Residence								
Rural	33.5	29.6	1.6	1.1	44.8	39.1	3.7	1.5
Urban	44.8	34.8	8.3	1.0	56.2	40.2	13.4	2.3
Type of House								
Pucca	47.8	34.7	10.8	1.5	58.2	41.4	13.7	2.6
Semi-Pucca	42.3	37.8	2.7	1.3	52.3	43.5	6.6	1.7
Kachcha	32.8	29.0	1.6	1.0	42.3	37.3	3.2	1.4
Religion								
Hindu	34.1	29.9	2.0	1.1	47.7	40.1	5.5	1.7
Other	34.9	29.6	2.7	0.0	47.1	31.5	13.5	1.8
Education								
Illiterate	33.6	30.2	1.4	0.9	45.4	40.7	2.6	1.6
Primary	42.1	34.9	3.6	2.3	53.0	45.6	5.8	1.3
Secondary	29.2	22.2	5.0	1.8	46.4	34.1	10.2	1.7
High School+	40.0	20.0	17.5	0.6	55.4	29.7	22.9	2.5
Age of Women								
15-19	2.31	0.0	1.7	0.5	4.6	0.0	3.9	0.5
20-29	20.0	15.6	2.6	1.2	30.8	20.8	8.1	1.7
30-39	50.6	46.2	1.8	1.0	65.7	57.1	6.0	2.0
40-44	58.2	53.9	1.1	1.1	68.2	63.8	2.5	1.4
Age at Consumn. of Marriage								
<18	35.1	31.4	1.6	1.1	48.3	42.3	3.8	1.7

(Contd...)

18-21	30.9	25.1	3.5	1.1	46.1	32.0	12.0	1.8
21+	27.3	18.2	6.8	0.0	44.2	22.5	20.3	1.1
Marriage Duration								
0-9	10.4	6.1	2.9	1.0	20.1	9.3	9.1	1.6
10-19	40.8	36.5	1.9	1.1	57.2	48.7	6.1	1.8
20+	56.8	52.9	0.9	1.0	68.0	63.3	2.5	1.7
Death of any Child								
Yes	35.5	32.1	1.3	1.1	49.3	43.5	3.5	1.7
No	33.4	28.8	2.4	1.0	47.0	37.9	7.1	1.7
Children Ever Born								
0	1.4	0.0	1.1	0.1	3.5	0.0	3.0	0.5
1	8.6	3.8	2.9	1.4	17.2	4.1	10.5	2.3
2	26.0	20.5	2.9	1.6	45.6	32.5	11.0	1.8
3+	46.3	42.1	1.8	1.0	61.7	54.9	4.5	1.8
No. of Living Children with Sex								
No Living Child	2.1	0.0	1.8	0.1	3.6	0.0	3.0	0.5
1 Liv. Child having 0 son	6.1	2.4	2.0	1.0	14.8	2.7	9.6	2.2
1 son	13.4	7.6	3.6	1.5	21.8	9.0	10.2	2.4
2+ Liv. Children having 0 son	13.0	7.6	3.2	1.5	20.3	9.9	8.7	1.5
1son	36.3	31.2	2.4	1.4	49.2	37.2	9.5	2.1
2+sons	52.6	48.5	1.6	1.0	69.4	63.3	3.9	1.6
All	34.1	29.9	2.0	1.1	47.7	9.4	6.1	1.7

Table 19: Unadjusted and Adjusted Contraceptive Prevalence Rate and Beta and Eta Coefficients as Obtained from MCA Analysis among Currently married Scheduled Tribes of Madhya Pradesh

		Unadjusted		*Adjusted*	
Characteristics		*CPR*	*Eta*	*CPR*	*Beta*
District Human Development Index		.075		.065	
	High	41.6		40.0	
	Medium	36.3		36.2	
	Poor	30.6		30.9	
Tribal Dominated Districts			.049		.056
	High	30.0		32.9	

(Contd...)

Medium	35.9		37.0	
Less	34.5		31.1	
Place of Residence		.055		.025
Rural	33.5		33.8	
Urban	44.8		39.1	
Type of House		.078		.055
Pucca	47.8		42.9	
Semi-Pucca	42.3		40.4	
Kachcha	32.8		33.2	
Religion		.003		.035
Hindu	34.1		34.4	
Other	34.9		23.9	
Education		.052		.075
Illiterate	33.6		32.8	
Primary	42.1		44.0	
Secondary	29.3		39.8	
High School+	40.0		46.5	
Age at Consummation of Marriage		.038		.035
<18	35.1		34.9	
18-21	30.9		31.6	
21+	27.3		21.6	
Death of any Child		.022		.073
Yes	35.5		29.3	
No	33.4		36.6	
No. of Living Children with Sex	.412		.273	
No Living Child	2.1		14.3	
1 Living Child having 0 son	6.1		16.9	
1 son	13.4		21.8	
2+ Living Children having 0 sons	13.0		15.8	
1 son	36.3		34.7	
2+ sons	52.5		46.6	

Chapter 6

Household Factors Affecting Infant Mortality in Scheduled Tribes of Madhya Pradesh

S. Nanda

In general, the infant mortality has been considered as one of very sophisticated issues for socio-economic development. Its components are neonatal deaths and post-neonatal deaths that are defined according to the time or period of life of the baby, when the event of death occurs. The former is deaths that occur within one month of the birth and these are mainly due to endogenous causes. The post-neonatal deaths are those that occur during the period of 2nd to 12th month of birth and are mainly due to exogenous factors. In the case of tribals, poverty-affected life-style and some deleterious social customs perpetuate the higher prevalence of infant deaths. So, it is highly warranted that many of the exogenous factors around the tribals should be thoroughly examined and interventions be worked out so as to bring down the infant deaths. Madhya Pradesh (M.P.), one of the central Indian states with highest proportion of scheduled tribes have continuously been experiencing higher infant deaths for last some decades. Study shows that about 86 infants die out of each 1000 live births occurred in last five years. This figure is worse in rural area where about 93 out of each 1000 children born in last 5 years die before celebrating their first birthday (NFHS-II, M.P. 2000). In case of the scheduled tribes of Madhya Pradesh, the situation is much grave, *i.e.*, out of each 1000 children born in last 5 years, more than 100 die before completing one year of birth (NFHS-II, M.P. 2000).

There have been studies (UN, 1973; Padmanabha, 1982; Nag, 1983; Jain, 1988; Nanda, 1998 and 2001) those have identified various exogenous factors such as poverty, household condition, health care and nutrition etc. responsible for the infant mortality. It is known that the physiological factors which are mainly responsible for neonatal deaths are little subject to control through public health measures and improvement in social and environmental conditions (U.N., 1973; Moriyama, 1967). Rather post-neonatal deaths being controlled by these factors, is considered more important to be studied. Padmanabha (1982) pointed out the inadequate social and medical amenities as responsible for high infant deaths in India. He showed that drinking water from well and non-electric source of lighting cause higher infant deaths both in urban and rural areas. Nag (1983) reported that though Kerala has lower economic development, but due to higher social development particularly education and medical facilities, the infant mortality rate (IMR) is lower.

Jain (1988) studied poverty as a selected index affecting infant deaths in rural India by taking per capita monthly expenditure. He also opined similarly as Padmanabha, in almost all states except few. In social amenities he considered drinking water, house type, number of rooms and electric facility which commonly affect IMR. Former three characteristics were found to have weak positive relationship with infant mortality. He observed inverse relationship between drinking water from tap and IMR for many states except some. However the electric facility showed a strong influence on IMR. He pointed out that the effect of poverty becomes more significant when other variables like female education, medical facilities etc. are included in the regression equation. Kanitkar and Murthy (1988) computed a standard of living index (SLI) by considering household assets and amenities (water, electricity, house type, toilet) as the socio-economic factors affecting infant mortality rate (IMR) in Orissa and Rajastan. Gondotra and Das (1988) considered the household amenities as 'status index' in the study of infant mortality in Gujurat. They concluded that the index has a negative association with IMR. Panda (1992) reported with that of electric facility to the households the child loss by pregnant woman decreases. Nanda *et. al.* (1999; 2000; 2001) in their study have tried to examine the impact of the household environment which they considered as the "micro determinants" on the infant death and could find out consistent correlation of toilet and electricity facility with the infant mortality. Against these backdrops, the main objective of this paper is to examine some of the selected household conditions affecting infant deaths in the scheduled tribes (STs) of Madhya Pradesh.

Data and Methodology

The data for this paper is obtained from the phase-II of National Family Health Survey (NFHS-II), Madhya Pradesh (M.P.), 1998-99. The total number of women interviewed in the state for the survey is 6,941. But, the relevant information for the present analyses have been extracted only for the scheduled tribe women in M.P. who have given birth to at least one child in the last five years preceding the survey.

To know the causal association between the selected household factors (independent variables) with the infant death, a logistic regression analysis has been carried out due to the dichotomy nature of the dependant variable (infant death). The main aim of studying these factors is to test the relative risk of getting infant deaths due to the presence/absence of the individual household factors as well as the cumulative impact on the former. For this analysis, the death of infants to women for all the births occurred during the last five years of survey has been dichotomised into two mutually exclusive categories, such as,

(a) those who did not have any infant death.

(b) women who have got any infant death.

Logistic Regression Model

In this model, the response (dependent) variable is mutually exclusive and exhaustive.

The Logit Model can be given as

$$\text{Log } P_1/P_2 = a + \sum b_i X_i \, ; \qquad i = 1, n \, ;$$

$$P_1 + P_2 = 1$$

where a is constant, Σb_i is the coefficient of X_i, P_1 denotes the estimated probability of occurrence of infant death and P_2 is the probability of no infant death. Here P_2 is the reference category.

In this study, four selected and most important household characteristics (variables) of the women have been considered for analysis, viz., type of place of residence, major source of drinking water, toilet facility and electricity facility. Each variable has been broken into two dummy variables to examine the relative influence on the response variables (see Table 1). For the variable, source of drinking water, the hand pump, tap and covered well have been consider as "safe" and rest others as "unsafe".

Table 1: Definition of Variables Used for Analysis

Variables used in the analysis	*Categorisation/definition*
Infant Death	No infant death = 0, Infant death = 1
Type of place of residence	Rural = 0, Urban = 1
Source of drinking water	Unsafe = 0, Safe = 1
Toilet facility	No = 0, Yes = 1
Electricity Facility	No = 0, Yes = 1

Analysis

Profile of Scheduled Tribe in M.P.

The simple percentage breakdown of scheduled tribe women by the household variables and infant mortality has been given in the Table 2. It showed that infant deaths has occurred to 92 per cent of women. About 94 per cent of all women lived in rural areas. Little less than half of all women collected drinking water from unsafe that is unhygienic sources such as pond, river, spring and open well etc. Another grave situation is that, about 97 per cent of all women did not have any toilet facility at all for which they had to go outside unhygienic open fields. Forty-six per cent of all scheduled tribe women in M.P. did not have the electricity facility at all which gives an impression that these women depend on kerosene or oil- based lantern or 'Dibri'.

Table 2: Percentage Distribution of Infant Mortality and Household Variables

Variables	*Percentage (N=667)*
Infant Mortality	
Yes	92.2
No	07.8
Type of place of residence	
Rural	93.6
Urban	06.4
Source of drinking water	
Unsafe	48.4
Safe	51.6
Toilet facility	
No	96.9
Yes	03.1
Electricity Facility	
No	46.0
Yes	54.0

Infant Mortality by Household Characteristics of Scheduled Tribe Women in M.P.

The Table 3 shows below, the distribution of infant deaths by different household characteristics of the scheduled tribe women. The bivariate table gives an idea of mortality differential by different categories of the household variables. It was found that all the women who got any infant death hailed from rural area. About 62 percent of all scheduled tribe women who got any infant death were using drinking water from unsafe sources. Another matter of grave concern is, the absence of toilet facility, for it was found that all the women who got any infant death were not having such facility. Half of all scheduled tribe women having any death of their infant(s), did not have electricity facility at all.

Table 3: Incidence of Infant Mortality by Different Household Variables

Background Variables	*Infant Mortality (%)*
Type of place of residence	
Rural	100
Urban	0
Source of drinking water	
Unsafe	61.5
Safe	38.5
Toilet facility	
No	100
Yes	0
Electricity Facility	
No	50
Yes	50
N	52

Correlates of Infant Mortality in Scheduled Tribes of M.P.

In order to substantiate the above findings and to find out probable correlation of between the selected household variables and the occurrence of infant mortality to the scheduled tribe women, a zero-order correlation analysis was performed (Table 4). To understand the relative risk of infant mortality vis-à-vis no infant mortality a logistic regression analysis was applied over the data. A set of selected household variables was regressed as independent variables. The results are shown in Table-5.

Zero-order Correlation Matrix

The Table 4 presents a matrix of zero-order correlation between the household variables and the infant mortality. It showed that the variables such as the place of residence and source of drinking water have got significant negative correlation with the infant mortality. Although the variables such as toilet facility and electricity facility also came out with negative correlation with the infant mortality, but they did not show this to a statistically significant level. It was found a condition almost always inherent in most of the social and demographic analysis that the potential predictor variables considered for this study have got some amount of inter-correlation between them.

Table 4: Zero Order Correlation Matrix among Infant Mortality and Household Variables

Variables	*Infant Mortality*	*Place of residence*	*Source of drinking water*	*Type of Toilet facility*	*Electricity Facility*
Infant Mortality	1.000				
Place of residence	-0.076*	1.000			
Source of drinking water	-0.076*	0.218*	1.000		
Type of toilet facility	-0.052	0.407*	0.175*	1.000	
Electricity Facility	-0.023	0.230*	0.261*	0.166*	1.000
N	667	667	667	667	667

* Correlation is significant at 95 % Confidence interval (2-tailed).

Logistic Regression Analysis

To work out the sole effect of each of the household variables on the infant mortality (dependant variable), a multivariate analysis was carried out. As the variable infant mortality is dichotomous in nature, hence a logistic regression was applied over the data. The Table 5 presents the summary result of the regression analysis. It was found that the odds of the infant death to women (ratio of those who lost vis-à-vis those who did not) was found to be lower in case of the women lived in urban areas in comparison to those lived in rural areas. This means that the likelihood of infant deaths is more in rural area. Likewise the relative risk of getting infant deaths are less when the drinking water is used from safe sources such as hand pump and pipe etc. It was found from the result that the probability of infant death is higher for the people who had not any toilet facility. In case of the variable, electric facility, a contradictory result was found, however it was not found statistically significant. A higher odds value of infant deaths was observed in case of the availability of electric facility.

Only the result for the variable, source of drinking water came out with a lower level of significance. Although the tested household variables could explain the variability of infant mortality to a smaller extent, it could be give some specific idea about the nature of differential impact of the variables on the infant death.

Table 5: Correlates of Infant Mortility* (Summary Result of Logistic Regression)

Background Variables	*Beta-coeff.*	*Odds Ratio*	*Sig.-T*
Type of place of residence			
Rural **			
Urban	- 6.2023	0.0020	0.6679
Source of drinking water			
Unsafe **			
Safe	- 0.4446	0.6411	0.1437
Toilet facility			
No **			
Yes	- 5.4107	0.0045	0.7796
Electricity Facility			
No **			
Yes	0.0796	1.0829	0.7886

Summary:

Total Number of selected cases:	667
Initial Log Likelihood Function	
-2 Log Likelihood :	365.19719
Method:	Enter
-2 Log Likelihood :	354.398
Cox & Snell - R squared :	0.016
Nagelkerke - R squared :	0.038
Constant :	- 2.2297

* **Dependent variable:** Infant Mortility:
No Infant Mortality = 0, Infant Mortality = 1
** **Reference Categories**

Conclusion

It is a grave fact that for last many decades, the infant mortality rate continues to be higher among the scheduled tribes of Madhya

Pradesh state. This paper has endeavoured to examine the possible influence of household factors on the infant mortality in the scheduled tribes of Madhya Pradesh. Some selected household characteristics such as source of drinking water, toilet facility, availability of electricity and place of residence (rural/urban) have been studied for the scheduled tribe women against the backdrop of the incidence of infant deaths. The data base studied here showed that majority of the scheduled tribe women has experienced some amount of child (infant) loss, and most of the women live in rural area and do not have toilet facility. Around half of all scheduled tribe women in Madhya Pradesh do not have access to safe drinking water and electricity facility.

Bivarite analysis (cross tabulation and correlation) showed that majority of the infant deaths have occurred to the women deprived of these basic household facilities and those lived in rural area. To find out the relative risk of infant deaths attributed to varied household conditions, a logistic regression analysis have been carried out. This also depicted a similar picture as the bivariate analyses, such as, the likelihood of getting infant deaths were lower for the women who have access to safe drinking water and toilet facility and those lived in rural area, except for the variable, electric facility. Although the magnitude of cumulative influence by the selected household variables was observed to be small, it certainly gives the nature of variability in infant death by the former. From the whole study, both from the bivariate as well as multivariate analyses, it was observed that the variable, "safe drinking water" showed consistent negative impact on the incidence of infant death. It gives an impression that, probably, intervention on this particular variable may bring down the infant mortality of the scheduled tribes of Madhya Pradesh to some extent.

REFERENCES

Bose, A. 1991. Demographic Diversity of India 1991 census. B.R. Publishing Corporation, New Delhi.

Gandotra, M.M. and Das, N. 1988. Infant Mortality: An analysis of recent births in Gujarat. In: Jain, A.K. and Visaria, P. (eds.): Infant Mortality in India. Sage Publications, New Delhi.

Govt. of India, Family Welfare Year Book: 1987-88, New Delhi.

Hiralal, R. B. and Russel, R.V. 1975. Tribes and Castes of the Central Provinces of India. Cosmo Publication, vol-3, New Delhi.

Jain, A. K. 1988. Determinants of Regional Variations in Infant Mortality in Rural India. In: Jain, A.K. and Visaria, P. (eds.): Infant Mortality in India. Sage Publications, New Delhi , pp. 127.

Kanitkar, T. and Murthy, B.N. 1988. Factors associated with Infant Mortality in Rajastan and Orissa. In: Jain, A.K. and Visaria, P. (eds.) Infant Mortality in India. Sage Publications, New Delhi, pp. 327.

Nanda, S. and Stephenson, R. 2001. Household Environment and Infant Mortality in India: A State Level Analysis with Special Focus to Orissa. Journal of Human Ecology, 12: 81-86

Nanda, S. and Ram, F. 2000. Teenage Motherhood, Child Survival and Child Health, International Women's Conference "Women's Status: Vision and Reality", New Delhi, Feb. 27- Mar. 3, 2000 (Conducted by McMaster University, Canada).

Nanda, S. et al. 1999. Utilisation of Antenatal Care (ANC) service by Scheduled Tribes in India. Journal of Human Ecology, 10: March.

Chapter 7

Some Factors Associated with Infant Mortality at District Level in Madhya Pradesh

S. N. Dwivedi

In India, a large number of important programs like Mother and Child Health Care (MCHC), Integrated Child Development Services (ICDS), and Universal Immunization Programs (UIP), regarding the health care of children, have been established. But, India still has high infant mortality. Also, the infant mortality rate (IMR) varies from one administrative unit (state/ district) to other administrative unit on a large scale. Therefore, the general question may be as to why IMR should differ from one to other administrative unit when the organizational set up for controlling infant mortality is almost same in all the units. This has attracted the attention of the concerning scientists for a long time. A number of studies, considering data from either SRS, Census or other large scale surveys or small scale surveys, have been attempted to know the reasons for the changing infant mortality. Some of them (Preston and Bhat, 1984; Pathak et al., 1989) are based on simply empirical evidences at state level or district level where as some of them (Dwivedi et al., 1990) have used appropriate techniques to study possible factors contributing to such changes. Dwivedi et al, (1990) utilized state level data and reported that the birth rate and the expenditure on health directly and indirectly both and literacy rate indirectly described the variations in infant mortality. Almost similar results were observed by Dwivedi and Singh.

Madhya Pradesh (M.P.) is situated in Central India and bounded on all sides by other states. M .P. is the largest state covering the largest area in the country and it has 45 districts. It has the largest population of scheduled tribes and a higher proportion of the scheduled caste. Together, these underprivileged constitute nearly one-third of the total population of M.P. Twenty three districts of M.P. are predominantly tribal. The economy of M.P. is primarily agricultural. Nearly 77 per cent of the population live in villages. M.P. is very rich in natural resources like iron, manganese, coal, limestone and tin. The infant mortality rate (IMR) in Madhya Pradesh (M.P.) has been always higher than the national level. Even currently, in the year 1989, it was 117 for M.P. and 91 for the India. Moreover, between the districts, wide variations are found. In this paper, an attempt is made to study reasons for high and low IMRs in various districts of M.P. based on empirical data available. Also, correlation and regression analyses were used as an attempt to know the available important factors at district level, which contribute in describing the changing level of the IMR.

Materials and Methods

The data pertain to 45 districts of Madhya Pradesh. These regarding infant mortality rate (IMR) and crude birth rate (CBR) for the year 1981; urban population percentage for the year 1991; percentage literacy, percentage S.C. population, percentage S. T. population and percentage Muslim population for the year 1981; number of village health guides per lakh population, number of hospitals per ten lakh population and number of sub-centres per lakh population for the year 1988, were considered in analysis. Since very few variables were reported at district level for the same year, different variables considered in the study relate to different points of time. This factor does not matter very much in relationship studies involving correlation and regression analysis. However, attempt was made to consider the data available for the closest year. The data were taken from Compendium of Madhya Pradesh Statistics (1989): Directorate of Economics and Statistics, Madhya Pradesh; Registrar General and Census Commissioner Report - Provisional population totals: Rural-Urban distribution, Paper-2 of 1991, New Delhi; and Census of India

(1981) – Occasional paper No.7 (1989): Fertility and child mortality estimates of M .P.

Considering IMR for the year 1981, out of all 45 districts of M.P., first group may be of those districts (16) whose IMR is higher to that of M.P. (IMR > 160). Second group may be of those districts (16) whose IMR is close to M.P. (140 < IMR < 160). Likewise, third group may be of those districts (13) whose IMR is below to M.P. (IMR < 140). Group-specific as well as irrespective of group, correlation and regression analysis (Kleinbaum et al., 1988; Neter et al., 1989) of data were carried out using BMDP package (Dixon, 1985).

The regression analysis used "best" subsets algorithms in which the "best" subsets according to a specified criterion are identified without requiring the fitting of all the possible subset regression models (Kleinbaum et al., 1988; Neter et al., 1989). The model including all variables under analysis is known as complete/ maximum model where as that including variables under a "best" subset is known as best model. The significance of correlation and regression coefficients was assessed using t-tests. The significance level was considered at less than or equal to 5 per cent.

Results

As presented in Table-l, out of all 45 districts of M.P., 16 districts were under first group whose IMR is higher to that of M.P. as well as of national (IMR > 160). Another 16 districts were under second group whose IMR is close to, M.P. Interestingly, each district in this group also has IMR higher than national level (140 < IMR < 160). Likewise, each of third group of remaining 13 districts has IMR below to M.P. It may however be mentioned that first seven of them have IMR above national level (120 < IMR < 140) whereas next four districts have IMR close to national level (100 < IMR < 120). However, remaining last two districts have IMR less than national level (IMR < 100). It is found that mainly districts in Sagar, Rewa, Hoshangabad and Jabalpur divisions experienced higher IMR (above the state level), where as, districts in Bhopal, Gwalior, Raipur, Bilaspur, Jabalpur and Ujjain divisions experienced IMR closure to that of state but higher than national level. Districts in Chambal and Ujjain divisions experienced IMR below state level but above the national level. One district from

Table 1: Socio-economic and Developmental Indicators for M.P. and Its Districts

	Indicators									
	1	2	3	4	5	6	7	8	9	10
M.P. (661.4)	150	38.0	23.20	27.87	14.01	23.0	4.80	50.88	12.35	13.57
(A) Districts with IMR higher than the state average (IMR>160)										
Shivpuri (11.3)*	179	41.6	15.20	20.51	19.20	10.0	2.75	80.53	9.73	15.75
Tikamgarh (9.4)	195	44.5	16.90	19.16	21.70	4.2	2.96	71.70	7.45	15.74
Chhatarpur (11.6)	182	42.2	19.28	20.31	22.90	3.4	3.70	54.31	12.05	11.12
Panna (6.9)	185	45.5	13.07	19.51	20.40	14.1	3.52	67.39	10.15	11.59
Sagar (16.5)	164	43.2	29.22	34.26	20.80	8.7	3.30	53.70	6.67	13.58
Damoh (9.0)	189	42.9	18.15	29.99	20.50	12.0	3.52	66.67	8.89	11.78
Satna (14 .6)	181	41.2	19.75	26.84	16.40	13.7	0.30	48.97	8.22	10.96
Rewa (15.5)	173	40.6	15.27	25.21	13.70	12.0	0.40	62.84	7.10	10.58
Shahdol (17.4)	164	35.6	21.12	19.41	7.10	47.4	0.37	48.22	16.67	15.92
Sidhi (13.7)	161	38.7	6.47	14.96	10.80	31.3	0.25	40.44	11.68	14.60
East Nimar (14.3)	161	39.7	27.51	30.60	10.70	25.7	13.25	55.32	9.79	11.05
Rajgarh (9.9)	170	39.0	16.81	26.28	10.70	48.5	0.86	57.88	40.40	35.86
Jabalpur (26.5)	188	35.0	45.53	41.02	12.20	17.4	5.59	38.94	6.04	8.00
Hoshangabad(12.7)	163	40.9	27.44	35.35	15.60	16.0	4.45	50.47	10.24	10.47
Narsimhapur (7.8)	162	36.9	14.88	33.23	15.60	12.9	0.21	51.80	11.54	10.38
Balaghat (13 .6)	193	34.3	9.52	34.00	7.20	21.8	2.25	69.56	11.76	13.75

(B) Districts with IMR close to that of M.P. (140<IMR<160)

	1	2	3	4	5	6	7	8	9	10
Datia (4.0)	156	40.0	22.63	27.20	24.60	1.4	3.64	67.75	10.00	14.00
Guna (13.1)	150	42.0	19.51	21.59	18.20	11.0	4.15	76.87	8.40	14.28
Ratlam (9.7)	143	38.2	31.88	29.46	14.00	21.5	10.19	40.10	11.34	10.21
Shajapur (10.3)	149	38.5	17.70	23.65	22.10	2.2	9.94	49.51	7.77	12.04
Jhabua (11.3)	144	42.7	8.65	10.99	8.30	83.5	2.27	28.76	24.78	18.05
Vidisha (9.7)	144	43.4	20.08	25.43	20.40	4.3	9.72	38.76	11.34	11.24
Betul (11.8)	158	40.7	18.71	27.95	10.50	36.2	2.15	41.10	18.64	16.19
Sehore (8.4)	146	40.8	18.00	23.28	20.30	9.1	9.64	49.17	5.95	11.07
Raisen (8.8)	157	42.6	15.88	23.01	16.70	15.4	8.84	57.27	10.23	11.70
Mandla (12.9)	153	33.6	7.67	22.92	5.30	60.4	0.13	68.68	29.46	22.17
Seoni (10.0)	149	35.1	9.46	26.99	10.60	36.4	5.21	54.20	15.00	16.60
Bilaspur (38.0)	145	34.1	17.08	28.60	17.30	23.4	1.62	62.11	12.90	4.18
Raigarh (17.2)	156	37.2	9.59	18.17	17.80	3.0	5.82	30.87	6.40	6.34
Rajnandgaon(14.4)	159	35.5	15.75	26.63	9.40	25.3	0.20	60.28	11.80	13.26
Raipur (39.0)	141	34.4	19.75	30.81	13.80	18.6	0.57	60.54	8.72	12.56
Gwalior (14.2)	151	40.7	58.94	39.63	20.50	2.8	5.80	37.82	7.04	12.82

(C) Districts with IMR below to M.P. (IMR<140)

	1	2	3	4	5	6	7	8	9	10
Mandasaur (15.6)	138	38.3	23.08	31.22	15.60	5.2	8.19	30.26	7.69	9.49
Dewas (10.3)	134	37.8	25.86	26.35	18.20	13.8	9.76	44.95	8.74	9.81
West Nimar (20.3)	137	39.7	15.06	22.81	10.20	43.3	5.91	50.84	19.70	20.05
Chhindwara (15.6)	138	35.6	23.18	28.19	11.80	33.4	0.60	31.28	17.31	14.36
Durg (24.0)	137	34.4	35.37	37.95	11.80	12.6	0.42	47.04	8.75	10.46
Bhinda (12.1)	129	40.2	20.67	31.35	21.20	0.1	3.41	69.26	6.61	15.37
Morena (17.1)	132	44.6	20.54	25.60	20.10	5.3	3.95	73.22	7.60	15.32
Ujjain 13.9)	106	37.2	39.74	32.99	24.10	1.9	11.04	38.42	5.04	8.56
Dhar (13.7)	116	39.4	13.14	20.21	7.00	52.1	4.90	64.89	20.44	19.93
Surguja (20.8)	115	33.4	12.04	16.40	5.20	54.8	2.98	47.12	26.44	21.39
Bastar (22.7)	118	34.3	17.13	14.25	5.50	67.8	0.65	46.83	32.16	23.04
Indore (18 .3)	84	35.1	9.32	48.98	15.60	4.7	11.71	17.43	3.83	4.15
Bhopal (13.5)	91	39.7	0.10	55.46	12.60	2.3	23.40	14.22	1.48	2.89

Indicators

l:Infant mortality rate (IMR), 2:Crude birth rate (CBR), 3:Urban population percentage, 4:Percentage literacy, 5:Percentage S.C. population, 6:Percentage S.T. Population, 7:Percentage Muslim population, 8:Number of village health guides per lakh population, 9:Number of hospitals per ten lakh population, 10:Number of sub-centres per lakh population.

*: Figure in parenthesis represents population in lakhs(1991).

each of Ujjain, Indore, Bilaspur and Raipur divisions experienced IMR close to national level. Indore and Bhopal districts from Indore and Bhopal divisions respectively may be highly developed districts having IMR below national level. It may be noted that Indore division consists of one district from each of the first two groups of districts where as remaining three from the third group, one from each of its sub-categories (Appendix-I).

To be more specific, Shivpuri, Tikamgarh, Chhatarpur, Panna, Sagar, Damoh, Satna, Rewa, Shahdol. Sidhi, East Nimar, Rajgarh, Jabalpur, Hoshangabad, Narsimhapur, and Balaghat districts had IMR higher than the state average. On the other hand, Datia, Guna, Ratlam, Shajapur, Jhabua, Vidisha, Betul, Sehore, Raisen, Mandla, Seoni, Bilaspur, Rajgarh, Rajnandgaon, Raipur and Gwalior districts had IMR close to that of M.P. but higher than national level. The districts Mandasaur, Dewas, West Nimar, Chhindwara, Durg, Bhind, and Morena districts experienced IMR below to M.P. but above the national level, whereas, Ujjain, Dhar, Surguja and Bastar districts experienced IMR close to national level. Only two districts Indore and Bhopal had IMR below the national level.

Group wise correlation of IMR with all the nine predictor variables crude birth rate (CBR), urban population percentage (UPP), percentage literacy (PL), percentage S.C. population (PSC), percentage S. T. population (PST), percentage Muslim population (PMP), number of village health guides per lakh population (NVL), number of hospitals per ten lakh population (NHTL) and number of sub-centres per lakh population (NSCL), are given in Table-II. As evident from the results, the districts with high IMR have high CBR ($p < .05$). Similarly the districts with high IMR have low urban population percentage. The relationship between IMR and literacy percentage is not statistically significant ($p > .05$). However, majority of the districts having higher IMR have lower literacy rate. A majority of the districts where IMR is high, have lower concentration of Muslim population. None of the remaining variables were significantly associated with IMR ($p > .05$). As in case of all districts considered together, similar observations were true in third group of districts. Surprisingly not a single variable was significantly associated with IMR in first and second groups of districts.

Table 2: Group wise Correlation of IMR with Other Variables and Respective Critical Values at 5% Level of Significance

Group	*Correlation of IMR with the variables*									*Critical Values (+/ -)*
	CBR	*UPP*	*PL*	*PSC*	*PST*	*PMP*	*NV*	*NH*	*NSC*	
I	0.19	-.04	-.01	0.33	-.43	-.04	0.17	-.30	-.24	0.50
II	0.03	-.09	-.02	-.07	-.11	-.22	-.35	-.28	-.37	0.50
III	0.19	-.75	-.54	0.01	0.13	-.65	0.49	0.17	0.33	0.55
Total	0.33	-.46	-.28	0.15	-.10	-.48	0.03	-.20	-.15	0.29

Table 3: Group wise Estimates[a] along with R^2- Values and Standard Error of the Estimate

Group	*Regression Coefficient of the variables*										*Std. error of estimate*
	CBR	*UPP*	*PL*	*PSC*	*PST*	*PMP*	*NV*	*NH*	*NSC*	R^2	
I	-.63	-.41	0.08	1.44	-.15	-.07	0.04	0.91	-.10	0.31	16.09
II	0.34	-.08	0.13	-.50	-.29	-1.46⁺	aa	0.50	-.07⁺	0.72	4.60
III	1.71	-1.92	2.36	-.37	-.51	-.45	aa	1.49	-.15	0.82	13.52
Total	2.92⁺	-.61	.57	-.07	-.28	-2.91*	.02	.60	-.18	0.56	18.82

a: Respective Intercepts of the models are 163.43, 162.28, 63.01 and 80.74.

aa: These variables did not enter in the model because of collinearity. +: $p<0.05$; *: $p< 0.01$.

Results regarding maximum regression model, that is, considering all the nine predictor-variables together in the model, are presented in Table-III. Similar to correlation analysis, these results for irrespective of group also reveal that crude birth rate is significantly positively associated with IMR where as percentage Muslim population is negatively associated ($p < .05$) even after eliminating the effects of other variables. In group-II, percentage Muslim population was again *f* significantly negatively associated. But, in place of crude birth rate, number of village health guides per lakh population was found negatively associated. In groups I and III, none of the variables was significantly associated with IMR. Coefficient of determination (R-Square value) is increasing from first group of districts to third group of districts being 0.31, 0.72 and 0.82 respectively. Thus, it is clear that level of IMR variation explained by these nine indicators depends on the level of IMR. However, considering all the districts together, this value comes to be only 0.56.

Table 4: Group wise Best Model and Respective R-square value and standard error of the estimate

Group	Best mode	R^2	standard error of estimate
I	IMR = 182.96 + -.39 PST[a]	0.19	11.46
II	IMR = 167.62–.10PST[a]–1.57PMP–.04NSC	0.59	4.20
III	IMR = 111.53–1.71UPP+2.05PL	0.77	9.63
Total	IMR = 191.11–.49UPP–2.77PMP–.87NH	0.48	18.82

a: $p>0.05$.

The results related to best model, considering best set of predictor variables, are presented in Table-4. The results show that only proportion of S. T. population in first group; this along with proportion of Muslim population and number of sub-centres per lakh population in second group; and only urban population and literate population proportions in third group were included. But, in case of considering all districts together, urban and Muslim population proportions along with number of hospitals per ten lakh population were included in the best model. This may be noted that between the groups similar pattern was noticed in R-square values but every time, as obvious, it was less in comparison to that for respective maximum model. But, standard errors of estimate were smaller in comparison to those observed with maximum model.

Discussions

The correlation analysis revealed that the districts with high IMR have high CBR ($p < .05$). Similar findings have been reported under various micro as well as macro level studies (Talwar, 1985; Singh et al., 1986; Pathak et al., 1989; Dwivedi et al., 1990). Similarly the districts with high IMR have low urban population percentage. The relationship between IMR and literacy percentage is not statistically significant ($p > .05$). However, majority of the districts having higher IMR have lower literacy rate. Pathak et al., (1989) considering male literacy in district level data and using composite index of development as well as Dwivedi et al[3] considering state level data and using path analysis showed that literacy status plays an important role in reducing the infant mortality rate. A majority of the districts where IMR is high, have lower concentration of Muslim population. None of the remaining variables were significantly associated with IMR (IMR> .05). As in case of all districts considered together, similar observations were true in third group of districts. Surprisingly not a single variable was significantly associated with IMR in first and second groups of districts.

The complete model results for irrespective of group reveal that crude birth rate is significantly positively associated with IMR where as percentage Muslim population is negatively associated ($p < .05$). In group-II, percentage Muslim population was again significantly negatively associated. But, in place of crude birth rate, number of village health guides per lakh population was found negatively associated. In groups I and III, none of the variables was significantly associated with IMR. Coefficient of determination (R-Square value) is increasing from first group of districts to third group of districts being 0.31, 0.72 and 0.82 respectively. Thus, it is clear that level of IMR variation explained by these nine indicators depends on the level of IMR. However, considering all the districts together, this value comes to be only 0.56. This indicates that having wide variation among the district level data on IMR, some more appropriate factors closely responsible for IMR need to be included in the model.

The results related to best model show that only proportion of S. T. in first group; this along with proportion of Muslim population and number of sub-centres per lakh population in second group; and only urban population and literate population proportions in third group were included. But, in case of considering all districts together, urban and Muslim population proportions along with number of hospitals per ten lakh population were included in the best model. This may be noted that between the groups similar pattern was noticed in R-square values but every time it was less in comparison to that for respective maximum model. But, standard errors of estimate were smaller in comparison to those observed with maximum model. Getting almost different variables in the best models for three groups of districts, this may be concluded that to help the policy makers more properly it is always better to analyze the district level data categorizing them in various groups as per varying level of the IMR, that is, variable under study.

In summary, predictor variables change with the level of infant mortality rate. Moreover, variables included in the best models also change from first group of districts to third group. Therefore, this may be concluded that this analysis may be useful to the policy makers for taking proper action among different categories of districts based on the level of IMR. Thus, this may be recommended that region wise studies and proper analysis of data collected under them may be very useful to the policy makers. Instead of the obvious limitations of the macro level studies, they provide important clues to help the policy makers.

REFERENCES

Dixon, W.J. 1985. Chief Editor. BMDP Statistical Software Manual. University of California Press, California.

Dwivedi, S.N., Dubey, K.K. and Shukla, D.K. 1990. Variations in infant mortality and some associated factors. In: Rao, V.K. and Radhaiah, G.N. (eds): Statistics in Health and Nutrition. NIN, Hyderabad, pp. 252-255.

Dwivedi, S.N. and Singh, R. Some factors in describing state level variations in several mortality indices in India: Through Component Analysis. Annals of the National Academy of Medical Sciences (India), 30: 207-218.

Kleinbaum, D.G., Kupper, L.L. and Muller, K.E. 1988. Applied Regression Analysis and Other Multivariate Methods. 2nd ed. PWS-Kent Publishing Co., Boston , pp. 80- 339.

Neter, J., Washerman, W. and Kutner, M.H. 1989. Applied Linear Regression Models. Second ed. Boston Irwin, 433-533.

Pathak, K.B., Ram, F. and Sirigh, B.S. 1989. Child mortality in the districts of Madhya Pradesh. Mimeographed, IIPS, Bombay, 1-12.

Preston, S.H. and Bhat, P.N.M. 1984. New evidence on fertility and mortality trends in India. Population and Development Review, 10.

Singh, S.N., Dwivedi, S.N. and Singh, K.N. 1986. Trends in neo-natal and post-natal mortality rates in Varanasi (Rural), Centre of Population Studies, B.H.U., mimeographed, 1-7.

Talwar, P.P.1985. Inter-relationship between infant mortality and fertility: Some evidence from Indian Studies. In: Socio- cultural Determinants of Fertility, ICMR, mimeographed, 1-11.

Appendix-1

Division	*Districts*
Chambal	Morena, Bhind
Gwalior	Gwalior, Datia, Shivpuri, Guna
Sagar	Tikamgarh, Chhatarpur, Panna, Sagar, Damoh
Rewa	Satna, Rewa, Shahdol, Sidhi
Ujjain	Mandsaur, Ratlam, Ujjain, Shajapur, Dewas
Indore	Jhabua, Dhar, Indore, West Nimar, East Nimar
Bhopal	Rajgarh, Vidisha, Bhopal, Sehore, Raisen, Betul
Hoshangabad	Hoshangabad
Jabalpur	Jabalpur, Narsimhapur, Mandla, Chhindwara, Seoni, Balaghat
Bilaspur	Surguja, Bilaspur, Raigarh
Raipur	Rajnandgaon, Durg, Raipur, Bastar

Chapter 8

The Status of Reproductive and Child Health (RCH) among Scheduled Tribe Population in Madhya Pradesh: An Observation from NFHS Survey in 1992-1998-99

D. Dey

The 1994 ICPD at Cairo provided an international consensus on a new approach to policies to achieve population stabilization. The concept of new approach, Reproductive and Child Health (RCH) in keeping with the evolution of an integrated approach to the programmes aimed at improving the health status of young women and children, which has been going on in the country.

The RCH programme incorporates the components covered under the Child Survival and Safe Motherhood (CSSM) and Universal Immunization Programme (UIP). It includes two additional components, one related to Sexually Transmitted Diseases (STD) and the other relating to Reproductive Track Infection (RTI). In short the programme integrates all interventions of fertility regulation, maternal and child health with reproductive health of both men and women. The services to be provided is client centered, demand driven high quality and based on the needs of the community arrived at through decentralized participatory planning and the target free approach.

The RCH programme provides special efforts at improving the

out-reach of services particularly for the vulnerable groups of population, tribes, urban slums and adolescents who have till now substantially been left out of the planning process. In Madhya Pradesh, high proportion (28 %) of total population is tribe as compared to only 8 per cent for the country as a whole (according to 1991 census). In this paper an attempt has been made to study RCH status among scheduled tribe population in Madhya Pradesh based on two National Family Health Survey (NFHS) data. The first survey (NFHS-1) is carried out in 1992-93 and the second survey (NFHS-2) is administered in 1998-99.

Several key indicators of RCH like age of first cohabitation, proportion of births of order 4 and above, contraceptive prevalence rate (CPR), antenatal care, Institutional and safe delivery, children immunisation and nutritional status of women and children etc. for scheduled tribe population of Madhya Pradesh are presented in Table-1 to 8.

Age at consummation of marriage is relevant for fertility study. The two surveys of NFHS measured age at first cohabitation with husband, which is taken as a proxy for age at consummation of marriage. The median age at first cohabitation for women age 20-49 for scheduled tribe population in Madhya Pradesh is seen as 15.9 in 1992-93. Surprisingly it reduced further a 0.2 point to 15.7 during 1998-99.

Mean ideal number of children by ever-married women among scheduled tribes is seen as 3.4 in both the surveys. The ideal family size of 3.4 children in the second survey consists of 1.8 sons, 1.3 daughters, and 0.3 children of either sex. Forty-four per cent scheduled tribe women wanted more sons than daughters. Ideal family size for whole population in the state is seen as 2.9 (1.5 sons, 1.0 daughter, 0.3 children of either sex) in 1998-99. It is further noticed that the mean ideal family size increases with age. The second survey shows that the ideal number was 3.1 for scheduled tribe women age 15-24 as compared to 3.9 for women age 45-49 (figures not shown in the table).

The median age of first birth is 18.8. in 1992-93 and it reduced further to 17.7 in 1998-99. About 43 per cent of births born during last three years proceeding to 1998-99 are of higher order (4+). The corresponding proportion for whole population in the state is 35 per cent. Several studies show that children are at increased risk of dying if the interval between births is less than 24 months. Short birth intervals also adversely affect mothers' health. It is seen that one-quarter of all births among scheduled tribes occurred within 24 months. The proportion increased to 31 per cent in 1998-99. It seems that there is an urgent need to discourage births from high-risk mothers like births during teenagers or delivering 4th and higher order births or too close births. Discouraging births from high-risk mothers not only reduce fertility but also reduce maternal and infant mortality.

Total fertility rate (TFR) among scheduled tribe is seen as high as 4.05 in 1992-93 and 3.69 in 1998-99. The total wanted fertility (in case if all unwanted births are prevented) among tribes is 3.62 in the first and 2.83 in the second survey of NFHS. This means that even if all unwanted births could be eliminated, TFR is 12 per cent higher than replacement level of fertility (TFR, 2.1) among scheduled tribes of Madhya Pradesh in 1998-99. The TFR and wanted TFR for whole population of the state is 3.3 and 2.4 respectively.

Table-1 provides information on current use of family planning methods by currently married women among scheduled tribes of Madhya Pradesh. It is observed that a big chunk of currently married women (70 % in 1992-93 and 67 % in 1998-99) are not currently using any method of family planning. Non-users among whole population of the state are 56 per cent in 1998-99. Proportion of women currently using any modern method is found as 30 per cent in 1992-93. The proportion increased marginally by 5 per cent to 31 in 1998-99. As seen in other places, female sterilization dominates among different methods. The share of female sterilization in contraceptive prevalence has increased from 70 to 85 per cent from first survey to the second survey. Spacing methods (Pill, IUD, and Condom) are found neglected. Hardly, 2.2 per cent women in 1992-93 and 1 per cent in 1998-99 used any spacing method. Unmet need of family planning is seen as 19 per cent in 1992-93 and decreased by 25 per cent to 14.5 in 1998-99. This means that about 15 per cent of women are not currently using any method of family planning and at the same time either they don't want any child more or don't want at least for 2 years. It can be mentioned that the scheduled-tribe women have lowest (Sch. Tribe, 47% Sch. Caste, 56%, Other Backward Caste, 63%, Others, 72%) total demand of family planning (met and unmet need together) and only 69 per cent of the demand is satisfied (figures not shown in the table). If all of the women who say they want to space or limit their births were to use family planning, the contraceptive prevalence rate among scheduled tribes in the state would increase from 31 per cent to 46 per cent.

The neonatal, post-neonatal and infant mortality rates are found very high among scheduled tribes (Table-2). The three rates are seen as 60, 43, and 103 respectively in 1992-93 and 69, 32, and 101 during 1998-99. It is noticed that neonatal mortality increased by 15 per cent and post-neonatal mortality rate decreased by 26 per cent during the two-survey period. Consequently IMR reduced marginally by 2 per cent during the same period. The under-five mortality increased by 8 per cent from 167 in 1992-93 to 180 in 1998-1999. The infant and child mortality for whole population is also very high. The four rates, neonatal, post-neonatal, infant, and under-five mortality rates are seen as 60, 32, 93, and 145 respectively in 1998-99.

The vaccination of children against six serious but preventable diseases, namely, tuberculosis, diphtheria, pertussis, tetanus, poliomyelitis, and measles has been taken a decisive role in reducing morbidity, mortality and disabilities among children. It is seen that among scheduled tribes of Madhya Pradesh a high proportion (43 %) of children age 12-23 months did not receive any vaccination in 1992-93. Encouragingly the proportion reduced to 26 per cent in 1998-99. But, the proportion who are fully vaccinated decreased from 19 to 11 by 42 per cent during the two surveys (Table 3). For the state as a whole, 22 per cent received full vaccination and 14 per cent did not receive any vaccination in 1998-99.

Vitamin A deficiency among children is one of the most common nutrition deficiency disorders. Table-3 shows that less than one-fifth (18 %) of children age 12-35 months received at least one dose of Vitamin A in 1998-99. The corresponding proportion for the state is 24 per cent. It seems a large majority of children in Madhya Pradesh did not receive Vitamin A supplementation at all. Also, diarrhoea is one of the most important killer of children under age five. Deaths from diarrhoea are often caused by dehydration due to loss of water and electrolytes. Majority of dehydration related deaths can be prevented by prompt administration oral rehydration therapy (ORT). It is seen more than half of the children did not receive any of the types of oral rehydration therapies (ORT) when sick with diarrhoea. Oral rehydration salt (ORS) packets are given to one-third (34 % in 1998-99) of children age 1-35 months who suffered from diarrhoea during the two weeks preceding the survey.

Antenatal care (ANC) refers to pregnancy-related health care provided by a doctor or a health worker in a medical facility or at home. From Table-4 it can be seen that about three-fifth (59 % in 1992-93 and 56 % in 1998-99) of scheduled tribe women in Madhya Pradesh received no antenatal checkup. Sixty-two per cent of the scheduled tribe mothers did not receive any TT injection/syrup and 35 per cent did not receive IFA tablets/syrup in 1992-93. The corresponding figures for 1998-99 is 48 and 36 per cent respectively. It can be mentioned that non-compliance of TT injection reduced by 23 per cent and. non-compliance of IFA tablets/syrup increased by 3 per cent during the two-survey period.

Table-5 presents place of delivery, postpartum check-ups and initiation of breast-feeding among scheduled tribe women in Madhya Pradesh. It is seen that 90 per cent of the births (94 % in 1992-93 and 91 % in 1998-99) are delivered at home. For the state corresponding proportion is 79 per cent. Less than one-fifth of the deliveries (18 % in 1992-93 and 14 % in 1998-99) are only assisted by any health professional. Hardly 7 per cent of non-institutional births were followed by a check-up within two months of the delivery. Initiation of breast-feeding immediately after childbirth is important because it benefits both the mother and the infant. It is seen among scheduled tribes of Madhya Pradesh only 15 per cent of children started breast-feeding within one hour of birth. There is hardly any change in the proportion during the two-survey period.

Nutritional status of scheduled tribe women in Madhya Pradesh is observed poor as can be seen from Table-6. NFHS-2 collected weight and height data to calculate several indicators of women's nutritional status. A woman's height is used to identify women at risk of having a difficult delivery. Short stature (less than 145 cm.) is often related to small pelvic size. The Table shows that 11 per cent of ever married women among scheduled tribes are under 145 cm. in height. Another index, which is body mass index (BMI), relates a woman's weight to her height. It is used to assess both thinness and obesity. The BMI is defined as the weight in kilograms divided by the height in meters squared (Kg/m^2). Chronic energy deficiency is usually indicated by a BMI of less than 18.5. About half (49 %) of the tribal women have a BMI below 18.5 indicating a high prevalence of nutritional deficiency. In the whole population of the state corresponding proportion is 38 per cent.

Anaemia, which is characterized by a low level of hemoglobin in the blood, is generally referred as iron deficiency anemia. It is responsible for underlying cause of maternal and perinatal mortality. Measurements of anemic were taken in the field using HemoCue system. Seventy per cent of ever-married women among scheduled tribe population in Madhya Pradesh have some degree of anaemia. The corresponding proportion for the state is 54 per cent. It seems there is urgent need to undertake anaemia prevention programme (like iron-fortification programme) among scheduled tribe population in Madhya Pradesh.

The nutritional status among children is measured by three summary indices, weight-for-age, height-for-age and weight-for-height. The three indices of nutritional status are expressed in standard deviations units (Z-scores) from the median for the international reference population. Children who are more than two standard deviations below the reference median on any of the indices are considered to be undernourished. In case of the first index (weight-for-age) is called underweight. In case of the 2nd index (height-for-age) it is considered as stunted (short for their age). The percentage in this category indicates prevalence of chronic under-nutrition. In case of the third index (weight-for-height) it is considered too thin or wasted. The percentage in this category indicates the prevalence of acute under-nutrition. Table-7 shows that among scheduled tribes in Madhya Pradesh more than three-fifth of the children (61 % in 1992-93 and 64 % in 1998-99) are underweight. Further, NFHS-2 data shows that 60 per cent of the children age 3 years among scheduled tribes are stunted and 25 per cent are wasted. Also, more than four-fifths (84 %) of the children age 6-35 months have some degree of anaemia. The proportion of underweight, stunted, wasted, and anaemic children for the whole population in the state are 55, 51, 20, and 75 per cent.

The NFHS-2 data provided data on AIDS and reproductive health problem of women. AIDS is an illness, which weakens the immune system and leads to death through secondary infection such as tuberculosis and pneumonia. AIDS prevalence in our country are increasing in alarming proportion. The NFHS-2 data shows that only 5 per cent of the scheduled tribe women have heard about AIDS as can be seen from Table-8. The corresponding proportion for the state is 23 per cent. Further, among women who have heard about AIDS, 60 per cent do not know any way to avoid infection. It seems there is an urgent need to disseminate information about AIDS and means to avoid AIDS in the community. The table also shows that 43 per cent of currently married scheduled tribe women have at least one reproductive health problem related to vaginal discharge, urination or intercourse. There is need to educate women regarding the symptoms and consequences of reproductive health problems.

The study shows that reproductive and child health (RCH) status among scheduled tribe population in Madhya Pradesh is very poor. The population is characterized by high fertility and mortality and less use of family planning method. Antenatal and postnatal cares are dismissal. Nutritional status of women and children are very poor. Reproductive health problems are widespread in the community. Urgent steps are needed to improve their situation.

REFERENCES

International Institute for Population Sciences (IIPS) and ORC Macro. 2001. National Family Health Survey (NFHS-2), India, 1998-99, Madhya Pradesh. IIPS, Mumbai.

Population Research Centre, Directorate of Economics and Statistics, Bhopal (PRC, Bhopal) and International Institute for Population Sciences (IIPS). 1995. National Family Health Survey (MCH and Family Planning), Madhya Pradesh 1992-93. Bombay: PRC, Bhopal and IIPS.

Table 1: Fertility and Contraceptive Prevalence Indicators among Scheduled Tribe Population of Madhya Pradesh in 1992-93 and 1998-99

Characteristics	*NFHS-1 1992-93*	*NFHS-2 1998-99*	*Percentage Variation 1992-93 to 1998-99*
Median age at first cohabitation with husband among women age 20-49 years	15.9	15.7	-1.3
Mean ideal number of children	3.4	3.4	0.0
Median age at first birth among women 20-49 years	18.8	17.7	-5.9
Proportion of births during last three years of order 4 and above	-	42.6	-
Proportion of births during last five years having birth interval less than 2 yrs	24.9	30.8	23.7
Total fertility rate (TFR)	4.05	3.69	-8.9
Total wanted fertility rate	3.62	2.83	-21.8
Proportion of currently married women currently not using any modern method	69.8	67.1	-3.9
Proportion of currently married women currently using any modern method	29.5	31.1	5.4
Proportion of female sterilization in total contraceptive prevalence	70.2	84.8	20.8
Unmet need of family planning	19.2	14.5	-24.5

Table 2: Neonatal, Postneonatal, Infant, and Under-five Mortality Rates among Scheduled Tribe Population of Madhya Pradesh in 1992-93 and 1998-99

Characteristics	*NFHS-1 1992-93*	*NFHS-2 1998-99*	*Percentage Variation 1992-93 to 1998-99*
Neonatal mortality rate	60.2	69.4	15.3
Postneonatal mortality rate	42.9	31.7	-26.1
Infant mortality rate (IMR)	103.1	101.0	-2.0
Under-five mortality rate	166.6	179.6	7.8

Table 3: Childhood Vaccination, Vitamin-A Supplementation and Treatment of Diarrhoea among Scheduled Tribe Population of Madhya Pradesh in 1992-93 and 1998-99

Characteristics	*NFHS-1 1992-93*	*NFHS-2 1998-99*	*Percentage Variation 1992-93 to 1998-99*
Proportion of children age 12-23 months who are fully vaccinated	19.3	11.1	-42.5
Proportion of children age 12-23 months who have not received any vaccination	43.2	26.2	-39.4
Percentage of children age 12-35 months who received at least one dose of vitamin A	-	18.0	-
Percentage of children under age 3* who had diarrhoea in past two weeks received no oral rehydration therapy (ORT)	54.1	55.2	1.8

* under age 4 in 1992-93.

Table 4: Antenatal Check-ups among Scheduled Tribe Population of Madhya Pradesh in 1992-93 and 1998-99

Characteristics	*NFHS-1 1992-93*	*NFHS-2 1998-99*	*Percentage Variation 1992-93 to 1998-99*
Proportion of mothers having no antenatal check-up during the three* years preceding the survey	59.2	55.7	-6.3
Proportion of mothers not received any TT injection/syrup during the three years* preceding the survey	62.4	47.8	-23.4
Proportion of mothers not received IFA tablets/ syrup during the three years* preceding the survey	34.6	35.7	3.2

* during four years in 1992-93.

Table 5: Home and Safe Delivery, Postpartum Check-ups, and Initiation of Breast-feeding among Scheduled Tribe Women of Madhya Pradesh in 1992-93 and 1998-99

Characteristics	*NFHS-1 1992-93*	*NFHS-2 1998-99*	*Percentage Variation 1992-93 to 1998-99*
Proportion of Home delivery among births during the three* years preceding the survey	93.9	91.0	-3.1
Proportion of Delivery assisted by health professional (Doctor/ ANM/ LHV/ Nurse) during the three* years preceding the survey	18.4	13.9	-24.5
Proportion of non-institutional births during the three years* preceding the survey for which post-partum check-up was received within two months of birth	-	7.3	-

* during four years in 1992-93.

Table 6: Nutritional Status of Women among Scheduled Tribe Population of Madhya Pradesh in 1992-93 and 1998-99

Characteristics	*NFHS-1 1992-93*	*NFHS-2 1998-99*	*Percentage Variation 1992-93 to 1998-99*
Percentage of ever-married women with height below 145 cm.	-	10.9	-
Proportion of ever-married women with Chronic nutritional deficiency (BMI <18.5 Kg/m^2)	-	49.2	-
Proportion of ever-married women have some degree of anaemic	-	70.3	-

Table 7: Nutritional Status of Children among Scheduled Tribe Population of Madhya Pradesh in 1992-93 and 1998-99

Characteristics	*NFHS-1 1992-93*	*NFHS-2 1998-99*	*Percentage Variation 1992-93 to 1998-99*
Proportion of underweight children under age three* years	61.5	64.5	4.9
Proportion of Stunted (chronic undernutrition) children under age three years	-	59.9	-
Proportion of wasted (acute malnutrition) children under age three years	-	24.7	-
Proportion of children 6-35 months with anaemia	-	83.9	-

* under age four years in 1992-93.

Table 8: Knowledge about AIDS and Prevalence of Reproductive Health Problem of Women among Scheduled Tribe Population of Madhya Pradesh in 1992-93 and 1998-99

Characteristics	*NFHS-1 1992-93*	*NFHS-2 1998-99*	*Percentage Variation 1992-93 to 1998-99*
Proportion of ever-married women have knowledge about AIDS	-	5.2	-
Proportion of ever-married women having any reproductive health problem	-	42.8	-

Chapter 9

Reproductive and Child Health Status of the Underprivileged in Central India

F. Ram, U. Ram and D. Govil

Under various provisions, the constitution of India offers several rights to the people who have been isolated for centuries from the main stream. For instance, article 46 declares: "The State shall promote with special care educational and economic interests of the weaker sections of the people and in particular of Schedule Caste and Schedule Tribes, and shall protect them against all forms of social injustice and exploitation."

Health is (and must be) considered as the basic human right and not merely a social good. Thus health of an individual becomes most important in any human population and almost becomes a precondition for achieving efficient human resource development. More than half a century has elapsed since we attained independence, however, not much has been achieved in the area of health in general and for a larger proportion of the under privileged group in particular (such as Scheduled Castes and Tribes). This fact becomes even more important when we realize that many popular programs have been launched and implemented from time to time to address the special needs of these people at various levels. As is evident, all our past efforts have somehow not led to the better utilization of public services by this group of the population.

The life style, dietary pattern, social behavior as well as health behavior are prescribed by the deep-rooted traditions that are more pronounced amongst tribal populations where outside influences, education and urbanization are minimal (Chatterjee, 1993). Tribes in India are no exception to this. As we know, most tribes have their own distinct but unique, cultural milieu and life style. In addition to this they also have many deep routed practices of indigenous system of medicine (probably resulting into higher mortality levels and poor reproductive health of these people). In view of this, the task of improving their health status appears to be even more difficult to attain and remains a bigger challenge for programmers and mangers in the health sectors. Under the revised RCH approach[1], the Govt. of India has adopted decentralized process for planning various programs and is now using bottom to top approach based on the community need assessment. The revised approach is also seen as a holistic move where the needs of the local people occupy top rank in the priority list of the planners. In short, it can be said that the new RCH approach, in true sense, is made for the people, by the people and of the people. In the next stage, New Population Policy- 2000 (NPP-2000) was launched. The NPP-2000 document rightly identifies all the tribes as underserved groups. The document further emphasizes on need to provide special focus to address the social, economic and health status (particularly RCH) issues of these underserved. It is hoped that this would be an important step to bring them into the mainstream of the development process of the nation.

In view of the above background, in the present paper we attempt to explore the reproductive and health status of the tribal population in the undivided state of Madhya Pradesh (MP). It may be mentioned that, In India, tribal population constitutes around 8 per cent of the nation's total population. As per the 1991 census, the scheduled tribes were enumerated at about 67.76 million (excluding the state of Jammu and Kashmir, Census of India, 1991). Besides being the largest state in terms of population size, of the northern state, MP also had maximum share of tribal population in the state's total population

---

[1] In April 1996, Government of India after accepting the recommendations of the International Conference of Population and Development held at Cairo in 1994, made its family planning program target free.

(23.27 per cent) during 1991. It was thus decided to carry out the analysis for the state of MP. In the present paper, we therefore attempt to examine some of the issues related to the reproductive health of the women, children's health, family planning practices and incidence of reproductive tract infections among the SC an ST in MP.

The specific objectives of the present research are as below:

1. To understand overall social, demographic and health scenario of the SC and ST;
2. To study the levels of utilization of various reproductive and child health services including ante-natal, natal and post-natal care, reproductive morbidity, vaccination, incidence of diarrhea and pneumonia amongst the SC and ST;
3. To study the contraceptive uses by the SC and ST;
4. To study the prevalence of selected reproductive tract infections amongst SC and ST; finally
5. To examine the differentials in the utilization of RCH including contraceptive practices across SC and ST.

Before starting the analysis we would like to mention that the analysis in the present paper is carried out separately for state as a whole and separately for the selected 14 districts in the state. The paper also attempts to understand the possible explanations for poor coverage of the reproductive and child health care coverage in these groups. Further, we would like to state that the selection of the district for the present analysis was purposive. The districts were selected on the basis of the relative share of the ST Population in the total population of the districts in 1991. It was decided to include only those districts where percentage of ST population was 25 per cent or more. Fourteen of the 43 districts in the state fulfill this criterion and all of them have been included in our analysis.

Data Sets Used and their Limitation

The data for the present analysis has been taken from the two sources. For the state level analysis, data is taken from the National Family Health Survey-I and II for the State of MP (popularly known as NFHS I and NFHS II). For the district level analysis data is taken from the Reproductive and Child Health – Rapid Household Surveys (known as RCH-RHS) of the respective district. It may be mentioned that the information in National Family and Health Survey I and II were conducted during 1992-93 and 1998-99 respectively. The data in NFHS I and II was collected form the ever married women in age group 13-49 years. In all, a total of 6254 and 6941 women were interviewed in the NFHS I and II respectively. Out of the total interviewed women in NFHS I, about 7 per cent were SC and 26.8 per cent were ST. The corresponding figures for NFHS II were 15 and 27 per cent respectively. As may be clear, the Schedule Castes were proportionately less in the sample in comparison of ST Sample and hence it becomes difficult to say if they represent the SC population of the state. This warrants for some amount of caution while drawing any inferences on certain parameters for the SC's and should be kept in mind throughout the paper. The RCH-RHS surveys were conducted during 1998-99 and the information was obtained from about 1000 households from each of the district.

State Level Analysis

The analysis in this section is based on the data drawn from the NFHS I and II for the MP. The relevant data on this section is presented in Tables 1 through 5.

Profile of the SC and ST

Table 1 gives the data on the selected indicators of social, demographic and health status of the SC and ST population in Madhya Pradesh. It may be seen that out of the total households and women contacted in NFHS I, the share of SC and ST was more or less similar at about 7 and 27 per cent. In NFHS II too, the per cent of SC and ST households as well as women was similar at about 16 and 23 per cent respectively. As one would expect, very few of the SC and ST women were literate. The per cent of literate women in SC was about 18 per cent during 1992-93, which increased marginally to nearly 20 per cent during 1998-99. The literacy rate among women was even lower for ST women during both the periods (9 and 14 per cent respectively).

With respect to the fertility indicators it may be seen that the total fertility rate (TFR, average number of children per woman) for

SC declined from 4.71 during 1992-93 to 3.87 during 1998-99 (decline by 0.84 children per woman in about 6 years). The corresponding decline was slower for the ST (0.36) from 4.05 to 3.69 children per woman. The data also reveals that the mean number of children ever born (CEB) to the ever-married women (EMW) aged 40-49 too was higher for the SC as compared to the ST (approximately 5.7 as against of 5.0 in 1992-93 and 1998-99). It may be pointed here that the couple protection rate (CPR) was also higher among SC as compared to the ST during both the periods and also the improvement in CPR levels were slightly rapid for SC.

Coming to the mortality indicators, it may be seen that the Infant Mortality Rate (IMR) is high for both SC and ST (well over 100 infant deaths per 1000 live births). The IMR was 124 for SC and 103 for ST during 1992-93, which declined to approximately 101 for both SC and ST during the next six years, indicating that the gap between the two has virtually disappeared. Contrary to this, the levels of child mortality were very different in both groups. For example, the CMR was 50 for SC and 71 for ST during 1992-93, gap of about 20 points, which widened during 1998-99 (26 points).

The data also indicates that the per cent of women with two living children and do not desire any additional child, was more or less similar in both the groups, particularly in 1992-93 (about 38 per cent). However, during 1998-99 this proportion increased marginally for ST whereas the increase was relatively more for SC (almost half of the SC and 42 per cent of ST women with two living children did not want any additional child).

It is interesting to note that although SC's had higher levels of CPR, the gaps between actual and wanted fertility for SC too were relatively high. For example, wanted fertility for SC was lower by almost one child than the actual fertility during both periods. The corresponding gaps though initially were narrower among ST they had widened over time (from less than 0.5 child to 0.9 child in six years). The data on the fertility preference indicates that, on an average, both SC and ST women prefer to have more sons than daughters. Further, reported number of desired sons and daughters seem to be quite similar in both the groups.

Some of the studies carried out in the past have revealed that majority of the women belonging to the lower socio economic strata of the society have relatively poor nourishment levels (Ghosh, 1987). It has also been found that within the household, food is distributed more in accordance with the status and position of the individuals than their nutritional requirements (women and female children usually receiving the leftovers). The data given in the table 1 too seem to support this finding since about half of the SC women and nearly 70 per cent of ST women during 1998-99 had some type of anemia.

Utilization of RCH Services by the Women

Antenatal, Natal and Post Natal Care

The Table 2 gives relevant data on the selected indicators of ante natal (ANC), natal (NC) and post natal care (PNC). It may be mentioned here that the data for NFHS I refers to all the live births during the four years preceding the survey whereas in NFHS II, it refers to the all births during the three years period preceding the survey date.

It may be noticed that in about 43 per cent and 59 per cent of the cases among SC and ST respectively mothers did not receive ANC. Though the corresponding figures declined during next 6 years they were still remain at the unacceptably higher levels, particularly for the ST since 37 per cent of them during 1992-93 and about 56 per cent during 1998-99 mothers did not receive ANC. In the remaining cases, majority of the mothers received ANC at the institution from either doctor or trained health professional. Nonetheless, there were about 14 and 20 per cent of the mothers in SC and ST during 1992-93 who received ANC at home from the health worker(s). Interestingly, share of mother received ANC at home declined marginally to 10 per cent for SC and to about 12 per cent among ST (indicating more rapid decline by about 8 per cent points in 6 years).

With regards to various components of ANC, the data reveals that about 62 per cent of ST women in 1992-93 did not receive TT Injection, which came down to 48 per cent during 1998-99. In case of SC, the share of mother with no TT injection declined from 49 per cent to around 30 during the same period. Only about 45 to 49 per cent of SC mothers and 35 to 36 per cent of the ST mother were distributed iron and folic acid (IFA) tablets, reflecting very moderate improvement indeed. It may thus be concluded that the ANC coverage in the study populations continues to be at rather lower levels.

Table 2 also includes data on the place of delivery and type of assistance received in case of home deliveries. Few observations may be made from the data. Firstly, majority of the deliveries in the study population took place at homes (81 to 84 per cent among SC and as high as 93-94 per cent among ST). In other words, only about 7 per cent of the deliveries among ST and about 15 per cent or so among SC occurred in institutions, primarily in the public institutions. Secondly, the per cent of institutional deliveries was slightly higher for SC than it was for ST. Thirdly, majority of the home deliveries in both the groups were attended by an untrained person (generally by relatives). For example, only about one-third of the total home deliveries among SC during 1992-93 and about a quarter of them during 1998-99 was attended by a trained health professional. Further, the per cent of home deliveries assisted by a trained person was even lower for the ST (18 and 14 per cent respectively). Lastly, though the per cent of home deliveries conducted by untrained person has declined during the six years for both the groups, they still continue to be at high level. Only in about one-tenth of the cases during 1998-99 for SC and about 7 per cent in ST mothers came for postnatal care.

Family Planning Practices

Table 3 shows the family planning use by the currently married women from both the surveys. In the same table we have also included data on the unmet need for the family planning as stated by the women at the time of survey. Also the data on the selected reproductive morbidity (namely, urinary tract infection and abnormal vaginal discharge) is also included in the same table.

Broadly speaking, the data on per cent of current users hardly show any variation across the two groups as well over time. Nevertheless, per cent of FP users (mainly sterilization users) has increased marginally (from 33 to 38 per cent for SC and from 30 to 33 per cent for ST). Further, the extent of total unmet need of family planning services revealed that the availability and accessibility of these services remain far from the reach of the women as about 21 and 19 per cent for SC and ST women during 1992-93 reported having unmet need. However, the extent of unmet need appeared to have declined slightly over time (to 19 and 15 in six years). The further break-up of unmet need by that for limiting and spacing indicated that the extent of unmet need for limiting[2] and spacing[3] was more or less similar.

In case of reproductive morbidity, it can be observed that little less than a quarter of the surveyed women reported positive symptoms of urinary tract infection. Nearly one-third of the women in both the groups were also reportedly suffered from the vaginal discharge.

Utilization of Child Care Services

Table 4 provides the information on the immunization status of the children aged 12-23 months at the time of survey. Though there is no clear pattern as such emerging from the data in this table as far as the immunization coverage among the children, few broad observations may be made. First and foremost, about 43-45 per cent of the SC/ST children did not receive any vaccination during 1992-93. However, the corresponding per cent declined drastically during 1998-99 to as low as 12 per cent for SC children whereas it remained at a relatively higher levels (26 per cent) for ST. Secondly, the proportion of children who received complete immunization (that is BCG, all three doses of DPT/OPV and measles) declined over time from 25 per cent to 18 per cent for SC and from 19 to 11 per cent for ST. Nonetheless, the per cent of children with complete immunization is higher for SC than ST at both the points of time. It may thus be said that relatively higher proportions of the SC children than the ST children during both the periods received complete vaccination and also the gaps between the two groups have remained at more or less similar levels (difference of 6 to 7 per cent).

---

[2] The unmet need for limiting is the demand for family planning methods by women who are neither pregnant nor ammenohric and are not using any family planning method and who do not want to have any more children in the future.

[3] The unmet need for spacing is the need for family planning methods by women who are neither pregnant nor ammenohric and are not using any family planning method and they want to wait two or more years for their next birth, or unsure about it.

Thirdly, the per cent of children who received individual vaccines was always higher for SC than the ST. Further, the data indicated wider coverage over time for both the groups as far as the per cent of children received BCG is concerned. The data also revealed that during 1992-93, the gaps between per cent of children received DPT 1, DPT 2 and DPT 3 were relatively narrower for SC (ranging between 41 to 50 per cent) whereas it was much wider in case of ST (ranging between 29 to 50 per cent). In other words, it appears that the SC children who received DPT 1 had greater chances of getting DPT 2 and DPT 3 whereas it was not so in case of the ST children. Contrary to this, fewer children (both SC and ST) seem to have received the subsequent doses to DPT in NFHS II as compared to the NFHS I. This observation becomes important in view of the fact that the per cent of SC children who received first DPT dose was higher in during 1998-99 than it was 6 years back. Similar observations may be made for Polio 1, 2 and 3 as well. Lastly, per cent of SC children received measles remained at the same level during 1992-93 to 1998-99 (in the vicinity of one-third). In case of the ST children, per cent children received measles during 1998-99 actually declined to almost half the level of 1992-93 (from 35 per cent to just about 19 per cent).

Anemia and Diarrhea and Pneumonia among Children

It should be mentioned that the data on anemia is available only for 1998-99. The data in the Table 5 clearly brings out that majority of SC and ST children in the state suffered from anemia during 1998-99; the situation was more serious in later. As may be noted out of every 10 children, 7 among SC and 8 among ST children were found to be suffering from any type of anemia (that is mild to severe). Further, majority of the children suffered from moderate type of anemia.

With regards to the incidence of diarrhea and pneumonia, the incidence of diarrhea seem to have increased significantly from 4-6 per cent during 1992-93 to 30 per cent in SC and 26 per cent in ST during 1998-99. Similarly, the levels of pneumonia too seem to have gone up during the same period for both the groups of children (from 7-8 per cent in during 1992-93 to about 23-25 per cent in the next six years).

District Level Analysis

The analysis in this section is taken from Rapid Household Survey under Reproductive and Child Health (often referred as RHS-RCH) conducted during 1998-99 in the 505 districts in all India. However, for the convenience of the reader we would refer to it as RHS in the analysis to follow. For our paper we have taken the data for the districts of the Madhya Pradesh. The analysis in this section is restricted to only fourteen districts in the state for the reasons mentioned earlier.

Profile of the SC and ST

Table 6 provides the data on the share of SC and ST population to the district's total population from 1991 census along with the share of SC-ST households and eligible women in the RHS in the total sample. As may be seen from the data that the per cent share of the SC in the district's total population during 1991 varied from a lowest of 3 per cent in the Jhabua districts to the high of 12 in the Chhindawara district. The corresponding range for the ST is 25 per cent in Rajanandgaon district to 86 per cent in Jhabua district. Coming to the distribution of households in RHS it may be noted that out of the approximately 1000 sample the per cent of SC households varied from a lowest of about 5 per cent in Jhabua and Bastar to 16 to 17 per cent in East Nimar, Seoni and Sidhi. Nevertheless, the range of per cent ST population varied from a lowest of about 14.5 per cent in Shahdol to as high as over 82 per cent in Jhabua. The same Table also encompasses the data on the share of eligible women from SC and ST in the total sample. It may be mentioned that the observations on this are very similar to the one mentioned for household population.

The female literacy rates and the mean number of children ever born (CEB), children surviving (CS) and children dead (CD) to the women aged 15-44 years of age for the selected districts is provided in Table 7. It is interesting to note that the female literacy rates vary widely across the districts. For example, only just about 5-7 per cent of the SC females in Raigarh and Sidhi were literate. On the other hand, in Betul and Chindwara nearly half of the SC females were literate. The literacy levels amongst ST women too varied substantially across the districts, though the levels were much lower than they were for SC women. As may be seen, 80 per cent or more of the ST women in the selected districts were illiterate. As a matter of fact, in 6 of the districts (Sidhi, Jhabua, West Nimar, Dhar, Bastar and Shahdol) 9 in every 10 ST women were illiterate. It may be mentioned that there is no clear pattern in the female literacy levels and the share of the SC-ST women in the district. In other words, we do not necessarily see better female literacy levels of SC women in the districts with higher share of SC women or vice versa. Similarly for ST women, literacy levels are not necessarily better in the districts with higher share of ST women.

It may be observed that out of the 14 districts, in as many as 8 districts mean number of CEB for SC women was 3 or more children whereas in the remaining 6 districts it was very close to 3 children per woman. In case of ST there were only four districts (namely Raigarh, Mandla, Chhindwara and Bastar), the mean number of CEB was less than three and it was well over three for rest of the districts. There were only four districts in which mean CEB was higher for SC than ST. It is important to note that the mean number of children dead was one child or more for SC in Jhabua. Incidentally, the district has relatively high mean CEB (4.4). Once again the mean number of children dead (CD) was approximately one or more child in Jhabua and here too the mean CEB was rather high (4.3 children per woman). Interestingly the mean number of CD was either zero or negligible for SC and ST in Shahdol (the district also has relatively lower mean number of CEB).

Utilization of RCH Services by the Women

Antenatal Care (ANC)

Table 8 gives data related to ANC availed by the women during her last pregnancy that occurred during three years period preceding the survey date and ended either as stillbirth or live birth. The data in Table 8a reveals that a large number of SC and ST women did not receive any antenatal care. It is unbelievable to note that over 95 per cent of the SC women in Sidhi did not receive any ANC. In case of the other districts, except for Betul, the share of SC women who did not receive any ANC varied from about one-third in East Nimar and

Dhar to 60 per cent or so in Raigarh and Jhabua districts. Once again Sidhi seem to be lagging behind terribly as far as the per cent ST women with no ANC is concerned (almost 9 in every 10 ST women in the district did not receive any ANC). Further, nearly 42 to 79 per cent of the ST women in other districts did not receive any ANC. In fact, the per cent share of ST women with no ANC was well over 60 for as many as 8 districts. It may thus be concluded that in majority of instances the per cent of women with no ANC was quite high for both SC and ST women. However, the situation was relatively better in case of the former (out of 14 districts in the analysis, per cent with no ANC was lower for SC than ST in as many as 12 districts whereas in one district, namely Mandla they were similar and in Sidhi it was higher for SC).

The data suggests that many women (SC as well as ST) received ANC at homes from the health workers. For example, the per cent of SC women who received ANC from the health workers was 10 per cent in Jhabua and 20 per cent or so in Raigarh, Seoṇi and Dhar. In case of the remaining districts, it was between 36-37 per cent in Betul, East Nimar and Shahdol to as high as 75 per cent in Sidhi. On the other hand, the per cent women who received ANC from the health workers at home was lowest in Rajnandgaon (28 per cent) and was close to 50 per cent for most of the districts whereas it was highest in Bastar (over 78 per cent).

One distinct feature emerging from the data on place of ANC is that despite variations, large proportion of the pregnant women (both SC and ST) in majority of the districts received ANC at their homes from the health workers. The data further reveals that in relatively larger proportions of the ST women than SC received ANC at home from the health workers in as many as 11 districts. However, the gap was unusually wide in districts such as Jhabua, Bastar, Dhar, Raigarh and Seoni. On the other hand they were of smaller order in the remaining districts whereas in Chhindwara proportion of women with ANC at home from health worker was relatively higher for SC. It is also noted that the corresponding gaps between the two groups were negligible in Mandla, Rajnandgaon, Sidhi and Surguja.

It may also be noticed from the same Table that out of the total women who received ANC, majority received at an institution, more so in case of the SC women. As may be seen, amongst SC women in seven districts, 90 per cent or more received ANC at an institution. They are, Bastar, Chhindwara, Dhar, Jhabua, Raigarh, Rajnandgaon and Seoni. As a matter of fact the figure was almost 100 per cent in Bastar and Chhindwara. However, in the remaining half it varied between 35 per cent in Mandla to 82 per cent East Nimar.

Coming to the ST women, the data clearly suggests that the per cent of women who received ANC at institution was though higher, it was lower than that of the SC for all of the 14 districts. Nevertheless, the corresponding range was between about 33-36 per cent in Mandla, Surguja and West Nimar to 64-68 per cent in East Nimar, Jhabua, Rajnandgaon and Seoni to about 72 per cent in Raigarh. The data also indicates that majority of these women received it from the Government Institutions since relatively fewer women received ANC from private institutions. In other words, Government institutions continue to be the important source (supplier) in meeting the ANC needs of the people in the populations under study.

In addition to the ANC at home by the health workers, the data in Table 8b gives information pertaining to whether the women received TT injection and IFA tablets or not. As may be seen, the per cent of women who were not protected against Tetanus varied substantially across the districts for both SC and ST women. Further, though the per cent of women not protected against tetanus was higher amongst ST than SC, the gaps across district were wider for SC than they were for ST. It may be observed that Seoni followed by Betul had lowest per cent of the SC women who did not receive TT injection (11 and 15 per cent). On the other hand, Jhabua (over 54 per cent) followed by Surguja (50 per cent) had largest proportions of women who did not receive TT. In case of ST women, it may be noted that the per cent of women who did not get TT injection ranged from a lowest of about 35-36 per cent in Rajnandgaon and Seoni to as high as over 77 per cent in Shahdol.

The data further indicates that more than two-thirds of the ST women in Chhindawara, Sidhi, Mandla, East Nimar, Seoni and Rajnandgaon districts received two or more doses of TT, whereas in rest of the districts the coverage was relatively lower (particularly in West Nimar, Jhabua and Betul, less than 50 per cent only). Amongst

SC women, over 80 per cent of them in Rajnandgaon received two or more doses of TT. In fact there were as many as 8 districts where more than two-thirds of the women received two or more doses of TT whereas it was less than 50 per cent in West Nimar. With regards to the IFA tablets, it may be said from the data in the last two columns of the Table 8b that more SC women than ST in all the districts under analysis were distributed IFA tablets. It may also be noticed that the per cent of women given IFA tablets was about 25-28 per cent in Shahdol and Sidhi for SC women and ranged between 41 to 73 per cent in rest of the districts. On the other hand, it appears that only a handful of ST women in Shahdol (about 9 per cent) and Sidhi (19 per cent or so) received IFA tablets. However, the corresponding figure varied between about 30 to 50 per cent in as many as 8 districts and between 52 to 56 per cent in the remaining four districts. Thus it can be stated that on the whole, coverage for IFA and TT seem to be relatively poorer amongst ST women.

Natal Care (NC)

The data on the selected Natal Care indicators such as place of delivery and types of assistance received in case of home deliveries is presented in Table 9. At the outset it may be mentioned that though the share of institutional deliveries is very little for all the districts for both SC and ST groups relatively speaking it was better amongst former. It may be observed from the table that the institutional deliveries has not yet found their ways in the study population, since most of the deliveries in all the 14 districts included in the analysis occurred in homes. In other words, only few of the births in the reference period took place in the institutions (both Government and Private). For example, the per cent of institutional deliveries in SC was about 5 to 10 per cent in 5 districts whereas in another five districts it was between 11 to 20 per cent. In case of the remaining 4 districts, per cent of institutional deliveries was around 21 to 24 per cent. In case of ST, the per cent of institutional deliveries was 15 per cent or less for all the districts. In fact, the corresponding figure was below 5 per cent in 5 districts.

The situation does not appear any better when it comes to the type of assistance available in case of home deliveries since most of them were assisted by an untrained person. For example, trained persons assisted merely 3 per cent or fewer home deliveries, in SC and ST in Sidhi. The per cent of home deliveries assisted by trained person for ST was 4 per cent in Jhabua, 7 per cent in Mandla and 8 per cent in Betul. Similarly, between 10 to 20 per cent of the home deliveries in Betul (only SC), Bastar and Raigarh (both SC and ST) were assisted by trained persons. Further, a quarter or more of the home deliveries were assisted by a trained person in Chhindwara (only SC), East Nimar (only SC), Rajnandgaon (only SC), Seoni (both SC and ST) and in Shahdol and Surguja (ST only).

The data further indicates that often it is the traditional birth attendants and/or relatives who are conducting these home deliveries. This is true for SC and ST groups. This probably indicates that either there is lack of knowledge of availability of the trained personnel for conducting home deliveries or their accessibility is very limited.

Post Natal Care (PNC)

The last two columns of Table 9b give data on the post delivery follow-up of the women. As may be seen, unlike ANC and NC, the care during the postnatal period appears to be the least popular practice. This seems to be the case for both SC and ST women. For example, in most of the districts included in the analysis, percentage of women who had post delivery follow-up was very less for both SC and ST women. Nevertheless, in Betul, around 24 per cent of SC women and in Mandla 27 per cent of ST women had PNC whereas in Sidhi and Shahdol it is only 2 per cent for the groups.

Complications Experienced by the Women during Pregnancy, Childbirth and Postnatal Period

Table 10 contains data on the per cent of women who experienced complications during the ante-natal, natal and post-natal period. Firstly, it looks that relatively larger proportions of the women suffered from some kind of health complications during the antenatal period. This is true for both SC and ST women in almost all the districts. As may be noted, about 46 to nearly 90 per cent of the SC women across the districts suffered from some type of health complication(s) during pregnancy. Similarly, for ST women too, the percentage reporting experiencing pregnancy complications ranged between 40 per cent in Shahdol to 79 per cent in Betul. It appears that relatively fewer ST women than SC women reported to have experienced health complication during pregnancy. For natal complications, the data indicates that they too are relatively common in both the groups.

Further, the per cent of women who suffered from any health complication during the PNC period though was high amongst both SC and ST, it was particularly higher in later. For example, the per cent of SC women who suffered any health complications during PNC ranged between a lowest of 21 per cent in Rajnandgaon to a highest of 83 per cent in Betul followed by West Nimar (about 79 per cent). On the other hand, the corresponding range for ST was between 17-18 per cent in Shahdol and Rajnandgaon to 68-69 per cent in Betul and West Nimar.

Utilization of Immunization Services

Tables 11 and 12 give relevant data on the immunization coverage and incidence of Diarrhea and Pneumonia among children aged 9-36 months at the time of survey date respectively. At the out set we would like to state that the data on the per cent of the children vaccinated for DPT and Polio refers to the Third doses of the vaccine. In other words, the children who have received all three doses of DPT and Polio are included in the table.

Speaking of individual vaccine coverage, the data clearly indicates that the BCG coverage appears to be better in most of the districts particularly for SC children since in 10 districts 75 per cent or more children were vaccinated against the BCG. Nevertheless, the corresponding per cent was slightly lower in Bastar, Shahdol, Sidhi and Surguja (varying between 54 to 65 per cent). In case of ST children, the BCG coverage was lowest at 35 per cent in Jhabua and 39 per cent in Shahdol. In the remaining districts, two-thirds or more children were vaccinated for BCG in 8 districts. Three broad observations may be made on the coverage of DPT and Polio. Firstly, the per cent of children protected against Diphtheria, Pertusis, Typhoid and Polio was even better than the coverage for BCG in most of the instances for both the groups. Secondly, the extent of DPT and Polio coverage were quite similar in most of the districts and is also true for both the groups as well. Thirdly, in majority of the districts under analysis, over 85 per cent of the children were vaccinated for DPT and Polio. This statement is also true for the two groups of children. Lastly, in Mandla and Shahdol all the children were given all three doses of DPT and Polio.

It seems that the coverage for measles was rather poor in most of the districts in both the groups in comparison to the coverage for the other vaccines. Further, the situation in this respect looks to be more disadvantageous for the children belonging to the ST group in particular. As may be seen, only about 18 per cent of the ST children in Jhabua and between a quarter and one-thirds of them in Dhar, Shahdol, Sidhi, Surguja, West Nimar and Chhindwara districts were protected against measles. Nevertheless, the per cent of ST children protected against this disease was slightly better in the other districts. On the other hand, though the coverage was better amongst SC children it was poor in few districts like Bastar, Chhindwara, Jhabua, Sidhi, Surguja and West Nimar where half or fewer children were vaccinated against measles.

In the same Table we have also given the per cent of children who have received all[4] the required vaccines and those who have not received any of the vaccine. The data as usual is presented separately for SC and ST children. Few points emerge from the data. We have summarized the data in the Statement-1. As may be noted there were seven districts in which half or more SC children received all the vaccinations whereas in case of ST it was true in only Betul and Mandla districts. On the other hand, West Nimar was the only district where less than a quarter of the SC children received all the vaccines whereas the number of districts in this category was six for ST children. Contrary to this, in five districts and one district respectively more than 30 per cent of the ST and SC children respectively did not covered in the vaccination program at all. Further, there were seven districts where 10 per cent of fewer SC children did not get any vaccine whereas it was true for only Rajnadgaon and Surguja districts in case of ST children.

[4] BCG + 3 DPT+ 3Polio + Measles.

Summary of the coverage of complete vaccination.

	SC	ST
	Per cent Children with Complete Vaccination	
Below 25 per cent	West Nimar (1)	Chhindwara, Dhar, Jhabua, Shahdol, Sidhi and West Nimar (6)
25 to less than 50	Bastar, Chhindwara, Dhar, Jhabua, Sidhi & Surguja (6)	Bastar, East Nimar, Raigarh, rajnandgaon and Seoni (5)
50 to less than 75	Betul, East Nimar, Mandla, Raigarh, Rajnandgaon and Shahdol (6)	Betul and Mandla (2)
Above 75 per cent	Seoni (1)	-
	Per cent Children with no Vaccination at All	
Below 10 per cent	Betul, Dhar, East Nimar, Raigarh, Rajnandgaon, Seoni and Surguja (7)	Rajnandgaon & Surguja (2)
10 to less than 20	Chhindwara, Jhabua, Mandla and West Nimar (4)	Bastar, East Nimar, Mandla and Seoni (4)
20 to less than 30	Bastar and Shahdol (2)	Betul, Chhindwara and Raigarh (3)
Above 30 per cent	Sidhi (1)	Dhar, Jhabua, Shahdol, Sidhi and West Nimar (5)
Total no. of districts	14	14

Note: Figure in parenthesis gives number of districts in each category.

Incidence of Diarrhea and Pneumonia among Children

District wise results in Table 12 shows that the per cent of women who reported that their children suffered from diarrhea during the past three months period prior to the survey date varied from a low of only about 2 per cent in Sidhi to as high as nearly 48 per cent Dhar followed by 38 per cent in Chhindwara and 33 per cent in Seoni and West Nimar. The corresponding range for ST was about 7 per cent Sidhi and Shahdol to 26-30 per cent in Dhar, Chhindwara, East Nimar and Seoni. Coming to the pneumonia, the data indicates that the the disease is more common in West Nimar as nearly half of the SC and ST women in the districts reported that their children suffered from it during the reference period. In addition to this, the per cent of women whose children suffered from pneumonia was also higher for SC in Seoni and Dhar (about 40 per cent) and Seoni (46 per cent) and Surguja and Chhindwara (about 31 per cent each). In contrast to this, the per cent of women whose children suffered from pneumonia was much lower in Shahdol (4 per cent in SC and 12 per cent in ST).

Family Planning Use

Information regarding family planning use (including traditional methods), commonly used method, and unmet need for limiting and spacing at the time of survey is compiled in Tables 13 and 14. As may be noted that in Raigarh, Rajnandgaon, Shahdol, Surguja and West Nimar districts, firstly fewer couples were using any family planning[5] (the per cent users varied between about 31 to 45 per cent) and secondly their share was quite similar across SC and ST couples. On the other hand, in the remaining districts, the per cent of FP users was relatively high for both SC (in the range of 50 to 63 per cent) and ST (30 to 40 per cent for most of the districts) couples and also the gap between the two groups were notable. It may also be said that the more SC couples than their ST counterparts were using any FP and holds true for all districts except Rajnandgaon.

In accordance with the common notion, here too female sterilization emerges to be the most commonly used family planning method as majority of the couples (both SC and ST) have reported using it. In addition to this, with only four exceptions of Mandla for SC, Bastar, Mandla and Betul for ST, more than three-fourth of SC and ST couples were using female sterilization. In fact, all of the SC couples in Dhar were using female sterilization.

The data in Table 14 on the unmet need for family planning clearly brings out that unmet need for family planning services range from a lowest of about 9 per cent in Betul to as high as 56 per cent in Surguja for SC whereas it varied between 13 per cent in Mandla to 61 per cent

[5] Any Family Planning Method : Traditional and Modern Methods.

in Surguja for ST. It is interesting to note that in Raigarh, Sidhi and Surguja districts for both SC and ST couples and in Bastar for ST couples, the proportion of couples having unmet need for family planning for ST was higher than the per cent couples using any FP method. This means that the level of FP use in these districts could be enhanced to twice the level of current FP use. It may also be noted that the extent of unmet need of family planning seems to be wider for ST couples than it is for the SC couples.

The data further indicated that on the whole, extent of unmet need is more for spacing[6] than that of the limiting and also there seem to exist variations across the districts. The data reveals that the extent of unmet need for limiting[7] varied between about a mere of 1-2 per cent for both SC and ST in Mandla to nearly 18 per cent for SC in Ragarh and Jhabua and 21 per cent for ST in Raigarh and Sidhi. On the other hand, the corresponding range for spacing was observed to be between 2-3 per cent in Betul to about 39-41 per cent in Surguja for both SC and ST. This clearly indicates that the gaps were wider across districts for unmet need for spacing than they were for limiting.

Prevalence of RTI

Tables 15 and 16 contain relevant data on the per cent of women suffered from selected RTI during the past three months prior to the survey date. The data once again is given separately for SC and ST women for all the 14 districts. As may be noted, around 6-8 per cent of the SC women in Rajnadgaon, Seoni, Bastar and Mandla suffered from the burning sensation while urinating. On the other hand, per cent of SC women who suffered from burning sensation while urinating was close to a quarter in East Nimar and over 21 per cent in Dhar. In the remaining districts it was in the range of 11 to 16 per

---

[6] The unmet need for spacing is the proportion of currently married women who are neither menopause nor had hysterectomy nor are currently pregnant and are not currently using any family planning method and who want more children but after one or more year.

[7] The Unmet need for limitation is the proportion of currently married women who are neither menopause nor had hysterectomy nor are currently pregnant and are not currently using any family planning method and who do not want to have another child instead of want more children.

cent. Further, there were 7 districts where per cent of ST women who suffered from burning sensation while urinating was less than 10 per cent (between 3 to 9 per cent). At the same time, it was between 10 to 20 per cent for the remaining districts. It is important to note that the difference between the two groups were not significant.

The data also indicates that about 10 to 17 per cent of the SC women in all the districts (except Raigarh- less than one, Jhabua- 7 per cent and Bastar- 8 per cent) reportedly suffered from the pain during intercourse. On the other hand, for ST women, corresponding per cent was less than 10 per cent in as many as 8 districts whereas in the remaining 6 districts it ranged between 11 to 17 per cent. Once again the differences across two groups were very little. Contrary to this, relatively larger proportions of the women seemed to have suffered from the vaginal discharge during the reference period. This appears to be true for most of the districts. For example, the per cent of women who suffered from vaginal discharge was less than 10 per cent for both SC and ST in six districts (Bastar, Mandla, Raigarh, Rajnandgaon, Seoni and Shahdol). On the other hand, it was close to 20-22 per cent in Betul, Chhindwara, Jhabua, Sidhi and West Nimar for ST women. The per cent ST women who suffered from vaginal discharge was 28 per cent in East Nimar and Surguja and nearly 38 per cent in Dhar. The corresponding figures for SC women ranged between 16 per cent in Betul to about 27-28 per cent in West Nimar and Sidhi.

The last 4 columns of the same Table give the per cent of women who suffered from all of the above three and with at least one of the three sicknesses during the reference period. It is found that though the per cent of women who suffered from all of the three sicknesses, on the whole, was relatively lower for all the districts for both SC and ST women (less than 10 per cent of women in all districts). On the other hand, the per cent of women who suffered from at least one of the three sicknesses was less than 10 per cent in Raigarh and Rajnandgaon for both SC and ST and in Bastar for ST women only. Further, it was observed to be between 11 to 20 per cent in 4 districts for SC and ST women. In the remaining, it was over 20 per cent. In fact, the per cent of such women was about 46 and 39 per cent respectively in Dhar and East Nimar for SC and about 32 to 35 per cent in Jhabua, Sidhi, West Nimar and Dhar for ST women.

All those women who suffered from vaginal discharge were further asked whether they had also experienced either or both itching and ulcers along with the discharge. Furthermore, they were also asked on if during discharge they also got lower abdominal pain and/or fever. The data on this is presented in Table 16a and 16b. The data reveals that although in most of the districts, large proportions of the women had neither itching nor ulcers, there were few who suffered either one of the two or both. Further, the share of such women varied across districts as well as across SC-ST groups. It may be observed that about 27 per cent of the SC women in Chhindwara suffered from both itching and ulcer. Once again, in Chhindwara, over 35 per cent of the ST women suffered from ulcers as well and another about 18 per cent suffered from itching. In West Nimar, about 29 and 37 per cent of the SC and ST women respectively suffered with itching along with the discharge. There were some other districts where per cent of women who suffered from itching was relatively higher, particularly amongst ST. In contrast to this, fewer women suffered from ulcers with discharge, particularly amongst SC.

It may also be seen from Table 16b that large proportions of the SC and ST women also suffered from lower abdominal pain and had fever during discharge. This was true for almost all the districts. Although there were gaps across districts as well as across two groups it may be noted the proportions were quite substantial in majority of the districts. For example, the per cent of women who had lower abdominal pain during discharge was less than 50 per cent for SC women in only Sidhi and West Nimar whereas in rest of the districts it was over 50 per cent. In fact, all of the SC women who suffered from discharge in Rajnandgaon, also suffered from lower abdominal pains as well. In case of the SC women, the per cent suffering from lower abdominal pain was lowest in Mandla and Surguja (close to 39 per cent) whereas it was over 60 per cent for as many as six districts. Similarly, around 18-20 per cent of the SC women in Surguja and West Nimar and about a third of them in Bastar, Dhar, East Nimar, Jhabua, Mandla and Sidhi also had fever during the discharge. In the remaining districts, their share was over 40 per cent and it was over 85 per cent in Shahdol. On the other hand, per cent of women who had fever with discharge was between 35 to 45 per cent in most of the districts whereas it was least in Surguja (at about 19 per cent) and highest in Chhindwara (at 65 per cent) followed by Seoni (59 per cent). It may also be noted that the per cent women who had fever with discharge was higher amongst ST women as compared to the SC women in most of the districts whereas reverse was true for the share of women who had lower abdominal pain with discharge.

Conclusion

In the present paper, attempt has been made to examine the reproductive and child health status in the SC and ST population in Madhya Pradesh. It is well known fact that utilization of health care services is still low in MP but its access to underprivileged group of population (SC and ST) is unreasonably low. Despite various special programme of development and for easy accessibility of primary health care, analysis indicates very poor coverage – be it ANC, safe delivery, immunization or family planning. Due to low social development (low female literacy) and poor coverage under RCH, IMR and Child Mortality is still very high.

Analysis very clearly indicates the need of training of the large number of Dai from the same community who will be easily accessible to these communities. These Dai can also act as link persons for referral and educate the community about the importance of ANC, immunization and care of skill persons at the time of delivery. Syndromic approach also revealed quite high level of reproductive morbidity (RTI/STI) in the study population. The trained Dai can help in promoting hygienic practices in general and during menstrual period in particular. This may accelerate the utilization of RCH services and reduce the reproductive morbidity.

REFERENCES

Chatterjee, K.K. 1993. Health Status of Tribal Women. Social Change, 23: 53-55.

Census of India, 1991. Paper 1 of 1992, Vol. II, Series 1.

Ghosh, S. 1987. Women Role in Health and Development. Health for Millions, Vol XIII (1&2), Feb. & April; pp. 2-7.

Government of India, National Population Policy 2000. Departmrnt of Family Welfare, Ministry of Health & Family Welfare, New Delhi.

National Family Health Survey, 1992-1993 & 1998-1999. International Institute for Population Sciences, Mumbai.

Reproductive and Child Health Survey, 1998 &1999: Ministry of Health and Family Welfare, Government of India, New Delhi.

Table 1: Selected Background Characteristics of the Schedule Caste (SC) and Schedule Tribe (ST) in Madhya Pradesh, 1992-93 and 1998-99.

Selected Indicators	SC		ST	
	1992-93	1998-99	1992-93	1998-99
Share of SC-ST in the total sample				
Households	7.2	16.1	27.5	23.7
Eligible Women (EW)	7.0	15.1	26.8	22.6
Total no. of EW in the sample	440	1087	1675	1600
Selected Demographic and Social Indicators				
TFR	4.7	3.9	4.1	3.7
CPR (any)	33.2	37.7	30.2	32.9
IMR	124.1	101.5	103.1	101.1
CMR	50.0	60.7	70.8	87.4
Mean CEB to EMW (40-49)	5.69	5.80	5.02	4.99
Women with 2 living children not desiring additional child	37.3	48.8	37.9	41.7
Actual minus Wanted Fertility	1.29	1.31	0.43	0.86
Mean no. of Son desired	NA	1.6	NA	1.8
Mean no. of Daughters desired	NA	1.1	NA	1.3
% Female Literate	17.5	19.6	8.9	13.5
Women suffering from Anemia				
Mild	NA	37.9	NA	46.5
Moderate	NA	11.4	NA	22.4
Sever	NA	1.2	NA	1.3
Any Anemia	NA	50.5	NA	70.3

Source: National Family Health Survey- I and II for Madhya Pradesh.

Table 2: Percentage Distribution of Eligible Women by Utilization of Antenatal Care (ANC), Natal Care (NC) and Postnatal Care (PNC) Services

Indicators	*SC*		*ST*	
	1992-93	*1998-99*	*1992-93*	*1998-99*
Antenatal Care				
Whether received ANC				
Received at home from HW	13.5	10.2	20.2	12.2
Received at Govt./Pvt. Inst'n	41.2	51.5	19.3	31.6
Not received ANC	43.4	37.5	59.2	55.7
Whether Received TT Injection				
No	48.6	29.9	62.4	47.8
Yes				
One Dose	8.0	13.3	10.0	17.5
Two or More Doses	42.9	56.1	27.4	33.8
Percent given IFA Tablets	45.4	49.0	34.6	35.7
Natal Care				
Place of Delivery				
Public Institution	12.2	9.9	3.1	7.0
Private Institution	3.3	6.2	0.9	0.3
Home	81.3	84.0	93.9	92.7
Type of Assistance during Delivery				
Trained Personal	32.5	25.7	18.4	13.9
Untrained Personal (TBA/Rel)	75.3	73.6	71.7	85.5
Percent Received PNC with in two months of the birth	NA	10.0	NA	7.3

Source: Same as Table 1.

Table 3: Percentage Family Planning Users and Unmet Need and Prevalence of Tract Infection among Eligible Women

Indicators	*SC*		*ST*	
	1992-93	*1998-99*	*1992-93*	*1998-99*
Per cent couple using contraceptive				
Any method	33.2	37.7	30.2	32.9
Female sterilization	23.1	32.5	21.2	27.9
Per cent having unmet need				
For spacing	11.7	9.7	13.4	7.7
For limiting	9.4	8.9	5.8	6.8
Total unmet need	21.2	18.6	19.2	14.5
Per cent women suffered from				
Urinary tract infection	NA	23.6	NA	22.8
Abnormal vaginal discharge	NA	35.7	NA	32.8

Source: Same as Table 1.

Table 4: Percentage of Children Aged 12-23 Months Old at the Time of Survey Who are Vaccinated

Percentage children vaccinated for	*SC*		*ST*	
	1992-93	*1998-99*	*1992-93*	*1998-99*
BCG	45.7	66.5	48.0	53.8
DPT				
DPT 1	50.3	62.8	50.3	43.3
DPT 2	47.4	50.6	38.5	30.6
DPT 3	41.1	33.1	28.7	18.4
OPV				
OPV 1	53.8	87.7	53.6	72.8
OPV 2	52.1	82.1	43.9	62.5
OPV 3	45.7	58.7	30.1	42.1
Measles	32.6	33.2	34.6	18.8
Per cent Children With Complete Immunization	24.6	17.9	19.3	11.1
No Vaccine	44.6	11.7	43.2	26.2

Source: Same as Table 1.

Table 5: Percentage of Children with Anemia and Suffered from Diarrhea, Pneumonia within Last Three Months before the Survey

Indicators	*SC*		*ST*	
	1992-93	*1998-99*	*1992-93*	*1998-99*
A. Whether had Anemia				
Yes	NA	71.4	NA	83.9
No	NA	26.8	NA	16.1
B. Type of Anemia				
Mild	NA	22.4	NA	20.0
Moderate	NA	45.7	NA	57.8
Severe	NA	3.3	NA	6.1
Children Suffered with				
Diarrhea	3.8	30.4	5.6	26.2
Pneumonia	6.4	22.9	8.0	24.9

Source: Same as Table 1.

Table 6: Base of SC and ST by Districts, M.P.

Districts	*Per cent of SC and ST in the Total Sample*				*Per cent of SC/ST in the Total Population, 1991*	
	Households		*Eligible Women*			
	SC	ST	SC	ST	SC	ST
Bastar	5.5	59.2	5.0 (4.8)	59.6 (568)	5.9	67.4
Betul	12.9	25.3	11.5 (86)	25.2 (188)	10.8	37.5
Chhindwara	10.0	28.0	8.0 (59)	27.6 (202)	12.2	34.5
Dhar	10.5	54.5	6.4 (60)	58.7 (554)	6.9	53.5
East Nimar	15.8	24.7	14.8 (136)	23.1 (213)	11.4	26.8
Jhabua	5.3	82.3	4.6 (44)	83.1 (789)	3.1	85.7
Mandla	8.7	54.4	8.8 (69)	52.2 (409)	5.2	60.8
Raigarh	13.1	44.8	14 (126)	41.8 (375)	11.4	47.7

(*Contd...*)

Rajnandgaon	10.6	33.8	8.4 (77)	35.1 (320)	10.3	25.2
Seoni	15.9	31.2	17.0 (144)	30.3 (256)	10.8	37.0
Shahdol	7.6	14.5	7.6 (71)	14.0 (131)	7.7	46.6
Sidhi	17.0	21.0	16.3 (168)	19.5 (201)	11.4	30.4
Surguja	8.4	40.4	16.3 (168)	38.9 (328)	5.5	53.7
West Nimar	9.4	39.0	9.6 (105)	39.8 (436)	9.8	46.2

Source: Reproductive and Child Health-Rapid Household Survey, 1998-99.

Table 7: Selected Socio-Demographic Indicators for SC/ST for the Districts

Districts	*Female Literacy rate*		*Mean no. of CEB Age 40-49*		*Mean no. of CS*		*Mean no. of CD*	
	SC	*ST*	*SC*	*ST*	*SC*	*ST*	*SC*	*ST*
Bastar	23.8	9.0	2.8	2.8	2.4	2.5	0.4	0.3
Betul	47.7	18.6	3.2	3.3	3.0	2.9	0.2	0.4
Chhindwara	47.5	17.7	3.7	2.8	3.0	2.6	0.7	0.2
Dhar	26.2	8.3	3.4	3.5	2.7	2.9	0.7	0.6
East Nimar	30.7	17.8	3.0	3.7	2.5	3.0	0.5	0.7
Jhabua	12.5	8.0	4.4	4.3	3.4	3.4	1.0	0.9
Mandla	20.0	17.1	2.9	2.8	2.4	2.5	0.5	0.3
Raigarh	5.6	10.4	2.8	2.7	2.4	2.4	0.4	0.3
Rajnandgaon	28.6	21.9	2.8	3.0	2.3	2.5	0.5	0.5
Seoni	46.5	20.3	2.9	3.1	2.6	2.7	0.3	0.4
Shahdol	12.7	9.2	2.9	3.0	2.8	3.0	0.1	0.0
Sidhi	7.1	7.2	3.8	3.5	3.1	2.7	0.7	0.8
Surguja	15.6	14.9	3.1	3.1	2.6	2.4	0.5	0.7
West Nimar	26.4	8.3	3.4	3.8	2.9	3.2	0.5	0.6

Source: Same as Table 6.

Table 8a: Per cent of Women by Source of the Utilization of ANC Services

Districts	*Per cent of Women who received ANC Care by source**						*Not received ANC*	
	Home by HW		*Public Institution*		*Private Institution*			
	SC	*ST*	*SC*	*ST*	*SC*	*ST*	*SC*	*ST*
Bastar	54.5	78.3	100.0	46.3	0.0	5.1	47.6	66.5
Betul	35.5	50.0	57.7	46.1	6.6	1.9	14.6	57.2
Chhindwara	58.8	50.0	70.5	32.5	29.4	25.0	39.2	66.1
Dhar	22.2	54.4	72.2	47.9	22.1	10.9	33.3	53.8
East Nimar	37.5	45.4	55.0	51.5	27.5	16.6	32.2	41.5
Jhabua	10.0	46.0	80.0	48.8	10.0	18.7	58.3	62.9
Mandla	65.0	64.5	25.0	29.1	10.0	4.1	48.2	49.1
Raigarh	20.0	45.6	70.0	60.8	20.0	10.8	60.7	72.4
Rajnandgaon	25.0	27.6	65.0	55.8	25.0	8.5	42.8	67.8
Seoni	20.0	41.6	74.2	24.1	17.1	10.4	38.6	63.0
Shahdol	37.5	46.1	62.5	38.4	0.0	15.3	41.6	79.2
Sidhi	75.0	70.0	25.0	30.0	25.0	10.0	95.2	91.5
Surguja	50.0	54.8	37.5	30.6	8.3	4.8	41.6	62.2
West Nimar	47.3	59.1	34.2	25.3	13.1	11.2	39.2	47.1

* Per cent will not add up to 100 due to multiple responses.
Source: Same as Table 6.

Table 8b: Utilization of ANC Services Contd...............

Districts	*No. of Tetanus Toxoid injection**				*No TT injection*		*% given IFA tablets*	
	1		2					
	SC	ST	SC	ST	SC	ST	SC	ST
Bastar	14.3	23.7	64.3	56.4	33.3	46.2	61.9	54.8
Betul	14.3	32.6	71.4	48.8	14.6	54.2	68.3	37.5
Chhindwara	25.0	19.7	70.0	78.7	28.6	48.3	53.6	43.2
Dhar	10.0	34.3	70.0	61.1	25.9	44.6	66.7	44.3

(*Contd...*)

East Nimar	21.3	25.8	78.7	71.2	20.3	41.6	72.9	55.8
Jhabua	27.3	48.0	63.6	48.7	54.2	67.9	45.8	31.2
Mandla	36.4	15.9	63.6	75.6	45.0	36.4	45.0	53.8
Raigarh	18.8	27.8	53.1	60.0	37.3	46.1	41.2	42.5
Rajnandgaon	19.2	26.9	80.6	66.7	23.5	35.9	67.6	52.4
Seoni	19.6	25.0	72.5	69.0	10.5	35.4	54.4	46.9
Shahdol	14.3	45.5	71.4	54.5	41.7	77.4	25.0	9.4
Sidhi	16.7	19.6	79.2	76.5	43.5	56.8	28.2	18.6
Surguja	27.8	23.1	50.0	55.4	50.0	50.4	52.8	44.4
West Nimar	20.0	25.9	47.5	48.3	28.6	49.3	53.6	39.3

* Percent distribution of women who have received TT Injection. Percentage will not add up to 100 because of " Do Not Remember" response.

Source: Same as Table 6.

Table 9a: Percentage Distribution of Women by Place of Delivery and Type of Assistance Received at Home Delivery

Districts	*Place of delivery*					
	Home		*Public institution*		*Private institution*	
	SC	*ST*	*SC*	*ST*	*SC*	*ST*
Bastar	90.5	95.5	9.5	3.4	0.0	1.0
Betul	75.6	91.7	19.5	7.3	4.9	1.0
Chhindwara	82.1	98.3	17.9	1.7	0.0	0.0
Dhar	92.6	89.2	3.7	7.6	3.7	3.2
East Nimar	79.7	95.6	11.9	1.8	8.5	2.7
Jhabua	87.5	85.0	NA	5.3	12.5	9.7
Mandla	95.0	95.5	5.0	4.5	NA	NA
Raigarh	90.2	97.0	NA	NA	9.8	3.0
Rajnandgaon	82.4	93.8	5.9	2.8	11.8	3.4
Seoni	78.9	94.6	15.8	3.1	5.3	2.3
Shahdol	87.5	88.7	12.5	11.3	NA	NA
Sidhi	91.8	95.8	2.4	1.7	5.9	2.5
Surguja	86.1	93.3	8.3	5.2	5.6	1.5
West Nimar	78.6	94.8	16.1	4.4	5.4	0.9

Source: Same as Table 6

Table 9b: Percentage Distribution of Women by Type of Assistance Received at Home Delivery

Districts	*Delivery by type of assistance*				*Per cent of EW, had PNC*	
	Trained person		*Untrained person*			
	SC	*ST*	*SC*	*ST*	*SC*	*ST*
Bastar	10.5	14.1	89.5	85.9	9.5	13.8
Betul	19.4	8.0	80.6	92.0	24.4	21.9
Chhindwara	26.1	23.5	73.9	76.5	7.2	5.9
Dhar	24.0	18.1	76.0	81.9	3.7	11.1
East Nimar	25.5	22.2	74.5	77.8	22.0	13.3
Jhabua	14.3	4.0	85.7	96.0	9.1	3.4
Mandla	NA	7.1	100.0	92.9	10.0	26.5
Raigarh	19.6	11.1	80.4	88.9	22.2	24.2
Rajnandgaon	32.1	11.0	67.9	89.0	5.9	6.2
Seoni	31.1	32.5	68.9	67.5	7.0	13.1
Shahdol	19.0	29.8	81.0	70.2	4.2	1.9
Sidhi	2.6	0.9	97.4	99.1	2.4	2.5
Surguja	22.6	26.2	77.4	73.8	11.1	14.1
West Nimar	27.3	13.4	72.7	86.6	16.1	19.7

Source: Same as Table 6.

Table 10: Incidence of Pregnancy, Delivery and Post Delivery Complications among Women

Districts	*Per cent of women who experienced any*					
	Pregnancy complications		*Delivery complications*		*Post delivery complications*	
	SC	ST	SC	ST	SC	ST
Bastar	85.7	58.6	76.2	41.7	28.6	29.3
Betul	92.7	79.2	75.6	64.6	82.9	67.7
Chhindwara	69.6	73.9	39.1	34.8	42.9	41.5
Dhar	74.1	62.7	11.1	7.6	66.7	51.3
East Nimar	64.4	60.2	57.6	65.5	71.2	59.3

(Contd...)

Jhabua	83.3	74.9	NA	4.2	58.4	65.0
Mandla	90.0	63.6	50.0	46.2	40.0	38.6
Raigarh	72.5	67.1	43.1	42.5	41.2	43.1
Rajnandgaon	55.9	37.9	32.4	22.8	20.6	17.9
Seoni	71.9	75.4	54.4	63.1	57.9	60.8
Shahdol	45.8	39.6	45.8	7.5	33.3	17.0
Sidhi	71.8	58.5	36.5	51.7	54.1	51.7
Surguja	61.1	51.9	80.6	81.5	50.0	39.3
West Nimar	66.1	61.6	66.1	60.7	78.6	69.0

Source: Same as Table 6.

Table 11a: Utilization of Immunization Services among Children Aged 9 to 36 Months at the Time of Survey

Districts	BCG		3 Doses of DPT		3 Doses of Polio		Measles	
	SC	ST	SC	ST	SC	ST	SC	ST
Bastar	64.7	65.7	90.9	81.8	90.9	80.5	41.2	56.0
Betul	86.7	72.2	85.7	94.0	92.9	92.7	90.0	68.1
Chhindwara	80.0	53.8	85.7	65.9	81.3	73.6	50.0	31.3
Dhar	91.3	52.7	73.7	71.6	76.2	78.0	60.9	26.1
East Nimar	80.9	75.0	87.2	77.0	94.9	80.9	61.7	41.7
Jhabua	75.0	34.7	72.7	57.4	69.2	61.4	40.0	18.1
Mandla	78.6	77.5	100.0	94.4	100.0	90.5	71.4	72.2
Raigarh	85.0	71.1	92.1	91.7	94.4	89.2	75.0	54.8
Rajnandgaon	89.7	72.5	92.6	77.3	89.3	79.8	58.6	54.2
Seoni	95.1	78.4	92.3	78.2	87.5	66.7	85.4	62.2
Shahdol	64.7	38.6	100.0	94.4	100.0	92.8	58.8	29.5
Sidhi	53.6	46.4	69.2	77.4	72.4	8.9	39.3	25.0
Surguja	55.6	67.1	86.7	68.5	60.9	65.3	44.4	38.8
West Nimar	74.1	49.0	68.8	80.8	76.2	77.6	25.9	25.8

Source: Same as Table 6.

Table 11b: Utilization of Immunization Services

Districts	Per cent received			
	Complete immunization		No vaccine	
	SC	ST	SC	ST
Bastar	35.3	38.9	29.4	12.5
Betul	73.3	65.3	3.3	22.2
Chhindwara	40.0	20.0	10.0	27.5
Dhar	43.5	18.7	8.7	32.8
East Nimar	57.4	36.9	8.5	15.5
Jhabua	25.0	9.6	15.0	44.6
Mandla	64.3	67.8	14.3	17.8
Raigarh	62.5	44.4	5.0	20.0
Rajnandgaon	55.2	45.8	3.4	6.7
Seoni	75.6	45.9	2.4	12.2
Shahdol	52.9	20.5	23.5	38.6
Sidhi	25.0	22.6	32.1	44.0
Surguja	33.3	25.4	7.4	4.7
West Nimar	22.2	20.5	11.1	33.8

Table 12: Per cent of Women whose Children Suffered from Diarrhea and Pneumonia during Two Month Prior to Survey

Districts	*Per cent Children Suffered from*			
	Diarrhea		*Pneumonia*	
	SC	*ST*	*SC*	*ST*
Bastar	21.1	11.1	10.5	16.7
Betul	7.3	14.7	19.5	26.3
Chhindwara	38.5	28.1	34.6	31.6
Dhar	48.1	29.9	40.7	26.2
East Nimar	17.5	25.5	26.3	29.1

(Contd...)

Jhabua	27.3	21.6	22.7	20.7
Mandla	15.0	9.9	15.0	23.7
Raigarh	11.8	12.4	29.4	19.9
Rajnandgaon	8.8	10.4	11.8	12.5
Seoni	32.7	25.6	40.0	45.6
Shahdol	13.0	7.7	4.3	11.5
Sidhi	2.4	7.2	8.3	18.0
Surguja	5.6	9.1	25.0	31.1
West Nimar	32.7	19.5	54.5	49.3

Source: Same as Table 6.

Table 13: Family Planning Prevalence among Women

Districts	Per cent using any FP methods		Per cent of Tuberectomy in users of total FP users	
	SC	ST	SC	ST
Baster	50.0	31.1	76.2	64.8
Betul	62.5	46.9	76.0	73.8
Chhindwara	60.0	41.4	93.5	84.4
Dhar	60.7	42.0	100.0	85.9
East Nimar	59.5	46.2	90.3	94.2
Jhabua	56.3	24.4	77.8	87.8
Mandla	57.4	56.1	74.1	70.3
Raigarh	37.6	33.3	79.5	76.3
Rajnandgaon	43.1	47.2	89.3	81.0
Seoni	56.1	43.3	87.8	86.0
Shahdol	45.0	44.2	92.6	88.7
Sidhi	33.3	20.0	87.5	82.4
Surguja	35.7	31.1	84.0	82.6
West Nimar	44.4	42.2	84.1	84.9

Table 14: Extent of Unmet Need of Family Planning among the Eligible Women

Districts	*Per cent women with unmet need for*				*Total Unmet need*	
	Limiting		*Spacing*			
	SC	*ST*	*SC*	*ST*	*SC*	*ST*
Baster	14.6	18.5	8.3	24.5	22.9	43.0
Betul	7.0	14.9	1.9	3.0	8.9	18.0
Chhindwara	6.8	20.3	22.2	18.3	29.0	39.0
Dhar	6.6	13.7	23.2	16.6	29.8	30.0
East Nimar	9.5	11.3	14.7	24.0	24.2	35.0
Jhabua	18.3	4.6	6.9	15.3	25.2	20.0
Mandla	1.5	1.1	11.6	11.5	13.1	13.0
Raigarh	17.5	21.3	23.1	24.5	40.6	46.0
Rajnandgaon	13.0	10.3	10.4	13.4	23.0	24.0
Seoni	11.1	16.0	16.0	25.8	27.0	42.0
Shahdol	5.6	13.0	32.4	17.6	38.0	31.0
Sidhi	17.2	20.9	20.8	24.8	38.0	46.0
Surguja	17.0	20.2	39.2	41.2	56.0	61.0
West Nimar	10.5	8.9	20.0	26.4	30.0	35.0

Source: Same as Table 6.

Table 15: Incidence of Reproductive Tract Infection among Eligible Women

Districts	*Per cent of women suffered from:*									
	Urinary tract infection		*Any abnormal vaginal discharge*		*Abdominal pain during intercourse*		*Any of them*		*All three of them*	
	SC	ST	SC	ST	SC	ST	SC	ST	SC	ST
Baster	6.3	3.5	6.3	6.2	8.3	4.4	10.4	9.2	4.2	1.6

(Contd...)

Betul	16.3	13.8	19.8	16.0	17.4	12.2	27.9	19.1	9.3	9.6
Chhindwara	15.3	6.9	18.6	8.4	11.9	7.4	22.0	12.8	10.2	3.0
Dhar	21.3	19.1	37.7	26.8	16.4	16.6	45.9	34.8	8.2	8.8
East Nimar	24.1	15.5	27.0	22.1	16.1	14.1	38.7	29.1	7.3	7.5
Jhabua	13.6	17.3	20.5	23.0	6.8	10.8	25.0	31.6	2.3	5.6
Mandla	8.0	7.5	6.0	8.1	14.0	6.5	18.0	14.0	2.0	2.5
Raigarh	NA	4.3	NA	3.7	0.8	3.7	0.8	6.1	-	1.6
Rajnandgaon	6.5	2.5	1.3	2.8	1.3	1.9	6.5	3.1	-	1.6
Seoni	6.3	10.5	8.3	8.6	9.7	9.4	13.2	14.1	2.6	5.1
Shahdol	11.3	7.6	8.5	8.4	9.9	5.3	11.3	9.2	8.5	4.6
Sidhi	13.0	11.9	20.1	27.7	13.6	15.8	27.2	32.2	5.3	6.4
Surguja	10.9	9.1	28.6	22.0	10.4	8.5	31.2	27.1	6.5	3.4
West Nimar	15.1	16.3	22.6	26.8	12.3	13.8	34.0	35.1	4.7	5.3

Source: Same as Table 6.

Table 16 a: Percent of Women suffered from vaginal discharge by specific complications

Districts	*Percent of women suffered from itching or ulcer on both side of the vaginal area:*							
	Itching		*Ulcer*		*Both*		*None*	
	SC	*ST*	*SC*	*ST*	*SC*	*ST*	*SC*	*ST*
Baster	-	17.1	-	17.1	-	2.9	100.0	62.9
Betul	11.8	10.0	-	-	-	-	88.2	90.0
Chhindwara	9.1	17.6	18.2	35.3	27.3	-	45.5	47.1
Dhar	17.4	29.6	4.3	2.7	4.3	14.8	73.9	53.0
East Nimar	21.6	21.3	5.4	6.4	10.8	12.8	62.2	59.6
Jhabua	11.1	29.8	-	0.6	-	8.8	88.9	60.8
Mandla	-	19.2	-	-	-	-	100.0	80.8
Raigarh	-	21.4	-	21.4	-	-	-	57.1
Rajnandgaon	-	11.1	-	11.1	-	11.1	100.0	66.7

(Contd...)

Seoni	16.7	13.6	-	9.1	8.3	4.5	75.0	72.7
Shahdol	-	9.1	-	-	-	-	100.0	90.9
Sidhi	20.3	30.0	1.4	-	8.1	-	70.3	70.0
Surguja	4.5	18.1	-	1.4	-	-	95.5	80.6
West Nimar	29.2	36.9	-	1.7	4.2	6.8	66.7	54.7

Source: same as Table 6.

Table 16 b: Per cent of Women Suffered from Vaginal Discharge by specific Complications

Districts	*Per cent of women suffered from*			
	Lower abdominal pain		*Fever during discharge*	
	SC	*ST*	*SC*	*ST*
Baster	66.7	57.1	33.3	48.6
Betul	58.8	73.3	58.8	43.3
Chhindwara	90.9	76.5	54.5	64.7
Dhar	65.2	61.1	34.8	43.6
East Nimar	54.1	45.9	37.8	44.7
Jhabua	66.7	55.2	33.3	39.2
Mandla	-	38.5	33.3	38.5
Raigarh	-	64.3	-	28.6
Rajnandgaon	100.0	66.7	-	33.3
Seoni	58.3	59.1	41.7	59.1
Shahdol	83.3	72.7	85.2	27.3
Sidhi	44.1	50.0	38.2	46.4
Surguja	50.0	38.9	18.2	19.4
West Nimar	45.6	54.2	20.8	79.2

Source: Same as Table 6.

Chapter 10

Health and Nutritional Status of Tribal Population in Jhabua and Dhar Districts of Madhya Pradesh

A. Ranjan

The state of Madhya Pradesh is characterised by a very large tribal population. At the time of 1991 population census, the tribal population in the undivided Madhya Pradesh was 15.40 million, which was more than 23 per cent of the total population of the state. The state of Madhya Pradesh, as it existed at the 1991 population census has since been divided into the states of Chhattisgarh and Madhya Pradesh. Information available from the 1991 population census indicates that the tribal population in the new state of Madhya Pradesh was 9.68 million in 1991 which was almost one fifth of the population of the state. In terms of numbers, the new state of Madhya Pradesh still has the largest tribal population in the country.

Within Madhya Pradesh, the tribal population is almost entirely concentrated in its southern part, the region south of the river Narmada. Highest concentration of tribal population, is in district Jhabua where tribal population accounted for more than 85 per cent of the population of the district (Census 1991). In Dhar and Mandla districts, on the other hand, tribal population constituted more than 50 per cent of the population of the district. There were 11 districts in the state where the tribal population accounted for more than 20 per cent of the population of the district.

Tribal people are popularly known as forest people. Since ages, they have been nestling away from the historical 'perennial and nuclear areas' and placed in relatively isolated niches. This historical settlement pattern seems to have bearings even today. There is ample evidence to suggest that the social and cultural value system including values and status accorded to females is very significantly different in tribal communities than in the non-tribal communities, especially communities which have a very rigid caste system. Over generations, tribal communities have preferred to remain isolated from the main streams of social and economic development and have remained confined to forests which continue to be their main source of livelihood even today.

This paper analyses the health and nutritional status of tribal population in Jhabua and Dhar districts of Madhya Pradesh and explores their health seeking behaviour. Information about health and nutritional status of tribal population is usually available through nationally representative surveys like National Family Health Survey. Information available through these surveys provides, at best, only a macro view of the situation and that too in a residual context only. Such surveys are not designed to analysing the health and nutrition status of the tribal population and exploring their health seeking behaviour. In order to understand the specific health and nutritional needs of the tribal population in the right perspective, it is imperative that health and nutrition needs of the tribal people are assessed and analysed at the local level so as to plan and implement programmes that can address the felt needs of the people.

Data and Method

The present paper is based on the information collected through a survey of 300 tribal families in Jhabua and Dhar districts of Madhya Pradesh and focus group discussions with the representatives of tribal communities in these districts. The families surveyed were selected through a multistage sampling approach from 15 villages in one development block in each district selected randomly. Information from all the families surveyed was collected on the basis of a pre-designed and pre-tested information schedule from the head of the household as well as from one pregnant female in the family, if there was one at the time of the survey. The lay reporting of health information methodology developed by the World Health Organisation (WHO, 1978) was used for identifying the morbid conditions. On the other hand, the nutritional status of children of the families surveyed was assessed by following the guidelines and methodology developed by the United Nations (United Nations, 1986).

In addition to the household interviews, focus group discussions were also organized in all those villages where the household survey was carried out. Selected representatives of villages, numbering 10-15 including elected representatives of the people, government functionaries in the village and representatives of social services organisations functioning at the village level were invited to participate in the focus group discussions. The supervisor for the field survey acted as the facilitator for focus group discussions.

Characteristics of Families Surveyed

Basic features of the families surveyed are summarised in Table 1. Majority of the families surveyed belonged to the lowest social and economic strata of the society. Primary occupation of almost 9 out of every 10 families surveyed was agriculture. Average annual per capita income of the families surveyed was Rs. 2448 at current prices with almost one fifth of the families having an average annual per capita income of less than Rs. 1000; there were only about 5 per cent of the families surveyed where the average annual per capita income was more than Rs. 6000.

Extremely poor living conditions of the families surveyed is also reflected through the family belongings. Most common family belonging in the families surveyed was bicycle which was available in more than one fifth of the families, whereas the electric fan was available in about 15 per cent of the families surveyed. By contrast, colour television and refrigerator was available in less than 1 per cent of the families surveyed. Similarly, houses of more than 90 per cent of the families surveyed were mud houses and there was no separate kitchen. There was no latrine in two third of the houses, and 58 per cent of the houses surveyed had no electricity.

In the 300 families covered during the survey, 1698 individuals were enumerated. This gives an average size of approximately 5.66 individuals per family. Out of the 1698 individuals enumerated, 824 were females, which give a sex ratio of 943 females per 1000 males. According to the 2001 population census, the sex ratio of the combined population of Jhabua and Dhar districts was 970 females for every 1000 males, which indicates that there may be under enumeration of females in the survey.

The age-sex pyramid of the population surveyed was typically triangular in shape, which reflects persistent high fertility and high mortality conditions. More than 14 per cent of the population surveyed was below 5 years of age, while only 3.5 per cent was above 60 years of age. The dependency ratio was 931 dependants for every 1000 working age people. There were 835 young dependants (persons below 15 years of age) and 96 old dependants (persons above 55 years of age) for every 1000 population in the age group 15-54 years. Similarly, the child-woman ratio was 649 children of 0-4 years of age for every 1000 women in the age group 15-44 years. The births and deaths reported during the survey, on the other hand, indicate a crude birth rate of 30.62 live births for every 1000 population per year, a crude death rate of 13 deaths for every 1000 population per year and an infant mortality rate of 96 infant deaths for every 1000 live birth per year.

As regards education, more than 74 per cent of the population surveyed was found to be illiterate, the proportion being 87 per cent in case of females. Slightly more than one fifth of the population with age 6 years and more had been found to have ever gone to school. In females, this figure was less than 9 per cent. Just five per cent of the population above 6 years of age had education at least up to the high school level. In males, this proportion was 8.28 per cent but in females, this proportion was only 1.61 per cent, which shows that mass illiteracy conditions prevailed in the surveyed families.

Morbidity among Children

Information about current sickness and sickness during one month prior to the survey was collected for all children below five years of age. About one in every five children surveyed were found to be sick at the time of the survey, whereas more than 40 per cent of the children surveyed were found to have fallen sick during one month prior to the survey. The proportion of children found sick at the time of the survey or the proportion who were sick any time during one month prior to the survey was found to be slightly higher in male as compared to female children. Fever, resulting primarily from malaria, was the main cause of sickness among children. In case of children found sick at the time of survey, almost 70 per cent were suffering from fever normally associated with Malaria; this proportion was almost 90 per cent in children who were reported to be sick during one month prior to the survey. In addition to fever, cough, normally associated with acute respiratory infections, was found to be the second most common cause of morbidity in the children surveyed. More than 8 per cent of the children who were sick at the time of the survey were having cough and associated symptoms and this proportion was substantially higher in male than in female children.

In general, sickness reported in children surveyed was short duration sickness. In case of more than 42 per cent of the children who were sick at the time of the survey, duration of sickness was reported to be of less than 7 days. In only about 30 per cent of the children who were sick at the time of the survey, it was reported that the ailment was persisting for more than 15 days. The duration of sickness reported during the survey has been found to be substantially longer in male than in female children. More than 40 per cent of the male children found sick at the time of the survey were reported to be sick for more than 15 days. This proportion was only 16 per cent for female children.

In addition to the information on current sickness and sickness during one month prior to the survey, specific information related to diarrhoea, high fever and acute respiratory infections was also collected during the survey. Information available from different sources suggests that these morbid conditions are the most common morbid conditions in children and are the major causes of childhood mortality. In the present survey, more than one fifth of the children below 5 years of age had at least one bout of diarrhoea, 43 per cent had high fever and 44 per cent had cough sometime during one month prior to the survey. In case of children who had diarrhoea, total days of diarrhoea ranged between 1-3 days in almost half of the children whereas in about 28 per cent it lasted for more than 7 days. On the other hand, in almost 80 per cent of the children, who had high fever during the one month prior to the survey, the fever was associated with shivering while in case of 44 per cent of these children, high fever was associated with convulsions also. Similarly, among children having cough, more than two third had breathing problems whereas whooping cough was reported in 36 per cent of the children.

Nutritional Status of Children

The nutritional status of all children below 5 years of age identified during the survey was assessed on the basis of their height and weight. The height and weight of the child was used to estimate three indexes: weight-for-height, height-for-age and weight-for-age commonly used for measuring the nutritional status of children. The weight-for-height index is generally used as an indicator of "wasting" and is more commonly known as the body mass index. The height-for-age index, on the other hand, is the commonly used indicator for "stunting" in children, whereas the weight-for-age is a composite indicator of wasting and stunting. Weight-for-age is also the most widely used indicator for assessing the nutritional status. Once the three indexes were calculated for all children, they were compared with the corresponding values of a reference population by calculating the 'z' scores and estimating the proportion of children who fall below a given 'cut off' value of the 'z' score. The proportion of children falling below the cut off value of the 'z' score gave the prevalence of malnutrition. The data assembled by the United States National Centre for Health Statistics (United States, 1976) was used as the reference for estimating the prevalence of malnutrition following the recommendations of the World Health Organisation (Waterlow, at. el. 1977) and the cut off value of the 'z' score for estimating the prevalence of malnutrition was taken to be 2 for all the three indexes of nutritional status, as suggested in the guidelines developed by the United Nations for assessing the nutritional status (United Nations, 1990).

Information available through the present survey indicates that almost 21 per cent of the male and 17 per cent of the female children in the surveyed families were found to be 'wasted' at the time of the survey meaning that they were having significantly lower weight-for-height index than the reference population. Wasting is the best indicator of current and acute malnutrition in children. When the food intake is significantly reduced or infection is sufficiently serious, weight-for-height is the first indicator to be affected.

One known cause of the wasting or low weight-for-height index in children is food intake, inadequate to meet the energy needs of the child as in case of starvation or in a situation such as an infection in which increased energy requirements are not met. Another cause of wasting is the inadequate utilisation of available energy because of malabsorption of food as in case of fever and diarrhoea diseases. In the families surveyed, very high prevalence of fever has been currently reported as well as in the past. It appears that a primary reason for a very high proportion of malnourished children in the families surveyed is the prevalence of fever.

The prevalence of stunting in the surveyed children, on the other hand, was found to be very high (almost 72 per cent in male and 63 per cent in female children surveyed). Similarly, almost 72 per cent of male and 55 per cent of female children were found to be having lower weight-for-age as compared to the reference population. Main reason for very high values of these indexes appears to be the reference population used for the purpose of comparison. As remarked earlier, the reference population used for comparison is the American population. There is evidence to suggest that the height of an average Indian is substantially lower than the height of an average American. Because of this difference, the average value of height-for-age in the reference population is much higher.

Causes of stunting, however, are not very clear. Stunting is not as sensitive to serious inadequacies in the food intake as is wasting and seems to be the last indicator to be affected, if affected at all, in situations of acute starvation. There are evidences where a significant increase in the prevalence of stunting has been reported without any significant increase in the prevalence of wasting. As such, non-nutritional causes such as genetic effects, social and economic conditions, etc. have also been attributed as some of the causes of stunting.

Like the height-for-age, the weight-for-age is also not a good indicator of malnutrition in children because it is a composite indicator of wasting and stunting. A short child with a normal weight-for-height may have low weight-for-age or, conversely, a tall, wasted child may have normal weight-for-age. Moreover, this index does not tell whether the observed malnutrition is due to wasting or due to stunting. The weight-for-age index is also sensitive to the reference population used for the purpose of comparison.

Health Status of Women

During the survey, special emphasis was given on the information related to the health status of women. The respondents were specifically asked whether any female above 5 years of age was having any health related complication or problem at the time of the survey. In addition, the respondents were also enquired about any pregnant female in the family. When any female in the family was reported to be pregnant, a detailed pregnancy history was collected by interviewing the pregnant woman herself. Similarly, when any female in the family was found sick, detailed information was collected about the nature of the problem and the type of medical assistance received by the sick female. It may however be pointed out that the response received was significantly influenced by the prevailing perceptions about sickness and morbidity, particularly of women. It is well known that there are many disease conditions which are not perceived as morbid conditions by the people but which require medical attention and treatment, especially in traditional societies characterised where high morbidity and mortality levels exists and where general awareness about morbidity and their causes are low.

In the present survey, about 7 per cent of the females with at least 5 years of age were reported to be sick at the time of the survey. In the absence of proper investigation and diagnosis, this proportion may be viewed as an indication of the prevailing levels of morbidity in females of the surveyed families. Even more important is the observation that most of the reported morbidity was concentrated in the reproductive age group - of the total females reported to be sick at the time of the survey (more than 85 per cent belonged to the reproductive age group). On the other hand, more than 70 per cent of the reported sickness in females was due to two widely prevalent causes of morbidity - fever and pain in the abdomen. Fever alone accounted for half of the reported sickness in females above five years of age and this pattern is very similar to the pattern of morbidity observed in children below 5 years of age, either male or female. In addition, leucorrhoea and asthma were reported in about 10 per cent of the females who were reported to be sick at the time of the survey.

During the survey 24 pregnant women were identified. These women were requested to report all problems and complications that they were facing as the result of pregnancy. Two third of these pregnant women reported that they were having problems and complications as the result of pregnancy. Most of the pregnant women reported more than one problems and complications as the result of the pregnancy. The most common problem reported by pregnant women was weakness, closely followed by pain in the body and in the lower abdomen. In general the rate of pregnancy related complications in the women surveyed was very high despite the fact that general perception of females about reproductive health problems was poor. There was a general belief among the pregnant women surveyed that pregnancy is always associated with some problems and complications. These women were of the view that normally problems and complications associated with pregnancy were not regarded as serious enough for any attention or treatment.

Patterns of Treatment and Care

An important component of the health and nutritional status of any population is the patterns of treatment and care which is more popularly known as the health seeking behaviour. During the survey, information about treatment and care of the sick was collected for all those who were found sick at the time of the survey. Issues related to treatment and care that were covered during the survey included breast-feeding practices, immunisation status in women and children, nature of treatment during diarrhoea, fever and respiratory infections in children, patterns of treatment in women and children found sick at the time of the survey and attention and care during pregnancy. This section presents an overview of the situation that prevailed in the families surveyed.

Breast-feeding

Breast-feeding among the children surveyed was found to be nearly universal and quite prolonged. Nearly half of the children below 5 years of age were breast-feeding at the time of the survey. Among those who were not breast-feeding at the time of the survey, only 4 per cent were never breast fed whereas in more than one third, breast-feeding lasted for more than 18 months.

Immunisation

There was some substantial variation in the coverage of children below 5 years of age by different vaccines. Highest coverage of children was found to be in case of the first dose of oral polio vaccine. More than 78 per cent of the children below 5 years of age in the families surveyed were reported to have received the first dose of oral polio vaccines. The coverage of the second dose of oral polio vaccine was also very high; there was a drop of just 1.4 per cent between the first and second dose of this vaccine. But the gap between the second and third doses was found to be very large; while nearly 77 per cent of the children surveyed were found to have received the second dose of oral polio vaccine, this proportion was only 68 per cent in case of the third dose of the vaccine. Similarly, more than 72 per cent of the children surveyed had been found to have received the BCG vaccination.

Unlike the oral polio vaccine, the coverage of children below 5 years of age by the DPT vaccine has been found to be substantially lower; only about 56 per cent of the children surveyed were found to have received first dose of DPT vaccine and this proportion for the third dose of the vaccine was only about 47 per cent. Lowest coverage, however, had been found to be in case of measles vaccination; less than 40 per cent children below 5 years of age surveyed were found to have received the measles vaccination.

Sex differentials in vaccination of children in the surveyed families has been found to be quite interesting. In case of first doses of oral polio vaccine and DPT vaccine, the coverage rate was found to be higher in male than in female children. At the same time, the drop out between first and third doses of the same vaccine has also been found to be higher in male than in female children. As the result, the coverage rate of the third dose of both oral polio and DPT vaccines has been found to be higher in female as compared to male children. The drop out rate between first and third dose of oral polio vaccine was almost 17 per cent in male children but only about 9 per cent in female children; the corresponding proportions were 19 per cent and 12 per cent respectively for the DPT vaccine. On the other hand, the coverage rate of BCG vaccine was marginally higher while that of the measles vaccine was substantially higher in female as compared to male children.

Treatment of Sickness

A clear preference for a private doctor/hospital for the treatment of current and past sickness in the surveyed families was very much evident from the survey. In children below 5 years of age found sick at the time of the survey, more than 47 per cent were being treated at some private facility either in the village or in the nearby village/ town. In case of children, sick during one-month prior to the survey, this proportion was almost 63 per cent. In specific cases of diarrhoea, fever and coughs also, the preferred place of treatment was private health care facility.

Another important feature of the treatment pattern that was observed during the survey is that, a very substantial proportion of population who was found sick at the time of the survey or was sick during one month prior to the survey had either no treatment at all or some home treatment only. Among children below 5 years of age who were found sick at the time of the survey, this proportion was more than 37 per cent whereas in children who were sick sometimes during one month prior to the survey, this proportion was almost 20 per cent. On the other hand, three fourth of the women reported to be pregnant at the time of the survey and having some complications associated with pregnancy were found to be having no treatment and care for the problems that they were facing as the result of the pregnancy.

Since reproductive health is a major contributor to the over all health status of women, detailed information about care and attention during pregnancy was collected from women reported pregnant at the time of the survey. The situation that emerged in the surveyed families may be termed as alarming. Two third of the women reported to be pregnant at the time of the survey had no antenatal examination whereas only one fourth were examined only once during the pregnancy. Similarly, three fourth of the pregnant women had no tetanus toxoid immunisation, while blood pressure was measured and urine was examined respectively in less than 20 per cent and less than 5 per cent.

Observations from Focus Group Discussions

In addition to the quantitative information on the health and nutritional status of the population collected on the basis of household survey, focus group discussions were also organised in all villages where the household survey was carried out. The primary purpose of organising the focus group discussion was to provide the qualitative supplement to the quantitative information collected through the structured interviews. These focus group discussions focussed on the following broad topics:

- Diseases and morbid conditions prevalent in the village.
- Reasons for prevailing health and nutrition situation.
- Availability of health care facilities in the village and nearby villages.
- Means of transport.
- Nutritional status of children and factors associated with given nutritional status.
- Occupation and employment opportunities in the village.

Main observations of the focus group discussions are summarised below:

i. The disease profile that emerged from the focus group discussions was very similar to that emerged through the household survey. Fever, mostly associated with Malaria was found to be the most widely prevalent morbid condition in the villages surveyed.

ii. The villagers were not having any clear idea about the prevailing nutritional situation. However, the over all view was that the lack cf adequate diet was the main cause of poor nutritional status.

iii. In a number of villages, availability of safe drinking water was a major problem. This observation is supported by the fact that diseases of digestive system emerged as an important cause of morbidity in the household survey also. Hand pumps were installed in most of the villages but the use of the hand pumps was not popular, as water from even hand pumps was not found safe for human consumption. At some places, villagers were quite concerned about the near total neglect of traditional, time tested concepts of traditional, time tested ways and means of conserving and protecting water.

iv. Most of the participants in the focus group discussions were nearly totally ignorant about the need of balanced diet and proper dietary habits to combat malnutrition. Moreover, there were very limited options for improving the availability and quality of the food as the agriculture in the surveyed villages was traditional and the poverty was rampant in the villages surveyed.

v. Availability of basic minimum health care facility in every village was another issue that was raised by the villagers during the focus group discussion. Villagers were quite critical about the inability of the public administration to provide even the basic minimal health care facilities in the villages surveyed.

vi. Males were nearly totally indifferent about the health-related issues specific to females. There were very few participants in the focus group discussions who were really concerned about the health of women. Involvement of males in addressing female health issues, especially, reproductive health issues, emerged an important concern.

Conclusions

The findings of the survey presented and discussed in the forgoing pages provide some very valuable insight into the health and nutrition status of the tribal population of Jhabua and Dhar districts of Madhya Pradesh. It is clear from the information generated through the survey that the process of transition in the health and nutritional status of tribal population in the two districts is extremely slow despite all investments in the health sector. It appears that focussed efforts to accelerate the process of social and economic development are strongly needed to accelerate health transition in the population surveyed.

REFERENCES

United Nations, 1986. How to Weigh and Measure Children. New York, United Nations.

United Nations, 1990. Assessing the Nutritional Status of Young Children. New York, United Nations. National Household Survey Capability Programme.

United States, Public Health Service, Health Resources Administration, 1976. NCHS Growth Charts. Rockville, Maryland.

Waterlow, J.C. et al 1977. The presentation and use of height and weight data for comparing the nutritional status of groups of children under the age of 10 years. Bulletin of the World Health Organization, 55: 489-498.

World Health Organization, 1978. Lay Reporting of Health Information. World Health Organization, Geneva.

Table 1: Basic Characteristics of Families Surveyed

Number of families surveyed	300
Average annual per capita income at market prices	2448
Proportion of families having average annual per capita income of less than Rs 1000 at market prices	19.21
Family belongings	
Pressure cooker	4.62
Electric fan	14.85
Bicycle	21.12
Motor cycle/scooter	4.62
Radio/Tape recorded	8.91
Stitching machine	4.95
Television (B/W)	7.92
Television (colour)	0.33
Telephone	0.66
Refrigerator	0.66

(Contd...)

Car/Jeep	0.33
Tractor	0.66
Water pump	1.32
Thrasher	0.66
Bullock cart	8.25
Type of house	
Kuchcha	92.08
Pucca	4.29
Semi Pucca	3.63
Proportion of houses having separate kitchen	8.58
Proportion of houses having electricity	58.09
Source of drinking water	
Tap/well/hand pump in the house	18.14
Public tap/well/hand pump	72.93
Others	7.92
Proportion of houses having latrines	34.22

Table 2: Characteristics of Population Surveyed

Total population surveyed	
Total	1698
Male	874
Female	824
Average family size	5.7
Sex ratio of population surveyed (F/M)	943
Dependency ratio	
All	931
Young	835
Old	96
Child-woman ratio	646
Crude birth rate	31
Crude death rate	13
Infant mortality rate	96
Proportion of population above 6 years ever gone to school	
All	26
Male	38
Female	13
Occupational structure	
No work	45
Agriculture	39.35

(Contd...)

Labour	12.22
Business	2.06
Service	0.92
Others	0.14

Table 3:Morbidity and Nutritional Status of Children below 5 Years of Age

Children below 5 years of age		*All*	*Male*	*Female*
Found sick at the time of the survey		20.63	21.52	19.53
Fever		14.34	15.19	13.28
Cough		01.75	02.53	00.78
Abdominal pain		01.05	01.90	00.00
Others		03.49	01.90	05.47
Sick during one month prior to the survey		41.26	42.41	39.84
Having diarrhoea during one month prior to the survey		26.22	25.32	27.34
Total days of diarrhoea				
1-3 days		47.30	50.00	44.12
4-7 days		24.32	25.00	23.52
> 7 days		28.38	25.00	32.35
Having high fever and associated symptoms during one month prior to the survey		43.36	44.30	42.10
High fever with shivering		34.26	37.34	30.47
High fever with convulsions		19.23	21.52	16.41
Having acute respiratory infections during one month prior to the survey		44.06	46.20	41.41
Breathing problem		33.22	36.71	28.91
Whooping cough		16.08	17.72	14.06
Nutritional Status	Proportion “wasted”		20.89	16.50
	Proportion “stunted”		71.56	62.92
	Proportion low weight-for-age	71.85	54.95	

Table 4: Patterns of Morbidity in Females above 5 Years of Age

Proportion of women reported sick at the time of the survey	6.91
Pattern of sickness	
All	100.00
Fever	47.62
Leucorrhoea	9.52
Pain in abdomen	23.81
Asthma	9.52
Blood Pressure	4.76
Others	4.76
Age pattern of sickness	
All	100.00
5-14	9.52
15-49	85.71
50 and above	4.76

Table 5: Complications Associated with Pregnancy

Complications	*Proportion of pregnant women*
Bleeding	37.50
Weakness	66.67
High blood pressure	33.33
Swelling in the feet	45.83
High fever	54.17
Bad discharge	45.83
Pain in the back and the body	62.50
Pain in lower abdomen	62.50
Anaemia	45.83
Convulsions	54.17
Breach delivery	33.33
Others	41.67

Remarks: Figures do not add to 100 as the respondents reported multiple complications.

Table 6: Management and Treatment of Sickness in Children below 5 Years of Age

Particulars	*All*	*Male*	*Female*
Current sickness			
Taken to Vaidya/Hakeem	03.38	00.00	08.00
Taken to private doctor/hospital	47.36	55.88	36.00
Taken to government doctor/hospital	10.17	02.94	20.00
No treatment/home treatment	35.29	38.24	36.00
Sickness during one month prior to the survey			
Taken to Vaidya/Hakeem	00.79	00.00	01.85
Taken to private doctor/hospital	62.99	60.28	66.67
Taken to government doctor/hospital	15.75	12.33	20.37
No treatment/home treatment	19.69	26.03	11.11
Management of diarrhoea			
Proportion given ORS	25.33	22.50	28.57
Proportion continued breast-feeding	49.12	54.84	42.31
Proportion taken to Vaidya/Hakeem	02.67	00.00	05.71
Proportion taken to doctor/hospital	73.27	72.50	74.29
Treatment of high fever			
Proportion taken to Vaidya/Hakeem	00.00	00.00	00.00
Proportion taken to doctor/hospital	84.67	84.82	85.19
No treatment/Home treatment	15.33	15.72	14.81
Treatment of ARI			
Proportion taken to Vaidya/Hakeem	01.59	01.37	01.89
Proportion taken to doctor/hospital	76.19	76.71	75.47
No treatment/Home treatment	22.22	21.92	22.64

Table 7: Management and Treatment of Sickness in Women

Particulars	*Proportion*
Management and treatment of sickness in all women	
Consulted Vaidya/Hakeem	04.76
Consulted/attended private doctor/hospital	42.86
Consulted/attended government doctor/hospital	14.29
No treatment/Home treatment	38.10
Management and treatment of complications related to pregnancy	
Consulted Vaidya/Hakeem	00.00
Consulted/attended private doctor/hospital	12.50
Consulted/attended government doctor/hospital	12.51
No treatment/Home treatment	75.00
Antenatal examination during pregnancy	
Three times and more	04.17
Less than three times	25.00
No examination	66.67
Tetanus toxoid during pregnancy	
Two doses	04.17
One dose	16.67
None	75.00
Pregnant women having blood pressure check up	16.67
Pregnant women having urine examination	04.17

Chapter 11

Demography of Tribes: A Case Study of Sidhi District, M.P.

A. Kumar, H.N. Gautam & K.N.S. Yadava

Usually there are two traditions of demographic analysis. The first one is the technical or pure demography dealing with quantitative analysis of population phenomena covering both aspects of structural and dynamic. There has been a number of studies on such tradition and consequently sophisticated analytical techniques, laws and theories have been developed (Lorimer, 1959). It generates a second tradition, which focuses on the causes and consequences of population change, and, more specifically on the discussion of the related population problems. It may be called a social science approach of population study. According to Carr-Saunders (1922) all population problems have a single common root, the need and efforts of human societies to adjust their numbers and composition to the environment. Since the Second World War, increasing attention has been paid to the problem of under-development basing its analysis of interrelationship between population growth and economic development. Besides, there has been discussion on the association between population and levels of economic development both at the macro- and micro- levels.

For the present demographic analysis, the second approach has been followed. It is because of several reasons. First perspective of the survey was to correlate the indices of the demographic parameters with the process and planning for development, as it is generally recognized that demographic indices have to play a role in the nation's building. Population size, its composition and processes of change therein all are taken as basis of development. Programs such as the family planning, universal literacy, employment generation etc. of India intend to modify demographic attributes to cope with the developmental requirements. Needless to mention that the effectiveness of a developmental planning depends, to a great extent, on the demographic trends of the society – whether it is the question of controlling the size and quality of population or adoption of new and improved techniques, tools practices of raising production, in all physical, social and economic characteristics of the people concerned (Dasgupta, 1989 and Desai, 1975, 1990). As such the level of development of an area presents imprint of population characteristics, and therefore, may be evaluated in the perspective of the demographic situation of the area.

Needless to mention that the variation in the socioeconomic status of the people has been one of the major causes of inequality in the developing countries (Sundaram, 1983). Several studies attempted to analyse levels of regional development in Madhya Pradesh state of India and Sidhi district is placed in the category of very low developed districts (Agrawal and Khan 1983; Baghel, 1993; Dutta, 1980; Mishra and Chopra, 1979; Mishra and Gaikwad, 1979; Sharma, 1985; 1988).

In perspectives of the demographic differences between tribal and non-tribal population, and close association between population characteristics and the level of development, the objective of this study is to analyse the dynamics of growth of tribal population, emphasizing on the inter-tribal variation and to asses the relative position of tribal population in respect of certain demographic parameters in Sidhi district of M. P. Both primary and secondary sources of data have been utilized for this purpose.

The Data and Methodology

For this study population of tribes community of Sidhi district of Madhya Pradesh has been selected. The basic information has been extracted from census publications, particularly from District Census Handbook of Sidhi district of 1961, 1971, 1981 and 1991 censuses. These information have been supplemented by a sample survey entitled "A Demographic Survey of Tribes in Sidhi district, MP" during

1994-95. Located on the north-eastern extremity of the state, Sidhi district extends from 23 47' to 24 42' north latitudes and from 81 28' to 82 49' east longitudes and covers 10526 sq km of area. It is 2.37 per cent of the total area of the state. Total population of the district is 13,73,434 persons, about 2 per cent of total population of the state. Out of this a total of 4,18,004 persons belonged to tribes communities, which constituted 30.47 per cent of total population of the district. This proportion was found much higher than the state average of 23.27 per cent (Census of India, 1991). Thus it is one of the major tribal districts of the state.

The district is divided into eight developmental blocks and out of them Kusmi, Deosar and Chitrengi are known as tribes developmental blocks (TDB). There are two Integrated Tribal Development Projects functioning in the district. First one covers Kusmi block as a whole and 231 Tribal villages of Sidhi (87), Sihawal (23), Rampur (8), Majhauli (54) and Waidhan (59) blocks. Its headquarter is at Kusmi. Second project covers all villages of Deosar and Chitrengi blocks (Sharma, 1989). A large number of tribal communities were found residing in this district. Out of them six tribes were main namely, Gond, Baiga, Panika, Kol, Biar and Khairwar .

Since the objective of the sample survey was to interview tribal households of Sidhi district. Tribal people were distributed throughout the district with concentration in hilly and forested tracts. At the same time, not all tribes were found in one and the same settlement. The areas of their dominance are separate from each other but little is known about their spatial distribution. Under these constraints, it was very difficult to pre-decide the location of sample. Rather it was emphasized to contact households of all major tribes. In this process, tribal households residing in 87 villages of Sidhi were interviewed. A sample of 1528 households was enumerated comprising households of Gond, Kol, Baiga, Panika, Khairwar and Biar tribes.

Tribal Population, Density and Concentration Index

As pointed out earlier, the main thrust of the present study is to understand the demographic character of the tribal people of Sidhi district. It was found that the demographic character of the tribal people was quite distinct from the general population. For example, growth rate of tribal population during 1961-91 has been lower (2.5%) than that of total population (2.9%) in Sidhi district. The total fertility rate (4.0) per tribal woman was also lower than the total fertility rate of the state (5.3). Low propensity of migration among the tribal people is known fact. Sex ratio was comparatively high (985 females per 1000 males). Early marriage in tribal population, particularly among females was found prevalent. Literacy rate has been extremely low in spite of multifarious attack on illiteracy. All physically able males and females of this community work to earn livelihood. Consequently, participation rate among males (54.3%) and females (42.8%) was very high in comparison to the district and state averages. But most of economically active people were found engaged in agriculture (92.0%). Largest number of tribal people (85,561 persons) was in Chitrengi block followed by Deosar block (77,358 persons). Sidhi and Waidhan blocks also support more than 50 thousand tribal people. Block-wise tribal population is presented in Appendix 2.

Distribution of tribal population can also be looked in terms of the 'concentration index'. Proportion of tribal population of the block in total tribal population of the district is taken as the 'concentration index'. For instance, total tribal population of Chitrengi block was 85,561, about 20.5 per cent of total tribal population (4,18,004) of the district. This percentage is taken as the concentration index of Chitrengi block. Block wise index varied from 7.6 per cent of Sihawal block to 20.5 per cent of Chitrengi block. Thus, largest concentration of tribal population was found in eastern part of the district.

Both absolute number and concentration index, sometimes, fail to depict real picture. Both of them depend on the size of the Arial unit under consideration. For example, Chitrengi block possesses largest area among blocks of this district and constitutes 21.4 per cent of area of all blocks. It shares only 20.4 per cent of total tribal population, lower than its shared area. It means its large size of tribal population is in fact, not due to high concentration but is due to large areal extent. Whereas Deosar supports much higher proportion of tribal population (18.5%) on a lower proportion of area (12.6%). On average, 130 persons were found living per sq km of area in the district out of which 40 persons belonged to the tribal communities. This density of tribal population was found much higher than the state average of 27 persons. Average density of population in the state was 149 persons per sq km.

It is also evident that Gond and allied tribes constitute major share of the tribal population followed by the Baiga, Panika and Kol of the district. Other three tribes, viz. Agaria, Biar and Khairwar were numerically significant. Along with them, population of Pardhan, Oraon, Kawar, Bharia and Kamar tribes was between 100 and 300 each. Parja, Sawar and Bhil-Bhilla were more than 50 persons each (See Appendix 3).

Growth of Tribal Population

Annual average growth rate among the tribes of the district was 2.92 per cent while for the state was 2.56. For the total population including tribal population was 3.39 per cent. During the period (1961-1991) the growth of tribal population of this district was also found lower (113.62%) than the average growth (130.6%) of tribal population in the state. Comparison of growth in tribal population is presented in Appendix 4.

It is evident from the preceding discussion that growth varies spatially and temporally. It also varies from tribe to tribe. Since tribe wise breakup is not available for 1991, only 1981 census data has been used for this purpose. After the amendment made in 1976, a list of the number of tribes gone up to 31 whereas it was only 16 prior to this amendment. Data about 12 of them were available. Population of these tribes in 1961 and 1981 are given in Appendix 5.

Total tribal population grew by 58.26 per cent during 1961-81, recording average annual rate of 2.32 per cent. This rate was found lower than average rate for 1961-91. As discussed earlier, rate of annual growth was much lower during 1971-81(2.05%) than during 1961-71(2.59%). Out of the 12 tribes, which are considered here only seven recorded positive growth and remaining three tribes shown a declining trend. On state level also population of these tribes declined during this period.

Distribution of Tribal Population: Determinants

It is generally felt that the distribution of rural population is directly related to the capability and productivity of land (Mishra and

Sharma, 1983, Tiwary and Mishra, 1993). But it is not true in the case of tribal population. As mentioned earlier, tribal population have been pushed to some inhospitable environment and more so on a less suitable land for cultivation. With this view, relationship of the proportion of tribal population (Y = percentage of tribal population to total) with the following variables has been analyzed:

X1= percentage of net sown area to total area.

X2= percentage of area under forests.

X3= percentage of barren and uncultivable lands.

X4= percentage of area of major crops under high yielding variety of seeds.

X5= percentage of irrigated area to total cropped area.

Block-wise data of above variables for all eight blocks are processed and results are presented in Table 1.

Table 1: Correlation of Proportion of Tribes with Certain Variables

Variable	*x*	σ	Σ*xy*	*R*
Y	35.0	14.3	-	-
X1	37.4	13.9	-175.3	-0.88
X2	37.4	15.9	-1627.3	0.89
X3	7.2	6.7	24.3	-0.25
X4	11.0	13.3	9.2	0.05
X5	3.9	2.7	3.2	0.08

It is clear from Table 1 that the proportion of tribal population has direct and significant relation with the forested area (X2). It validates the character of tribals as 'VANAVASI'. This implies that most of the tribal population may concentrate in forests. Contrary to it, concentration of tribal population has been found negatively and significantly related with the proportion of net cropped area (X1). This indicates that the proportion of cropped area has been very limited among the major tribal areas and due to poor land capability, it may not be extended any more.

Some Demographic Indices Based on Sample Data

Based on sample observations some demographic indices are also computed. Due to small number of observation, it is difficult to make any generalization on the demographic scenario among the tribes community in the country. However, this sample study may provide some ideas about the recent trend in the growth of the tribal population in the study region, a central part of the country.

Crude Birth Rate and General Fertility Rate

Table 2 gives the Crude Birth Rate (CBR) and General Fertility Rate (GFR) in different castes of the tribes community. Not much difference has been noted in CBR of the different tribes. However, a higher value of these demographic measures were found among Kol, Panika and Gond tribes as compared to others. The CBR and GFR were found 37.2 and 127 respectively and these values are somewhat lower than the general rural population of the district and state. The Total Fertility Rate (TFR) (table not shown here) has been found in this sample as 3.99, a lower value than about 4.5 in rural population of the state (Dwivedi, 1995; Gupta and Baghel, 1992 and Pandey and Tiwary, 1995).

Table 2: Crude Birth Rate and General Fertility Rate among Tribes, 1995

Tribe	*Average mid year population*	*Children under 1 year of age*	*C B R*	*Number of women in child bearing age*	*GFR*
Kol	326	12	39.9	102	118
Panika	120	06	50.0	30	200
Khairwar	60	02	33.3	23	87
Biar	30	--	--	06	--
Baiga	108	04	37.0	249	129
Gond	861	32	37.2	33	121
All	1505	56	37.2	441	127

Family Planning Performance

The Government has made vigorous efforts to control the high growth of population and consequently a number of family planning programmes have been launched. To assess its effectiveness among tribals, four questions were asked about such family planning programmes during the sample survey. Results of these questions are presented in Table 3 below.

Table 3: Awareness about the Family Planning Programmes among Sample Tribal Households, 1995

Tribe	*Knowledge of Programmes*		*Acceptance*	
	Number	*%*	*Number*	*%*
Gond	103	78.0	51	38.6
Kol	37	77.1	08	16.7
Baiga	9	52.9	02	11.8
Panika	15	78.9	06	31.6
Khairwar	6	60.0	-	-
Biar	4	100.00	04	100.00
All	174	75.7	71	

It was found that information of family planning programmes has reached to more than three-fourth of households of the tribes. Only Baiga and Khairwar tribes were behind the average situation. Mostly they have got information from the medical and health personnel. However, a vast gap between knowing and accepting the family planning methods was observed. Only about 41 per cent of the total population who were knowing about the family planning adopted any measure to plan their family.

It was tried to know the reasons of not accepting family planning measures despite knowing about them. There are 103 persons who do not adopt them, though they are informed about them. Tribe-wise and caste-wise distribution of these persons is presented in Table 4 below. A major sections (about 45%) of the informed tribals fear that methods of family planning are injurious to health and reduces the working capacity drastically. Still one-tenth (about 12%) of them believe that these measures are against their religious faiths and about one third of these wanted more children.

Table 4: Reasons for not Accepting FPP by Informed Tribals, 1995

Tribe	*Wanted more children*		*Against religion*		*Harmful to health*		*Other reasons*	
	No	*%*	*No*	*%*	*No*	*%*	*No*	*%*
Gond	20	38.5	6	11.5	20	38.5	6	11.5
Kol	7	24.1	6	20.7	13	44.8	3	10.3
Baiga	1	14.3	-	-	6	85.7		
Panika	1	11.1	-	-	6	66.7	2	22.2
Khairwar	5	83.3	-	-	1	16.7		
Biar	-	-	-	-	-	-	-	-
All	34	33.0	12	11.7	46	44.7	11	10.6

Tribe Specific Death Rate

As tribes vary in socioeconomic and demographic characteristics from each other, it may lead to the variation in their mortality rate. The tribe specific death rates are presented in Table 5. Tribe-wise difference in death rate was found not significant. It ranged from 6.7 per thousand in Khairwar tribe to 8.6 in Gond.

Table 5: Tribe Specific Death Rates, 1995

Tribe	*Person*	*Male*	*Female*
Gond	8.6	7.2	10.1
Baiga	7.4	8.0	6.9
Kol	7.4	4.7	10.2
Panika	8.3	8.6	8.0

(Contd...)

Khairwar	6.7	7.1	6.3
Biar	7.6	7.4	8.1
All	8.0	6.7	9.3
Mean	7.7	7.1	8.3
S.D	0.7	1.3	1.6
C.V.	8.9	18.7	19.4

Cause Specific Death Rate

Classification of deaths according to the cause of death is presented in Table 6. The head of the household or some adult member of the household supplied the cause of death. In many cases, no medical diagnosis of the illness, which led to the patient's death was available. Therefore these causes of death are only intelligent guesses of the informants. Under this situation, no valid conclusion can be drawn from this Table. Besides old age, skin disease like small pox and diseases of digestive system like dysentery, diarrhoea and cholera and fever were found the major killers among the tribes community.

Table 6: Cause Specific Death Rates among Tribals, 1995

Cause of death	*% of Total death*	*Death rate per 10,000*
Old age	13.3	10.6
Small pox	11.7	9.3
Cholera, etc.	11.7	9.3
Fever	10.0	8.0
Jaundice	3.3	2.7
Paralysis	1.7	1.3
Poisoning	1.7	1.3
Electric shock	1.7	1.3
Snake biting	1.7	1.3
Unspecified	43.3	36.6

Conclusions

A brief demographic sketch of the tribes community residing in the Sidhi district of Madhya Pradesh State has been drawn in this paper. Findings are based both on primary and secondary sources of data. Census records have been used to study the trends, distribution and growth in tribes population during the past several decades in the state. The sample data collected during 1995 have been utilized to study some of the demographic parameters of the tribals. All the tribes communities showed more or less a similar pattern in demographic behaviour and demographic indices are found slightly lower than the average level of the state.

REFERENCES

Agarwal, P.C. and Khan, Z.T. 1983. Spatial Analysis of Regional Development in M.P. In: Pandey, P. (ed): Modern Geographical Trends. Today and Tomorrow, New Delhi, pp. 315-324.

Baghel, A. 1993. Tribal Fertility: A Case Study of Tribals of Gariaband Block of Raipur District. In: Phanse, V. (ed): Scenario of the Evaluation and Exploitation of Tribal Resources. G.A.C.C. Indore, pp. 53-60.

Carr-Saunders, A.M. 1922. The Population Problem: A Study in Human Evolution. The Clarendon Press, Oxford.

Dasgupta, S., 1989. Diffusion of Agricultural Innovations in village India. Wiley Eastern Limited, New Delhi.

Datta, T.N. 1980. Regional Variations in the Levels of Development of M.P. Geographical Review of India, 42: 254-260.

Desai, P.B.1975. A Survey of Research in Demography. Popular Prakasan, Bombay.

Dwivedi, G.K. 1995. Statistical Analysis of Demography and Development of Tribal of Sindh District (M.P.). Unpublished Ph.D. Thesis in Statistics, Rewa Unversity, Rewa.

Gupta, H.S. and Baghel, A. 1992. Regional Variation in Fertility in M.P. Transactions of Institute of Indian Geographers. 14: pp. 163-169.

Jain, C.K. and Sharma, S.K. 1994. Tribals of M.P.: Habitat and Economy. In: Gupta, G.P. (ed): Socio-cultural Environment of Tribal Landscapes. Ashant Publishers, Jaipur, pp. 225-245.

Lorimer, F. 1959. The Development of Demography. In: Houser, P.M. and

Duncan, O.D. (eds): The Study of Population. University of Chicago Press, Chicago, pp. 124-179.

Mishra, S.K. and Chopra, A. 1979. Dimensions of Inter-District Disparities in Level of Development in M.P. Indian Journal of Regional Science, 1: pp. 1-7.

Mishra, S. K. and Gaikwad, S.B. 1979. Impact of Economic Development on Welfare and Living Conditions of People of M.P. Indian Journal of Regional Science, X: 25-35.

Mishra, V.C. and Sharma, S.K. 1983. Population Growth and Agricultural Changes in M.P.: Analysis of their Correlates. National Geographer, 18: pp. 141-152.

Pandey, G.D. and Tiwary, R.S. 1995. Literacy and Demographic Characteristics: A Study of Association among the Tribals of M.P. In: Tiwary, S.K. (ed): Tribal Situation and Development in Central India. M.D. Publications Pvt. Ltd., New Delhi, pp. 61-68.

Sauvy, A. 1969. General Theory of Population. Weidenfeld and Nicolson, London.

Sharma, S. K. 1988. Regional Resource-Base and Pattern of Economic Development in M.P. In: Vidyanath, V. and Rao, M. (eds): Development of India's Resource-base. Gyan Pub.Co. New Delhi, pp. 123-44.

Sharma, S.K. 1989. Patterns of Immigration in M.P. Geographical Review of India, 51: pp. 61-75.

Sharma, S.K. 1995. Tribal Demography. In: Tiwary, S.K. (ed): Tribal Situation and Development in Central India. M.D. Publications Pvt Ltd., New Delhi: pp 51-61.

Sundaram, K.V. 1983. Geoaraphv of Under-development. Concept Pub. Co., New Delhi.

Tiwary, S.K. and Mishra, K. 1993. The Pattern of Prevalence of Mosquito-borne Diseases in Tribal Areas of Vindhyanchal-Baghelkhand Region of M.P. pp. 173-79.

Annexure 1: Sidhi District: Block wise Population and Density, 1991

Block	*Total Poputation*	*Area (sq. km)**	*% of Total District Poputation*	*% Share of Area*	*Density per sq.km*
Rampur	172394	778.87	12.55	8.83	221
Sidhi	216445	1021.74	15.76	11.59	212
Sihawal	167188	744.46	12.17	8.44	225
Majhauli	102135	734.60	7.44	8.33	139
Kushmib	51274	1438.49	3.73	16.31	36
Deosar	174711	1112.95	12.72	12.62	157
Chitrengi	195619	1889.24	14.24	21.42	104
Waidhan	293668	1097.57	21.38	12.45	268
District	1373434	10526.00	100.00	-	130

b-Including forest village Karwahi
*Area according to village papers
** According to survey of India
Source: Villagel Town Primary Census Abstract, 1991,obtained from N.I.C, M.P.State Unit, District Collectorate, Sidhi.

Annexure 2 : Sidhi District: Block- wise Population and Density of Tribes, 1991

Block	*Tribes Population*	*% of Total Block Population*	*% of Total Tribes Pop. of District*	*Density of Tribes (per sq km)*
Rampur	36451	21.14	8.72	47
Sidhi	60642	28.02	14.51	59
Sihiwal	31890	19.07	7.63	43
Majhauli	34118	33.40	8.16	46
Kusmi	33224	64.80	7.95	23
Chitrengi	85561	43.74	20.47	45
Deosar	77358	44.28	18.51	70
Waidhan	58760	25.58	14.06	54
District	418004	30.43	100.00	40

Annexure 3: Sidhi District: Population of Major Tribes, 1981

Tribe	*Person*	*Male*	*Female*	*Percentage of S.T. in Distt.*	*Percentage of S.T. in State*
Gond	147914	74918	72996	47.76	2.8
Baiga	32234	16404	15830	10.41	12.9
Panika	23283	11778	11505	7.52	43.9
Kol	16593	8414	8178	5.36	13.4
Agaria	8015	4121	3894	2.59	14.4
Khairwar	1573	794	779	0.51	10.9
Biar	4106	2133	1973	1.33	55.7
All tribes	309684	157109	152575	100.00	4.6

Source: Census of India 1981, Series 11, M.P. Part IX (VII) Special Tables for Scheduled Tribes.

Annexure 4: Sidhi District: Comparison of Growth of Tribal Population, 1961-91

Year	*Sidhi District*			*Madhya Pradesh*	
	Tribes Population	*% Growth of Tribes Population*	*% Growth of Total Population*	*%Growth of Total Population*	*%Growth of Tribes Population*
1961	195678				
1971	252737	29.16	33.90	28.7	25.59
1981	309684	22.53	27.51	25.3	42.92
1991	418004	34.98	38.67	26.8	28.46
1961-91	--	113.62	136.75	104.4	130.58

Source: District. Census Handbooks of Sidhi for 1961-81 and Computer- sheet for 1991.

Annexure 5: Sidhi District: Tribe- wise Growth of Population, 1961-81

Tribes	*Population*		*% Growth*	*Annual*
	1961	*1981*	*(1961-1981)*	*Growth Rate (percentage)*
All	195678	309684	58.26	2.32
Agaria	4676	8015	61.07	2.41
Baiga	20624	32234	56.29	2.26
Bhil	02	50	2400.00	17.46
Bharia	40	186	365.00	7.99
Biar	2378	4106	72.67	2.77
Gond	89327	147914	65.59	2.55
Khairwar	6724	1573	-76.61	-7.01
Kol	54079	16593	-69.32	-5.74
Manjhi	08	08	00.00	-
Nat etc.	52	NA	-	-
Panika	15659	23283	48.69	2.00
Rao	105	21	-80.00	-7.73

Source: District. Census Handbook, 1961 and Census of India 1981, M.P. Special Tables for Scheduled Tribes, Part ix (vii).

Chapter 12

Trends of Morbidity among Bharias of Patalkot, Madhya Pradesh

A.N. Sharma

The tribal groups in India form about 8.08 per cent of the total population of India. There are seventy-five primitive tribes in India. The health status of the primitive tribes depicts a different situation as compared to other backward castes. The deforestation, impact of urbanization, chances of expenses increases and generation of less income have altered their way of life adversely affecting their survival in their habitat. As such majority of the primitive tribal population, who live in dense forest do not have access to adequate health facilities and are prone to several diseases. The studies related to primitive tribes indicate high degree of morbidity rates etc.

The importance of the trends of morbidity and the like have drawn the attention of several workers, viz., Adair (1970), Agrawal (1973), Ahluwalia (1974), Sinha (1979), Mathur (1982) and Sharma (1994) etc. Here, attempt has been made to study the possible aspects of trends of morbidity among the primitive tribes of Bharia of Patalkot of Madhya Pradesh.

Materials and methods

The data have been collected from Bharias of Patalkot valley, Madhya Pradesh, India. The Bharias of Patalkot are one of the most primitive tribal populations of Madhya Pradesh. The 'Bharias' are the Dravidian tribe, they have forgotten their origin and several stories of the origin of the tribe are prevalent, based on the farfetched derivation of the name. They live in the villages of Patalkot a natural formation in Tamia Block of Chhindwara district of Madhya Pradesh, India. Patalkot is a bowl shaped formation situated on Satpura plateau and is located between 22^0-24' and 22^0-29' North Latitude and 78^0-43' and 78^0-50' East Longitude. The estimated total area of Patalkot is about 79 sq. kms. The shape of this natural formation is like a horse-shoe, surrounded on three sides directly by hilly ridges and open somewhat on the north west side towards Dudhi river. The approach to Patalkot from outside is extremely difficult due to straight ridges and uneven terrain within Patalkot area, there are neither any shops or weekly markets or modern health facilities. Bharias of this area climb the ridges and walk from 5 to 25 kms. on foot to attend weekly markets, government offices and modern medical facilities. The whole of the area becomes completely cut-off during rainy season, not only from outside, but within Patalkot movement is not possible. The member of Bharia tribe depends mainly for medical cure on folk medicines.

The present investigation is based on the observation and interview of 305 individuals of Bharia tribe of Patalkot. The present investigation has been conducted through an interview schedule. Simultaneously, group discussion and formal interview method have also been used. All the villages (12) and hamlets have been covered from Patalkot valley. One sample has been selected randomly from each available household. In this regard representation of approximate total population of Patalkot has been covered.

Results and Discussion

The Bharias of Patalkot are a classic example of isolated society. Their economy based on forest. They still practiced magico-religious acts and ethno-medicines for the cure of various diseases. The results related to trends of morbidity among Bharias of Patalkot are presented in the following tables:

Table 1 exhibits information regarding percentile frequency of sick individuals during last one year. It could be seen that 67.54 per cent of the Bharias of Patalkot sick from minor ailments during last one year.

Table 1: Showing Percentile Frequency of Sick Individuals during Last One Year

Population	*No. of sick individuals*	*No. of not sick individuals*	*Total*
Bharias of Patalkot	206 (67.54%)	99 (32.45%)	305 (99.99%)

Table 2 shows information regarding sickness during last one year. It could be stated from the Table that malaria affects maximum of individuals of the Bharias of Patalkot (29.84). The next ailment is fever among the Bharias of Patalkot (17.70) .The dysentery or diarrhoea (7.54), cold and cough (2.59), body pain and aches (3.28), stomach (1.96), chicken pox (1.31) and jaundice (0.98), pneumonia (0.66) etc. affect the health of Bharias of Patalkot.

Table 2 : Showing Information Regarding Sickness during Last One Year

Popln.	KINDS OF SICKNESS										
	P	D	M	J	Ch	T	F	CC	ENT	P	S
Bharlas of Patalkot	02 (.66)	23 (7.54)	91 (29.64)	03 (0.98)	04 (1.31)	01 (0.33)	54 (17.7)	09 (2.59)	03 (0.98)	10 (3.28)	06 (1.96)

P: Pneumonia, D: Dysentery or Diarrhoea, M: Malaria, J: Jaundice, Ch: Chicken pox, T:Typhoid, F: Fever, CC: Cold & Cough, ENT: Ear, Nose & Throat diseases, P: Pain & aches, S: Stomach ache.

Table 3 shows information regarding duration of sickness (if sick during last one year). It could be observed that 16.39 per cent of the Bharias of Patalkot are sick for 7 to 15 days, 16.06 per cent individuals are sick for 3 to 4 days, 13.77 per cent of the Bharias of Patalkot are sick for 5 to 6 days, 11.48 per cent are sick for 1 to 2 days, 6.56 per cent individuals are sick for 15 to 30 days and very few (3.28%) are sick for more than 30 days.

Table 3: Showing Information Regarding duration of Sickness (Last One Year)

Population	DURATION OF SICKNESS (No. of Days)					
	1-2	3-4	5-6	7-15	15-30	30 days & above
Bharias of Patalkot	35 (11.5)	49 (16.1)	42 (13.8)	50 (16.4)	20 (6.6)	10 (3.3)

Table 4 exhibits information regarding type of treatment received during last one year. It could be observed that Bharias of Patalkot received treatment more from folk healers (42.3) called Bhumika than private allopathic doctors (10.8), health staff (6.6) self treatment (6.2), Govt. Doctors (0.98) and Ayurvedic Doctors (0.66).

Table 4: Showing Information Regarding Type of Treatment Received during Last One Year

Population	TYPE OF' TREATMENT					
	Self	*Health staff*	*Pvt.Allopathic Doctor*	*Govt. Doctor*	*Ayurvedic Doctor*	*Folk Healer*
Bharias of Patalkot	19 (6.23)	20 (6.56)	33 (10.82)	03 (0.98)	02 (0.66)	129 (42.29)

It could be concluded from the above discussion that:

1. The 67.54 per cent of the Bharias of Patalkot fell sick from different ailment during last one year.
2. The malaria affects maximum of individuals (29.84) than fever (17.70), dysentery or diarrhoea (7.54), cold and cough (2.59), bodyache and aches (3.28), stomachache (1.96), chicken pox (1.31), jaundice (0.98), pneumonia (0.66), etc. among Bharias of Patalkot.
3. The sickness persists in maximum cases (16.39) 7 to 15 days, than 3 to 4 days (16.06), 5 to 6 days (13.77) than 3 to 4 days (16.06), 5 to 6 days (13.77) , 1 to 2 days (11.48), 15-30 days (6.56) and more than thirty days (3.38) among the Bharias of Patalkot.

4. The maximum of the Bharias of Patalkot fell sick (54.70) between one to fifteen days.
5. The Bharias of Patalkot received more treatment in different ailments from folk-healer (Bhumika) (42.29) as compared with private allopathic doctors (10.82), health staff (6.56), self treatment (6.2), Govt. doctors (0.98) and Ayurvedic doctors (0.66).

It may be concluded that malaria, fever, dysentery and diarrheas, skin diseases and nutritional disorders of various kind affect maximum of individuals of all age groups and sexes. The sickness persists in maximum of cases seven to fifteen days and folk healer (Bhumika) treats most of the patients in the Patalkot valley.

The results of the foregoing study indicates that Bharias of Patalkot suffered from extreme poverty, abundant magico-religious beliefs, taboos and unawareness regarding available medical facilities. The following health care strategies suggested to be actively pursued:

1. The level of health education, general literacy standard mould be uplifted through formal and informal devices to minimize superstitious beliefs, taboos and rigidity concerned utilization of available medical services.
2. The level of awareness regarding causes of health hazards, nutritional aspects and immunization should be improved through different mass-medias and programs.
3. The medical aid related to malaria, fever, measles, typhoid, dysentery and diarrhoea, skin diseases and nutritional disorders must be provided through para-medical staff or trained folk healers (Bhumikas) or local village health guide with each hamlet for such purposes by local or district medical authorities.

In brief, awareness regarding health and related aspects should be enhanced through different devices, so that health status of Bharias must be uplifted to a certain extend and fully enjoy the natural life. It may be stated that health profile, prevalent diseases and health seeking behaviour are vital tools for the socio-economic development of the isolated primitive societies.

REFERENCES

Adair, J. and Deuschle, K.W. (1970). *The People's Health: Anthropology and medicine in a Navajo community*. Appleton-Century Crofts, New York.

Agrawal, B.C. (1973). *Disease and medicine*. Unpublished Dissertation. Department of Anthropology, Lucknow University, Lucknow, India.

Ahluwalia, A. (1974). *Sociology of medicine in India. Survey of Research in Social Science*, Indian Council of Social Science Research, 2: 401-430.

Mathur, P.R.G. (1982). Anthropology of tribal medicine: Disease and Curing techniques among the tribals of North Wynad (Kerala). *Man in India*, 62: 295-312.

Sharma, A.N. (1994). *The Bharias of Patalkot: Socio-cultural, environmental determinants and promotion of health care*. M.K. Offset Printers and Publishers, Bhopal.

Sinha, R.K. (1979). Disease and disease-spirits among the Pandu tribe. *Journal of Social Research*, 22 : 89-96.

Chapter 13

Infant Mortality Rate as an Indicator of Health Status: A Review of Raipur District

J. Nanda and M. Mitra

Health is one of the most important indicators for any developing country as a whole of its socio-economic status. The rising per capita income has been associated with better health and lower infant mortality all over the world including India. In the International Conference on "Safe Motherhood" 'which was held in Nairobi, Kenya 1987, the attention of the international health community was closely focussed on death of women due to complications arising during pregnancy or childbirth for the first time. A second important moment was the 1990 World Summit for children sponsored by the United Nations and organized by UNICEF. In the World Summit one of seven major goals is the reduction of maternal mortality by half between 1990 and the year 2000. This goal has been reemphasized at the 1994 International Conference on Population and Development held in Cairo (1995), and in the Fourth World Conference on Women in Beijing (UNFPA-Report, 1997).

Infant mortality rate (IMR) is the number of infant deaths (children under age one) per thousand live births. The reduction of infant mortality is a major goal of both WHO and UNICEF as part of the strategy of health for all. Currently major efforts are being made to address the most important health problems of children which is diarrhea and related diseases (diseases for which immunization is possible) and malnutrition. These primarily affect the children after the first few months of life i.e., the neonatal period. Sometimes the neonatal deaths may be underestimated, since the reporting of neonatal deaths is often less accurate than that of past neonatal deaths.

Infant survival is closely linked to the timing, spacing, number of births and to the reproductive health of the mothers. Thus, early, late, numerous and closely spaced pregnancies are major contributors to high mortality and morbidity rates, especially, where health care facilities are scarce, infant mortality remains high, where couples often have more children than they otherwise would to ensure that a deserved number would survive (ICPD, UN Report, 1994).

The present paper consists of two parts: the first part is an analysis of neonatal and post-neonatal deaths at National and State level (M.P.). The second part is emphasized on the infant mortality of Raipuir district, a specific review data based on NFHS -1 (1992-1993) and NFHS -2 (1998-1999). Thus, the aim of the present paper is to report the IMR in Raipur with a specific reference to neonatal and post-neonatal deaths and to compare the IMR data with the state and national level.

Material and Method

The data for the present study has been taken from the secondary data, collected from NFHS-1 and NFHS-2 and the Census of India for the State of M.P. (1991). The data has been compared with IIPS, Mumbai, which is the first land mark in the development of the demographic database for India.

Analysis and Discussion

The data from NFHS-1 and 2 regarding IMR has been analyzed and given in Tables 1 and 2. All the female respondents in the NFHS survey were asked to give a complete history of their births; including the sex, date of birth, survival status, age at the time of the survey, age at death for each live birth, since the level of infant and child mortality are the basic indicators of the quality of life in a society. In India the IMR declined by 22 per cent during the last 15 years i.e., prior to NFHS survey. In all instances, urban mortality rates were lower than rural mortality rates. In NFHS-1, IMR of India was 78.5

per cent but in NFHS-2, IMR was 72 per cent. It declined very slowly during the six years. In M.P. IMR was 85.2 per cent and in NFHS-1, while it was 86 1 per cent in NFHS-2, again declined only about by 1 per cent. But IMR of Raipur was 121.1 in NFHS-1 and 112.1 per cent in NFHS-2 i.e. declined about 10 per cent during six years.

MP is the largest state by area and is having higher concentration of tribal population. Tribal people generally prefer their indigenous medical practice, and mostly the birth of the child takes place at home, without the help of doctors. This is one of the reasons of high IMR in the rural areas as compared to urban areas. M.P. is having the fifth highest rank by IMR in India as it comes under the "BIMORU STATES" (the states under this are: Bihar, M.P., Orissa, Rajasthan and U.P.). The Total Fertility Rate of Raipur is 4.33, which falls between India (3.35) and M.P (4.92).

As per 1991 Census, the population of Raipur was 39.08 lakhs and constitutes 5.91 per cent of the total population of M.P. The district has a higher population density of 184 persons per square kilometer as compared to 149 of the state. The annual exponential growth rate of the district during 1981-1991 was 2.38 per cent, which is exactly equal to that of the state. In Raipur 20 per cent of the population living in urban areas in comparison to 23 per cent at the state level. Sex ratio of the district is 993 females per thousand males, which is higher than that of the state. Currently married women in the age group 15-44 years per 1000 population comes to 177 as against 178 at the state level. In the state the proportion of ST population is 23.3 per cent and SC population is 14.50 per cent where as in Raipur district the ST population constituted 18.3 per cent and SC population constituted 14.4 per cent of the state. The literacy rate of the district is 48.1 per cent with 65.1 per cent for males and 31.0 per cent for females. These proportions are higher than that of the state.

From 1991 Census, Kerala, Bihar and Tamilnadu are the best performers on IMR (i.e., IMR values are the lowest) while M.P., Orissa and U.P. were the worst. Better performance of the Bihar in this regard is really surprising.

IMR is the direct result of what happens to the child due to feeding problem, carelessness of mother, infection to child etc. Neonatal and Perinatal Mortality are linked to the environment of the fetus of the womb i.e., they are directly related to the mother's health (biological) and to things that happen during or immediately after birth. Perinatal deaths i.e. death occurring between the 28th week of gestation. and one week after birth, can be very difficult to classify, but precise diagnosis is probably not important. The main causes of death are intra-uterine and birth asphyxia (low birth weight) due to either prematurity or intrauterine malnutrition, birth trauma and neonatal (uterine) infections.

Few general diseases are also prevalent in Raipur due to geographic as well as environmental impacts. Chattisgarh is separated from M.P. as a new state and is the most backward and tribal dominated area. Raipur is the capital of Chhattisgarh. It is really alarming to note that the neonatal mortality and perinatal mortality rates are very high in this region. This may be due to backwardness, lack of knowledge about childcare practices, traditional health care practices and lack of safe motherhood knowledge etc.

From the above analysis it has been seen that one of the major achievements of the 21st century is the unprecedented increase in human longevity. The number of infant deaths per thousand live births in India declined from the beginning of the new Millenium. IMR is not only influencing the total size of the population but also its composition by age and sex. The analysis of IMR is of vital interest to researchers and planners involved in the public health programs, policy makers and other agencies interested in public health. Therefore, there is an urgent need to promote infant health and survival to reduce disparities between and within developed and developing states and nations as early as possible with particular attention in eliminating the pattern of IMR especially among infant girls. There is also need to improve health and nutritional status of infants and lactating mothers and making mothers and people more aware to breast feeding as an infant survival strategy. It is also essential to promote antenatal checkup for the healthy child born as "healthy mother gives healthy child" proved itself a slogan.

REFERENCES

Census of India, 1991.

ICPD, UN Report, 1994.

National Family Health Survey (NFHS) 1 and 2 Report. IIPS, Mumbai.

UNEPA Report, 1997.

WHO, Repoıt, 1996.

Table 1: Infant Mortality of 0-1 Years Age Group

Region	*NN*	*PNN*	*IMR*
India (Total)	34.1	22.0	56.1
India (Urban)	52.9	32.2	85.0
India (Rural)	48.9	29.9	78.5
SC-U	45.0	35.7	80.6
SC-	66.9	46.0	112.9
ST-U	43.9	11.7	55.5
ST-R	55.6	38.1	93.7
MP-U	35.0	19.7	54.7
MP-R	57.7	35.2	92.9
MP- T	53.2	32.0	85.2
ST	60.2	42.9	103.1
SC	64.0	60.1	124.1
RAIPUR U/R	62.1	59.0	121.0

SC- Schedule caste, ST- Schedule Tribe, U- Urban, R- Rural.
Source: NFHS-1 (1992-1993).

Table 2: IMR, CBR, TFR

Region	*CBR*	*TFR*	*Population 1991*	*SC Population*	*ST Population*
INDIA-U	24.1	2.7	217611	-	-
INDIA-R	30.4	3.7	628692	-	-
INDIA-T	28.7	3.4	846303	-	-
MP-U	-	-	15339	2104285	746304
MP-R	-	-	50842	7522394	14652730

(Contd...)

MP-T	31.6	4.8	66181	9626679	15399034
RAIPUR-U	-	-	771622	91161	37221
RAIPUR-R	-	-	313420	472416	70806
RAIPUR-T	-	-	313420	472416	76806

Source: NFHS-II (1998-1999).

Table 3: Infant Mortality of 0-1 Years

Regions	*Neonatal death*	*Perinatal death*	*IMR*
India	48.0	28.1	72.0
MP	54.9	31.2	86.1
Raipur	68.2	42.0	112.0

Source: NFHS-2 (1998-1999).

Chapter 14

Socio-Demographic and Nutritional Status of Tribal Population in Three Ecological Zones of Madhya Pradesh

K.M. Rao, D.H. Rao, Y.N. Mathur, G. Radhaiah and N.P. Rao

The tribals, in general, are endogamous groups sharing common language and culture. They are living under varying geo-ecological setting of hills and forests and far removed from modem conveniences of life. In India, there are about 573 tribes with 67.8 million population constituting 8.1 % of the country's population (1991 census). Their concentration mainly in the central region comprises the states of Madhya Pradesh, Maharashtra, Orissa and Andhra Pradesh. Studies have shown that tribals living in different ecosystems have varying degrees of nutrition and health status (Satyanarayan et al., 1974; Rao and Satyanarayan, 1979; Gopaldas, 1987). Because of their large dependence on primitive agricultural practices like shifting cultivation, they often face uncertainty of food supply. Lack of proper health and educational facilities and their poor utilization, faulty feeding habits, certain belief systems prevalent among them, further aggravate the already poor health and nutritional situation.

Studies pertaining to tribal demography and health and nutritional status are very few. But there is general agreement that the health and nutrition of most of the tribal groups in India is very poor. The health and nutrition problems of different tribal groups are not of the same. Different tribal groups in India are characterized by their individual socio-cultural, socio-biological and socio-economic attributes and in a strict sense the tribal groups are distinct biological isolates (Ali, 2001). The health of these tribal populations is, as such, a function of the interaction between socio-cultural and socio-biological practices, genetic attributes and the environmental conditions. In this context proper understanding of tribal setting and a broad idea of tribal development in India become two essential pre-requisites for understanding of health status of tribal groups. Hence, the present study is an attempt to review the socio-demographic and nutritional and health status of the tribal population in different ecological settings of Madhya Pradesh.

Methodology

Multi-stage stratified random sampling procedure was adopted to obtain relevant information. All the districts of Mahdya Pradesh where the tribal population is more than 60% were selected and categorized into three strata taking into consideration, the relative contribution of agriculture and forest and a combination of both to their economy. From each of these three strata, one district was selected randomly. Thus three districts namely Jhabua, Bastar and Sarguja were selected. The major tribal groups living in these districts are the Bhils, Bhilala and the Patelias in Jhabua, Gonds, Kanwar, Khonds and Oraons in Sarguja and Maria and Muria Gonds, Bhattaras Dorlas in Bastar .

The blocks of the selected districts were stratified into two groups on the basis of information on (a) percentage of area under cultivation (b) percentage of area under forest. From each stratum one block was selected randomly. Thus two blocks from each district namely Jhabua and Kathiwada blocks from Jhabua district, Pharasgaon and Geedam blocks from Bastar district, pratappur and Khadgaon from Sarguja were selected for this study.

Six hundred households were covered from each block based on distance from health facility viz. (1) Villages located with 5 km. of PHC headquarters (2) Villages within 5 km. of sub-centre (3) Villages beyond 5 km. from PHC and sub-centre. All the inhabited households of the selected villages were included in the survey for operational convenience.

Information on demography and family economic status was collected from all the households, while 24-hour recall method of diet survey and socio-cultural practices was collected from one third of the households selected for demography. Making use of standard procedures (Weiner and Lourie, 1969) and equipment, body measurements namely height, weight, mid-upper arm circumference and skin fold at triceps was taken on all the subjects in the household. (Gomez et al., 1956) and Waterlow's et al. (1977) classifications were used for quantification of growth retardation among pre-school children. However, in the present study the demography and nutritional status of the tribals was discussed.

Results

A total of 3506 households which include 1099 in Jhabua, 1276 in Bastar and 1131 from Sarguja were covered. Similarly, individuals of different age and sex groups including 2277 from Jhabua, 5758 from Bastar and 3719 from Sarguja were covered for nutritional anthropometry.

Demography

The general distribution of the population by age is given in Table-1. This indicated that the percentage of child population (14 years) in Sarguja (37.6%) is less as compared to 45.3 per cent in Jhabua and 40.5 per cent in Bastar. Similarly, the proportion of population aged 50 years and above was 11.9 per cent in Sarguja, and is higher compared to Jhabua (8.9%) and Bastar (7.6%). However, the sex ratio was lowest in Sarguja (938) as compared to Jhabua (968) and Bastar (1001).

The demographic features according to regions are presented in Table-2. The results revealed that Sarguja had higher proportion of nuclear families (64.5%) followed by Bastar (57%) and Jhabua (52%). The average family size was smaller in Sarguja (4.4) and higher in Bastar (5.8%) and Jhabua (7.0%)

However, the per cent of children married earlier than 14 years was higher in Sarguja (5.2% in males and 18.9% in females) as against 3 per cent in other areas.

Though the literacy level, in general among tribals, is low with slightly higher proportion of males (25%) in Sarguja are literate as compared to the Bastar (7.8%) and Jabhua (11.8%). Migration of the tribals to the neighboring areas was found only in Jhabua. Forty two per cent of the families reported that they usually migrated to Gujarat and Rajasthan during lean agricultural periods and the period of migration ranged from 3-4 months in a year. A negligible percentage (0.2%) of households in Bastar also reported that they migrate in search of livelihood during lean seasons.

Economic Status

Agriculture was found to be main source of income for tribals of Bastar (69. 9%) and Sarguja (57.2%). The tribals of Jhabua however, depend on labour (56.2%). In addition, to these major sources, forest and livestock resources also contribute to their income. Income from forest appeared to dominate in Bastar (13.3%), while livestock in Jhabua (7.8%). In Sarguja, forest and livestock seemed to contribute equally (4.5%) to the total income (Table-3).

The percapita monthly income in the areas studied was (according to 1986 prices) Rs.32/- in Jhabua, Rs.28/- in Bastar and Rs.46/- in Sarguja. The percentage of tribal families with more than 5 acres of land was 20 per cent in Jhabua, 35 per cent in Bastar and 30 per cent in Sarguja. These lands are mostly rain dependent. The modern agricultural practices are minimal. Between these three areas Sarguja has a relatively higher income from agriculture due to better crop yield.

Livestock like poultry, sheep, goat and cattle form an important material asset in the tribal economy. Though its contribution to the total income was less compared to that of agriculture and labour, the significance in bartering, domestic consumption and rituals is considerable. It may be mentioned that for these tribals poultry often serve like ready cash, while sheep, goat and cattle are symbol of social prestige and exchanged during marriages.

Majority of the households collecting major forest produce of economic value. Prominent among these are Mohua, Tendu, Sal seeds, Amla and Chirongi. These are more abundant in the forest of Bastar.

Toddy tapping mainly for self-consumption was seen to be a major activity in Jhabua.

Housing Conditions

Tribal families live in houses built with local material like straw mud and wooden rafts. The roofs are low, and covered with of hand-made tiles. The floors are plastered with mud and previous. The dwelling invariably consists of a single room in which a portion is kept apart for cooking. Each dwelling has open area around, often surrounded by shrubs or bamboo sticks. Waste water is drained off into the backyard kitchen garden. Agricultural lands separate the huts from each other. The houses, generally, present a very clean look. They regularly sweep with brooms and plaster the floors with mud. Unprotected open wells formed the major source of drinking water as reported by 50 per cent of the families in Jhabua, 69 per cent in Bastar and 58 per cent in Sarguja. Safe drinking water through borewells is available to only about a third of the households in Jhabua, negligible proportion in Bastar (4%) and Sarguja (3%). A considerable proportion of households surveyed depends on rivers and ponds in Jhabua (19%), Bastar (27%) and Sarguja (39%).

Nutritional Status of Children

It may be emphasized here that while Gomez classification provides a measure of extent of problem of undernutrition in the community, Waterlow's classification attempts to provide a picture of the type of malnutrition, whether it is acute or chronic with duration implicit in it. The percentage of severely malnourished children was high (11.3%) in Jhabua followed by Bastar (9.8%) and lower in Sarguja (6.5%) (Table-4). Correspondingly the percentage of normal children were higher in Sarguja (24.5%) than Jhabua (16.2%) and Bastar (9.3%). The per cent of "at risk" children (75% of weight for age) was more or less similar (50%) in Bastar and Jhabua, while it was less in Sarguja (31.5%).

The percentage of preschoolers who are assessed as normal by Waterlow' s classification (Table-5) was high (48.1) in Sarguja as against 41.1 in Bastar and 26.7 in Jhabua. The per cent of stunted children were higher in Jhabua (59.8%) followed by Bastar (51.3%)

and Sarguja (46.3%). The percentage of children with stunted and wasted were also higher in Jhabua (8.3%) compared to other two areas.

To summarize, on the basis of weight for age deficit of children (Gomez classification), Sarguja emerges as the best district followed by Bastar and the Jhabua. Similarly, on the basis of Waterlow's classification Sarguja continues to hold better status than the other two areas. Children in Jhabua are worse off with greater extent undernutrition, higher stunting and wasting compared to other two districts.

Comments and Conclusions

Malnutrition is an obvious manifestation of food insecurity and not surprisingly, a nutritional survey is often one of the first steps taken by agencies looking for evidence of food scarce conditions in that area. Promotion of nutrition well being of people as envisaged in the action plan of Health for all by 2000 AD, is one of the essential elements of primary health care. Despite several efforts to combat malnutrition in the population particularly among low socio-economic groups in the rural and tribal areas, malnutrition continues to be an important public health problem. Poverty is the root cause of food insecurity and consequent undernutrition. The capability poverty measures (Vijayaraghavan and Rao, 1998), which makes use of non-income indicators of human development, indicate that 50 per cent of the Indian population is not capable of management of poverty. The role of non-nutritional factors like better health care, improved literacy especially among females appeared to be of considerable importance in controlling undernutrition.

The higher literacy, better socio-economic status and greater opportunities to interact with outside World due to mining activities was found in the tribals of Sarguja compared to other districts. In addition higher family planning acceptance (especially male sterilization) was observed in Sarguja. A reflection of this was found in favorable demographic situation of smaller family size (4.4) higher proportion of nuclear families (64.5%) and lower dependency ratio (37.6 children below 14 years).

Growth retardation, the hallmark of protein energy malnutrition in young children, was encountered in all the three districts to varying degrees. Children of Sarguja fared better, with relatively lower proportion of undernourished children manifesting stunting (46%) and wasting (2.1%) compared to Bastar (51% stunting and 3.7% wasting) and Jhabua (60% stunting and 5.2% wasting). As indicated already, the tribals of Jhabua depends more on labour and less on agriculture. The terrain in Jhabua was not conducive to agriculture. The per acre yields are quite low and depend on uncertain monsoon resulting often in migration. The result was low level of food consumption and more malnourished. However, in Bastar, the income from agriculture and forest and in Sarguja from agriculture and labour were relatively more stable resulting in better consumption levels which in turn led to better nutritional status when compared to Jhabua. Though there exist regional difference, the overall situation of health and nutrition in all these tribal groups is worse. These tribals facing uncertainty of food especially during lean seasons such as rainy and summer months. Distribution of subsidized food grains through public distribution system, provision of employment opportunities especially in lean periods and steps to strengthening of the availability of health care and their utilization may be the immediate needs for the upliftment of the tribal groups.

REFERENCES

Ali, A. 2001. Health Status of Tribals in India. An overview. Paper presented at National Seminar on Tribal Health in India: Present status and future strategies. National Institute of Health and Family Welfare, New Delhi, 9-11.

Gomez, F., Galvan, R., Frank, S., Cravioto, I., Chavez, R. and Vasquiz, I. 1956. Mortality in second and third degree malnutrition. *Journal of Tropical Pediatrics*, 2: 77.

Gopaldas, T. 1987. Nutritional Status of some selected tribes of Western and Central India. Proceedings of Nutrition Society, 33:76-93.

Rao, H. and Satyanarayana, D.K. 1979. Nutritional Status of Tribal preschool children of Andhra Pradesh. *Indian Journal of Nutrition and Dietetics*, 11: 328-334.

Satyanarayana, K., Hanumantha Rao, D., Susheela, T.P. 1974. Nutritional Status of people of Andaman and Nicobar Island. *Indian Journal of Medical Research,* 62: 662-671.

Vijayaraghavan, K. and Rao, D.H. 1998. Diet and Nutritional situation in rural India. 108: 243-253.

Waterlow, J.C. et al. 1977. Presentation and use of weight and weight date for comparing the nutritional status of groups of children under the age of 10 years. *Bulletin of WHO*, 55: 389-398.

Weiner, J.S. and Lourie, I.A. 1969. Human Biology -A guide to Field Methods, Hand Book. 9. Blackwell Scientific Publication, Oxford.

Table l: Percentage Distribution of Population Surveyed by Age in Three Districts

Age (Yrs.)	District		
	Jhabua	Bastar	Sarguja
<1	2.6	2.2	3.0
01-04	13.5	11.7	10.6
05-09	16.3	13.1	13.1
10-14	12.9	13.5	10.9
15-19	8.5	12.3	9.8
20-30	16.8	15.6	17.1
30-40	11.9	13.7	12.8
40-50	8.6	10.3	10.8
50-60	6.2	4.8	6.7
>60	2.7	2.8	5.2

Table 2: Some Demographic Features of the Areas Surveyed

S.No. Particulars	*District*		
	Jhabua	*Bastar*	*Sarguja*
1. Sex Ratio	968	1001	938
2. Type of Family : Nuclear	51.8	56.8	64.5
Joint	48.2	43.2	35.5
3. Average Family Size	7.0	5.8	4.4
4. Age at marriage (Male)			
10-14 years	2.3	3.0	5.2

(Contd...)

15-19 years	12.8	29.2	50.9
> 20 ears	8.6	88.5	97.5
5. Age at marriage (Female)			
10-14 years	1.5	2.2	18.9
15-19 years	25.1	44.1	85.7
>20 years	84.6	81.2	88.1
6. Literacy Status: Male	11.2	7.8	25.0
Female	3.0	1.0	3.4

Table 3: Socio-Economic Characteristics in the Three Districts

S.No. *Particulars*	*Districts*		
	Jhabua	*Bastar*	*Sarguja*
1. Percentage of Income from			
Agriculture	31.0	69.9	57.2
Forest	5.0	13.3	4.5
Livestock	7.8	0.3	4.6
Labour	56.2	16.5	33.7
2. Average percapita monthly income (Rs.) (according to 1986 prices)	32.0	28.0	46.0
3. No.of HHs possessing irrigated land (acres)			
No land	91.5	99.6	99.2
< 5 acres	7.6	0.4	0.4
5 acres	0.9	0.0	0.4
4. No.of HHs possessing unirrigated land (acres)			
No land	2.5	5.1	5.4
< 5 acres	77.6	59.5	64.8
5 acres	19.9	33.4	29.8
5. Percentage of expenditure on:			
Food	84.4	77.8	83.5
Consumable items	11.9	16.5	13.6
Non-Consumable item	3.7	5.7	2.9
6. Source of drinking water (HHs)			
Hand pump	31.0	4.0	2.9
Open well	49.7	68.8	58.4
River/Pond	19.3	27.2	38.7

Table 4: Percentage Distribution of Children (1-5 Years) by Gomez Classification

District	*No. of children*	*Gomez Grades*			
		Normal	*Mild*	*Moderate*	*Severe*
Jhabuaa	339	16.2	34.2	38.3	11.3
Bastarb	725	9.3	40.5	40.4	9.8
Sarguiac	363	24.5	44.0	25.0	6.5

Table 5: Percentage Distribution of Children (1-5 Years) by Waterlow's Classification

District	*No.of children*	*Nutritional Grades*			
		Normal	*Stunted*	*Wasted*	*Stunted & Wasted*
Jhabua	339	26.7	59.8	5.2	8.3
Bastarb	725	41.1	51.3	3.7	3.9
SarguiaD	363	48.1	46.3	2.1	3.5

Note: Tests of significance was carried out by chi-square test. Areas having one of the Superscripts common are not statistically significant.

Chapter 15

A Study of Socio-cultural Factors Affecting Reproductive Health among the Primitive Tribes of Madhya Pradesh

G. D. Pandey and R. S. Tiwari

Among all the States of India, Madhya Pradesh (undivided; including Chhatisgarh) has the largest population of tribals, about one fourth of the country's total tribal population. There are as many as 46 different tribal groups in the State among which Gonds, Bhils, Oraons, Bhilalas, Kols, Kanwars are prominent. These groups show considerable variation in population size, level of development, acculturation and assimilation. Their social and cultural traits, religious beliefs and norms as well as traditional economics pursuits vary from tribe to tribe and area to area (Pandey and Saxena, 1998; Pandey, 1988). Out of these 46 tribal groups, seven have been identified as the most backward or primitive tribes. They are Abujhmarias, Baigas, Hill Korwas, Bharias, Kamars, Saharias and Birhors inhabited in the different parts of the State (Tiwari, 1984). Besides, acute poverty (over 90% below poverty line) high illiteracy (over 90 % illiterate) is prevalent in these tribe. They lead a secluded life far removed from modern conveniences. They are vulnerable from nutritional standpoint. Because of their large dependence on primitive agricultural practice, like shifting cultivation they often face uncertainty of food supply. Lack of proper health and educational facilities, faulty feeding habits, certain irrational belief systems and special tribal mores that are likely to be prevalent among them, further aggregate their health and nutrition situation.

There is paucity of studies depicting association between their socio-cultural characteristics and reproductive health. Demographic studies carried out in these populations have revealed that most of the primitive tribes are lagging behind about three decades than the population characteristics of the State (Pandey, 1988). The fertility levels are lower and mortality levels are higher – resulting in slow or negative population growth. These observations have led the State Government to ban sterilization operations for Family Planning among them (Amanullah, 1988). The anthropological studies carried out in some of the primitive tribes have revealed prevalence of a number of socio-cultural practices in these populations which are likely to affect the reproductive health of their women. (Pandey and Tiwari, 1991; 1992; Pandey, 1992; 1993). It is in this context, such studies are highly desirable to see the relevance of these practices and their likely effect on reproductive health of the women. The information collected in such studies may be utilized to plan intervention programmes for these tribal groups, if needed. This paper, which is largely based on the observations collected by the Regional Medical Research Centre for Tribals (ICMR), Jabalpur has following objectives:

(i) To study the socio-demographic profile of the primitive Tribes,

(ii) To study Birth Related practices and Health Seeking Behaviour of the primitive Tribes, and

(iii) To study the Socio-Cultural practices having bearing on their reproductive health.

Methodology and Data

The Regional Medical Research Centre for Tribals, Jabalpur has collected valuable information on demographic, socio-cultural and health-related aspects of the primitive tribes of Madhya Pradesh under various studies carried out by the Centre during 1990-93. The data, though, not collected with the specific objectives is a byproduct of health and morbidity studies. These observations, though, do not show direct association of the socio-cultural characteristics on their reproductive health, but are invaluable and compel for further in depth investigations. This concept paper is largely based on the data collected in three primitive tribes of the State by the senior author as Principal Investigator during 1990-93 and describes mainly their socio-demographic characteristics, Birth Related practices and Health seeking behaviour. The primitive tribes studied are - (i) Hill Korwas of Sarguja district (ii) Kamars of Raipur district and (iii) Bharia of Patalkot area, Chhindwara district.

Results and Discussion

Demographic Characteristics

(i) Socio-Demographic Profile

As evident from Table-1 and Table-2, the main occupation of the majority of households is labour. Less than one per cent of the households are engaged in service or household industry. More than 90 per cent households are below the poverty line. Among the population characteristics, the sex ratio (No. of females per 1000 males) is more than 1000 in Kamar and Hill Korwa tribes. The mean age at marriage for femaies is around 15-16 years. The longevity, as indicated by the percentage of aged (60+) persons and Index of ageing is very low. The mean number of children born is also lower compared to the Indian population.

(ii) Age-Specific-Fertility and Fecundability

The cumulated number of children born to an eligible woman according to her age has been given in Table-3. It is evident from the table that, though the mean age at marriage of females does not differ considerably the cumulated fertility curve shows speed of family formation among the primitive tribes than the non-primitive tribe (Pandey and Tiwari, 1991). A number of reasons may be suggested behind the lower fertility in the primitive tribes like, different disease pattern, difference in breast-feeding practices etc. The reasons are required to be investigated. One of the reasons may be adolescent sterility. As evident from Table-4, primitive tribes, have higher proportion of adolescent sterile couples as compared to non-primitive tribes and non-tribals (Gupta et al., 1989).

Birth Related Practices

(i) Marriage

(a) The primitive tribes consider a girl of marriageable age if she attains menarche. The mean age at menarche in the girls is 13-14 years. The marriage is very simple. Usually, the parents of the boy have to bear all the expenditure. The parents of the girl do not spend a single paisa in their daughter's marriage; on the other hand they get benefited through the presents received from boy's parents.

(b) There is no custom of '*GAUNA*' (return marriage) in these tribes, as commonly observed in the non-tribal population. The couple starts cohabitating after the marriage. In general the tribes prefer to marry their daughters with the son of maternal uncle (Bharias and Hill korwas) and with the son of the sister of the girl's father (Kamars). This may have effect on their reproductive health by increasing the chance of hereditary diseases (Pandey, 1993). In the tribes under study, though premarital cohabitation is avoided, but in case it happens and resulted into a conception, the girl is permitted to marry her lover. Widow marriages are permitted. Divorce is simple.

Males can marry more than once if the earlier wife could not produce a child. In case of divorce, the children live with their father.

(ii) Cohabitation

Cohabitation is prohibited during the course of menstruation. The wife sleeps outside the house. After the menstruation period is over, Kamar women get massage of mixture of *haldi* (turmeric) powder and oil and then take bath. After this purification, they are permitted to sleep with their husbands. There is no restriction in cohabitation during the festivals, but since, husbands consume liquor heavily during these days, wives prefer not to sleep with their husbands. During the course of pregnancy, the cohabitation is prohibited. After the delivery, the cohabitation is prohibited for about four months, till the newborn is given supplementary food. They also try to avoid cohabitation, till the child is fed on the breast milk along with the supplementary food. Bharias believe that cohabitation after taking liquor results in weak pregnancy.

Pregnancy

If a female is young, discontinuation of menstruation is an indication of conception. Besides, vomiting, enlarged abdomen are also indications of conception. During the pregnancy, Kamar women do not consume liquor and do not see the eclipse or elephants, because it is believed that the shape of the baby to be born may get affected. Similar concepts have been also observed among the Bharia women.

They do not care for antenatal care. Women continue to do all their normal duties including fetching of water and cutting of wood. No special diet is given to the pregnant women. Among the Hill Korwas, taking of liquor and bones are prohibited during the pregnancy.

The tribal women can guess about the sex of the unborn child. In Kamars, the women can judge by examining the circumference of the wrist of the pregnant women. If the circumference appears large, then the conception will result in a female child. A Bharis women can guess the sex of the child to be born by observing the health of a pregnant women and/or movement of the baby in the womb. If a pregnant Bharia woman looks thin, she will deliver a male child, otherwise a female child.. Similarly, if the child in the womb starts movement after three months of conception, the out come of pregnancy will be a female child.

Intranatal Practices

They consider delivery as a natural phenomenon. The room is kept cleaned in advance in which delivery is to be conducted. In Bharias, the surfaces of walls of the room and flour are coated with the cowdung. For easy and less painful delivery, among the Kamars, the pregnant woman is given hot water for drinking as soon as the pain starts and she is asked to sit in the squatting position. Among the Bharias and Hill Korwas also, the delivery is conducted in squatting position. In this position they feel that the delivery is less painful and less time consuming. In Bharia tribe, as soon as the pain starts, few women start massaging the abdomen of the pregnant woman. During the pains at the time of delivery, the Bharia female is administered with a mixture of Haldi (turmeric), Gur (Jaggery) and water. Sometimes the pregnant woman is also served with *MAHUA KA*

RANG (Mahua boiled with water) to reduce the pain. Usually, elderly women and local traditional Dais help in conducting the deliveries. In complicated cases, the local traditional Healer (Badawa) is also called. In rest of the cases the ANM or Doctor from PHC is also called. The reasons behind the under-utilization of services of ANM in conducting deliveries are inhospitable terrain, lack of cash money in hand to pay their fees and of course, to some extent, lack of faith.

In Bharias, the umbilical cord is cut with the help of a sickle or blade. Little soil is put on the naval. If the cut is not dried, application of betel nut is suggested. The cord rapped in leaf is put in a deep pit in the house where the delivery had taken place. It is believed that, the depth of the pit is directly related with the delay of the next pregnancy. In the pit, they put seven kinds of grains, like Wheat, Gram, Maize etc. with the belief that this will lead to change the sex of the children in the next pregnancy. The pit is covered with soil and fire is put on the pit for about a month since delivery.

Among Hill Korwa tribe, the cord is cut with a bamboo piece in case of a male child and with a knife or blade in the case of a girl child (This is because the boy will grow up to hunt and gather food with the help of a bow and arrow made of bamboo). A thread is used for tying and mustard oil is applied to the affected area.

In Kamars, after the child is born, a mixture of mustard oil and ash is applied to the child's cord. The baby is given bath with hot water and is breast-fed immediately. Colostrums in all the three primitive tribes are not discarded and the child is breast-fed within hours of delivery.

Postnatal Practices

Just after delivery in Bharia tribe, the child is given bath with warm water and soap. The child is put in the smoke generated by putting king's cumin (Ajwain) on fire. The child is also given massage with the mustard oil. The mother is given bath with warm water. She is served with *dal* or gruel. She is also served with some nutritious food, if she affords. Up to two months of delivery, the mother is not permitted to eat green vegetables, Maize, Wheat, and Gram etc. since they believe that it affects the health of the child. A women who does not have sufficient breast milk is administered *papaya/chutni/urad dal/mahua* boiled with water. It is believed that these preparations help to enhance the breast milk. The child is breast fed as long as the mother continues lactating i.e. approximately 3-4 years.

In Hill Korwas, after delivery, the mother and the child are given a bath with warm water. The mother is then fermented with *haldi* (turmeric) powder and given some *haldi* powder mixed in water to drink and *kulthi dal* (a local lentil) and rice to eat. After about one hour of delivery, the child is breastfed. Colostrums is not discarded and fed to the new born. The children of these mothers who have no enough breast milk are fed-on goat milk. After six months, the child is given rice, *dal* etc. The mother continues to breast feed her child as long as four years.

In Kamars, the baby is given bath with hot water and is breastfed immediately. The mother is first given massage and then given bath with hot water. She is given rice along with starch to eat. She is not permitted to take sour things, green vegetables and cold water for a week after the delivery. The mother starts taking alcohol after 5-6 months of the delivery. A child starts taking supplementary food after a year. The supplementary diets are rice/starch/*dal*. A child is breast fed as and when he requires. The breast-feeding continues for about three years. The lactating mothers do not take any special diet. In case, if a mother has no sufficient breast milk, it is reported that she is administered lioness milk mixed with water. They also believe that most of the diseases of childhood like dysentery, diarrhoea can be cured by administering a small dose of alcohol.

No knowledge about the postnatal care among these tribes exists. A very small preparation of mothers are aware about the immunizations of the child and less than one per cent children were found immunized with incomplete doses of either of the vaccines. Some case studies in this regard, which are presented, in the subsequent sections will make the things more clear. Comparative details of socio-cultural practices having bearing on reproductive health have been given in Table-5.

Health Seeking Behaviour

Short descriptions of the health seeking behaviour of the primitive tribes, which have bearing on their reproductive health, are being discussed in this section.

Sickness and Treatment

The tribes believe that a person who can do his routine work is a healthy person otherwise he is sick. Usually, they believe that disease is a kind of punishment awarded by the God for person's misdeeds carried out in earlier births or in the present life. They also believe that people may become sick due to evil eyes. During the sickness, the first line of treatment is the traditional healer, if not cured then they approach the Health Worker /ANM/ allopathic doctor. The reason of preference for traditional healer is to make sure whether the disease is not due to some evil's eye. Majority of the population is unaware of PHC services. It is difficult for them to differentiate between a Doctor and a Nurse. Usually the PHC is visited in very serious cases, i.e. snake bites, bites by the wild beasts, accidents etc.

It is believed that certain diseases, like the traditional healer can only cure small pox, measles, leprosy etc. For other diseases, they approach to the private practitioner or medical shop of the nearest market. Usually, PHC is visited in very late stage as last option. To prevent births and also for abortions, they approach the traditional healer and they believe that, the magic man knows a number of herbs and roots which are effective in preventing births. To abort a pregnancy up to four months, concentrated *mahua* solution boiled with water is administered.

Antenatal Care

As these tribes are located in difficult hilly and forest areas, it is difficult for the health workers to visit these areas as frequently as they required. If in any case the ANM approaches the pregnant women, they do not hear her, they do not take the Iron and Folic acid tablets and throw them away. They also do not pay any attention for her advice to T.T. injections. An ANM serving the villages inhabited by Hill Korwa narrates her experience as,

'It is very difficult to convince these people'. They do not easily agree to get immunized. Pregnant women do not take iron tablets due to the fear that it will harm the foetus. And if a pregnant woman is persuaded to take the tablets 'she usually throws them away after my departure.' As mentioned earlier, these people consider delivery as a natural phenomenon, 'there is no need to pay special care as we do in animals.'

A few case studies are presented below to give an idea of the knowledge and attitude of the women belonging to the primitive tribal groups regarding immunization of the pregnant women or other antenatal services and family planning.

Case-1

Smt. Kusmi Bai (Hill Korwa tribe), a mother-in-law, aged 46 years whose daughter-in-law is currently five months pregnant, has this to say about ante-natal care: 'I have delivered so many children. Neither have I needed any medicine nor injections for myself not for my children. My daughter-in-law has conceived for the second time, she has no problems whatsoever. Evan if she has any, I will not go to the Government Dispensary, because they charge fees and we have no money for two square meals. Tell me, from where I will pay. It depends on God, since, it is by his grace that we get children. It is his desire to save or let them die.'

Case-II

Smt. Ruchiya Bai (Hill Korwa), aged 30 years and pregnant for about five months says: 'I have delivered five children, of whom two have died, I did not experience any problems during my earlier deliveries. Though, I know that some injections and the Nurse gives tablets during pregnancy. I did not think it necessary to visit the Government Dispensary for any problem.'

As in the case of antenatal care, the Hill Korwas have no knowledge about post-natal care. Out of the 641 children observed, only 2.5 per cent has received BCG, 2.0 per cent had receipt DPT and polio vaccines, and 1.0 per cent had been vaccinated against measles.

Case-III

Smt. Dhanesari Bai (Kamar tribe), aged 20 years narrates her experience about the services of ANM as: 'It makes no difference if a pregnant woman is given injections or medicines by an ANM. Last year my elder daughter-in-law who was given some tablets by the ANM, died during the delivery, later the child was also found dead. While, women who do not take her help survive and produce healthy children.'

Case-IV

Smt. Basanti Bai (Bharia tribe), aged 55 years says: 'I had delivered five children, but I never found any discomfort, I never visited Government hospital. Of course, there was some trouble during the first delivery, but the local magic man (*Jhumka*) made the things right.' Similarly, they do not believe in post-natal care and Family Planning. A case study may be quoted here to show how these people are taking the health services provided by the Government.

Case-V

Smt. Harafi Bai (Kamar tribe), aged 25 years, when asked about the treatment of her children, responds as: 'Children are given by the God, if I had done noble deeds, my children will live healthy and survive. In case I had done sins in past (including previous births) the God may take away my children as punishment and thus, they will die or will continue as diseased. I have three daughters, I want two sons, because sons are necessary to take care of us in the old age.'

Summary and Conclusion

From the study, it is clear that the primitive tribes of Madhya Pradesh studied in this paper, where 90 per cent population is living below poverty line and are illiterate, have a number of misconceptions, irrational beliefs etc. regarding Birth Related Practices and thus, affecting reproductive health of their women. The areas, where they are located are hilly, covered with forests are inapproachable in most of the months of the year. The health services are thin, due to some or other reasons. The resources, whatever available are not being fully utilized. It is highly desirable to have a thorough in depth study of their socio-cultural practices having bearing on their reproductive health, some of them might be beneficial, but the unscientific practices are required to be dispelled by proper intervention programs.

REFERENCES

Amanullah, M. 1988. MADHYA PRADESH KE ADIVASI KSHSTRON MEN PARIVAR NIYOJAN NISHEDH/PRATIBANDH (EK MULYANKAN ADHYAYAN). Tribal Research Institute, Bhopal.

Gupta, R.B., Pandey, P.L., Pandey, G.D. and Tiwari, R.S. 1989. Marriage patterns among the Bharia Tribe of Madhya Pradesh. *Indian Journal of Preventive and Social Medicine*, 20: 96-99.

Pande, P.L. 1993. High prevalence of Haemoglobinopathias and G6PD Deficiency among the Tribals of Madhya Pradesh: Need of Effective Genetic Counseling and Health Education program. *Tribal Health Bulletin*, 2: 1-6.

Pandey, G.D. 1993. Socio-Cultural Aspects of Health Care in Bharias – A Primitive Tribe of Madhya Pradesh. Regional Medical Research Centre for Tribals (ICMR), Jabalpur (Memio).

Pandey, G.D. 1999. A study of effect of social factors on human fertility and family planning with special reference to major primitive Tribes of Madhya Pradesh D.Litt. Dissertation, Rani Durgawati University, Jabalpur.

Pandey, G.D. 1992. Socio-Cultural Aspects of Health Care Among the Kamars. Regional Research Centre for Tribals, Jabalpur (Memio).

Pandey, G.D. and Tiwari, R.S. 1993. Socio-Cultural Characteristics and Health Seeking Behaviour of the Hill Korwas. *Journal of Family Welfare*, 39: 44-48.

Pandey, G.D. and Tiwari, R.S. 1991. Fertility in Hill-Korwas- A primitive Tribe of Madhya Pradesh. Man in India, 76: 325-329.

Pandey, G.D. and Saxena, B.N. 1998. District level planning for Health and Family welfare for Tribals. Demography India. 17 : 216-226.

Pandey, G.D. 1988. A study of Demographic Characteristics of Tribals in Rural Madhya Pradesh: Some observations for Health and Family Welfare Planning. *Indian Journal of Preventive Medicine*, 19: 119-138.

Tiwari, D.N. 1984. Primitive Tribes of Madhya Pradesh : Strategy for Development. Ministry of Home Affairs. Govt. of India, New Delhi.

Table 1: Household Characteristics of the Primitive Tribes Studied

Characteristics		*Tribe*			
		Kamar	*Bharia*	*Hill Korwa*	*Gonds*
(i)	Type of HH (%)				
	Nuclear	81.9	45.3	67.6	51.4
	Joint	18.1	54.7	32.4	48.6
(ii)	Mean HH Size	04.7	05.5	04.3	05.4
(iii)	Main Occupation				
	Own-Agriculture	07.5	38.6	31.6	72.1
	Labor	92.2	60.3	67.9	21.4
	Service or H.H. Industry	00.3	01.1	00.3	06.5
(iv)	Average Annual H.H Income (in Rs.)	3744.0	6321.0	3799.0	5644.0
(v)	% H.H. below poverty line	91.0	89.9	91.8	71.1

Non-primitive tribe.

Table 2: Population Characteristics of the Primitive Tribes Studied

Characteristics		*TRIBES*			
		Kamars	*Bharias*	*Hill Korwas*	*Gonds*
(i)	Sex Ratio (F/Mx1000)	1000.9	1068.0	945.4	956.9
(ii)	Literacy (%)				
	T	8.9	17.6	2.9	26.4
	M	13.0	29.3	4.5	40.7
	F	4.8	6.7	1.6	12.1
(iii)	Mean Age at Marriage				
	M	19.5	18.7	17.0	18.3
	F	15.8	15.6	14.9	15.5
(iv)	Age Composition (%)				
	O-14	41.9	40.1	33.4	38.4
	15-59	54.5	53.8	51.8	55.4

	60+	3.6	6.1	4.8	6.2
(v)	Median Age	20.7	22.3	23.8	21.3
(vi)	Dependency Ratio $\frac{[(0\text{-}14)+60]}{15\text{-}59} \times 100$	83.5	85.9	73.7	80.5
(vii)	Index of Ageing $(\frac{60+}{0\text{-}14} \times 100)$	8.6	15.2	14.4	16.1
(vii)	Mean No.of Children born per eligible couple	2.1	2.2	1.9	2.6

Table 3: Cumulated Average Number of Live Births to Eligible Couples by Age of Wife

Age of wife	Cumulative average No, of children born			
	Kamars	Bharias	Hill Korwas	Gonds*
15	0.55	0.20	0.00	0.00
20	1.68	1.25	1.20	0.90
25	2.50	2.15	1.60	2.00
30	3.00	2.95	2.50	3.10
35	3.33	3.55	2.70	3.90
40	3.55	3.85	2.80	4.80
45	3.73	3.90	2.90	5.10
50	3.80	4.00	3.00	5.30

-*- Non –primitive tribe.

Table 4: Age at Marriage, Interval for First Birth and Probability of Conception Leading to Live Birth

Age at Marriage	*Interval for First Birth (months)*				*Monthly Probability of conception leading to Live Birth*			
	(a)	(b)	(c)	(d)	(a)	(b)	(c)	(d)
12-13	44.9	52.2	70.8	37.1	0.0278	0.231	0.0162	0.02691
14-15	40.1	40.8	49.9	27.7	0.0322	0.0314	0.0244	0.0361
16-17	33.0	35.8	32.9	20.5	0.0417	0.0373	0.0418	0.0487
18-19	25.0	33.0	30.6	15.7	0.0625	0.0417	0.0463	0.0636

(a) : Kamars, (b): Bharias,(c):Hill Korwas, (d) Gonds (Non- primitive tribes).

Table 5: Socio-cultural Practices Affecting Reproductive Health among the Primitive Tribes

Practices	*Tribes*			*Likely affect on Reproductive health*
	Kamars	*Bharias*	*Hill Korwas*	
(a)	*(b)*	*(c)*	*(d)*	*(e)*
(i) Marriage (a) Mean age at marriage (years.) for Females	15.8	15.6	14.9	Most of the girls get married before 18 years and become mothers before the age of 20 years.
(b)Consaguinous marriages	Preferred	Preferred	Permitted	May lead to a number of genetic diseases. Observations have indicated high prevalence of sickle cell anaemia and G6PD deficiency in these tribes which may complicate their reproductive health.
(c) Widow marriages	Permitted	Permitted	Permitted	-
(d) Pre-marital conception	The girl is permitted to marry with the boy	Accepted and the girl is allowed to marry with boy.	The girl is permitted to marry with the boy.	-
(ii) Cohabitation	Certain irrational beliefs regarding menstruation and cohabitation. Co-habitation is avoided till the child is breastfed.	They believe that cohabitation in drunken state may lead to weak progeny. Co-habitation is prohibited for few months after delivery.	Cohabitation is prohibited/ avoided after delivery till the child is too young and depends on breast feeding.	The practices seem to be beneficial in avoiding conception and helpful in recovering health of the mother after delivery.

(Contd...)

(a)	*(b)*	*(c)*	*(d)*	*(e)*
(iii) Pregnancy	(i) Certain practices like seeing eclipses, elephants during pregnancy are prevalent.	(i) Practices like not to see eclipses are prevalent	(i) Practices not to see eclipses are prevalent	They consider pregnancy and delivery as natural phenomenon besides / certain irrational beliefs.
	(ii) No ante-natal care	(ii) No ante-natal care	(ii) No ante-natal care	
	(iii) No special diet	(iii) No special diet	(iii) No special diet	
	(iv) Pregnant woman does her duties until the labour pain starts	(iv) Pregnant woman does her duties until the labour pain starts	(iv) Pregnant woman does her duties until the labour pain starts	
	(v) They can guess the sex of the unborn child by examine circumference of the pregnant woman's wrist	(v) They can guess the sex of the child. If the pregnant woman appears thin, she will deliver a male child.		
	(vi) Pregnant women do not consume liquor		(v) Taking of liquor and bones are prohibited.	
(iv) Intranatal Care	(i) As soon as the lobar pain starts the pregnant woman is given hot water.	(i) As soon as the lobor pain starts the abdomen of the pregnant woman is given massage. They are also administered a mixture of Haldi, Gur and warm water. To reduce pain, sometimes the pregnant woman is required to drink concentrated Mahua liquor.		
	(ii) Delivery is conducted in	(ii) The delivery is conducted in	(ii) Delivery is conducted in	Conducting delivery in

(Contd...)

(a)	(b)	(c)	(d)	(e)
	squatting position	squatting position.	squatting position	squatting position seems to be less painful and more scientific. The administration of warm mixture may perhaps make easier delivery besides its nutritional contents.
	(iii) Elderly women and traditional Dais help. In complicated cases the traditional healer is also called	(iii) Elderly women and traditional Dais help. In complicated cases local traditional healer is called	Elderly ladies and Dais help.	
	(iv) The room is cleaned and plastered with the cow dung.	(iv) The room is cleaned and plastered with the cow dung.	(iii) The room is cleaned and plastered with the cow dung.	
	(v) A mixture of mustard oil and ash is applied on the child's cord. The cord is cut by an arrow. Sometimes stool of hair mixed with oil/water is also applied on the affected part	(v) The cord is cut with the help of sickle or blade some soil is put on the naval. If the cut is not dried, application of betel nut is suggested.	(iv) The còrd is cut with a bamboo piece or knife depending on the sex of the child. Mustard oil is applied to the affected part.	The extent of harm by putting things like stool of hair, ash, soil etc. on the affected part after cutting the navel cord.
	(vi) Colostrum is not discarded.	(vi) Colostrum is not discarded.	(v) Colostrum is not discarded.	It is a nice practice which is usually not found among the non-tribals.
(v) Postnatal care	(i) No postnatal care, like immunization to the children.	(i) No postnatal care, like immunization to the children.	(i) No postnatal care, like immunization to the children.	
	(ii) After giving bath with warm water, the mother and	(ii) After giving bath the child is put in the smoke generated	(ii) The mother and the child are given warm water. The	

(Contd...)

(a)	(b)	(c)	(d)	(e)
	the child is given massage with oil.	by putting king's cumin on fire. The child is given massage after given bath with warm water.	mother is fermented with turmeric powder.	
	(iii) Mother is served with some liquid food.	(iii) The mother is given some liquid food.	(iii) The mother is given some liquid food mixed with turmeric powder.	
	(iv) The mother is not permitted to take sour thing green vegetables and cold water for a week after delivery. The mother does not take alcohol for about 5-6 months after delivery.	(iv) Upto two months of delivery, the mother is not permitted to take green vegetables maize, wheat, gram etc., since they might affect the health of the child.	(iv) There is no restriction of mother's food.	KAP about the post-natal care services are required to be promoted and the irrational beliefs are required to be dispelled.
	(v) The child is breast fed as long as the mother continues lactating.	(v) The child is breast fed as long as the mother continues lactating.	(v) The child is breast fed as long as the mother continues lactating.	
	(vi) In case, mother has no sufficient breast milk she is administered lioness milk mixed with water and if the lioness milk is not available, then fish or crab are administered.	(vi) If the mother dose not has sufficient breast milk, she is administered papaya/urad dal/ mahua boiled with water.	(vi) If the mother does not have sufficient breast milk, the child is fed with the Goat milk.	
	(vii) Most of the child - hood diseases can be cured by administering a small dose of alcohol.			

Chapter 16

Fertility Differentials in Khairwars of Madhya Pradesh

G.D. Pandey and J. Roy

Though fertility is a biological phenomenon, its level varies according to socio-cultural characteristics of the population. Tribes are socio-culturally distinct from one another. Very few empirical studies on tribal fertility have been carried out. (Pandey, 1989; Pandey et al., 1996; Pandey et al., 2000; Roy, 2000 and Sinha, 1981). Tribe wise studies are needed to study variation in fertility level and associated socio-cultural factors. This paper attempts to study fertility differentials in Khairwars of Sidhi district of Madhya Pradesh.

The Tribe

Khairwar is considered to be closely connected with the Cheros (Russel et al. 1916). They are found in Sidhi, Panna, Shahdol, Chhatarpur, Satna and Rewa districts of Madhya Pradesh. The traditional occupation of the tribe is Catechu making from Khair wood (Acacia Catechu) and this occupation has given the name to the tribe. The tribe has a number of exogamous groups, named after plants and animals. Survey conducted by Government of Madhya Pradesh among Khairwar revealed a negative growth of population and high infant mortality in some of the villages of Kusmi block of Sidhi district (Shukla, 1986).

Materials and Methods

The paper is an outcome of the study carried out among the

Khairwars of Sidhi district by Regional Medical Research Centre for Tribals (I.C.M.R.), Jabalpur in 1992-94. The sample includes 558 eligible Khairwar women drawn from four blocks (Singraulli, Devsar, Kusmi and Chitrangi) of Sidhi district, Madhya Pradesh. In this survey, a couple was defined eligible, if both the partners were living together and the wife's age was less than 50 years on the reference date of survey, have not used any contraceptive method till the reference date of survey and have not attended menopause (Bhende and Kanitkar, 1985). Information was collected by visiting households using structured questionnaires. The index of fertility used in the study is the number of children born per eligible couple.

It was observed that 84 per cent of the study population was illiterate (7^+ years), 42 per cent population were below 14 years of age and 8 per cent were of 60^+ years. Nearly two third of the population (62%) was engaged in agriculture, followed by agriculture labour (34%). The sex ratio was found to be 949 and Infant Mortality Rate (IMR) was 142. The annual household income was Rs. 9628.00, much lower than the defined poverty line (Rs. 11000). (Table-1).

Results and Discussions

As evident from Table-2 that the number of children born per eligible couple is 2.74, which is lower than that of M.P. (3.33) (NFHS-2). Variation of fertility and associated socio-economic factors is discussed below.

Literacy of Husband

Since, in this study, most of the wives of the eligible couples were illiterate, education level of husband was taken as a factor associated with the fertility in the wife. The observations have indicated that the mean number of children born to the wives of illiterate husbands is 2.91 and it is higher than the women whose husbands were literate (2.28). This difference has been found statistically significant ($Z=2.99$, $P<0.05$).

Occupation of Husband

Most of the women in the study area were housewives (non-workers). So occupation of husband has been taken as a factor affecting fertility in the tribe. For analysis, two broad groups of occupation have been made, namely, agriculture (engaged with any kind of agricultural activities either as owner of the land or as agricultural labour) and non-agriculture (engaged in labour, household industry, service etc.).

As it is evident from Table-2, the mean number of children born to a wife is higher (2.85) where husbands were engaged in agriculture and it is lower (2.46) for other group of wives. This difference has not been found statistically significant. ($Z=1.79$ $P > 0.05$).

Type of Household

Association of fertility performance of a female with the type of household, she belongs has been shown in Table-2. It is evident that the mean number of children born is higher (3.12) to the females belonging to nuclear households, than those belonging to joint (2.14) households. The difference in fertility according to the type of household was statistically significant. ($Z = 4.76$, $P < 0.05$).

Annual Income

To see the association of household income and fertility, the females were grouped according to their annual household income: i) females of households with income below poverty line i.e. below Rs. 11000/- and ii) females of households with income above poverty line i.e. Rs. 11000/-. It has been observed that the females with annual household income above poverty line have slightly higher fertility (2.91) than the other group of females (2.58). This difference in fertility levels was insignificant ($Z = 1.42$, $P > 0.05$).

Land Holding

It is evident from the Table 2 that a large number of couples did not possess any land (34.4%). The average number of children born to the females, belonging to the households having land is 3.11 while it is 1.77 children for females with no agricultural land. This difference was statistically significant ($Z = 7.04$, $P < 0.05$).

Age at Marriage

Several studies have revealed that age at marriage of women

affects her fertility performance. (Bhargava; 1984 and Agarwal, 1961) The data for Khairwar women reveals that mean number of children born to the woman who married at an early age is highest (3.40) compared to the other group of females. The average number of children gradually decreases, as the age at marriage increases from 12 years to 17 years. This difference is statistically significant.

Age Difference between Husband and Wife

To see whether the difference in ages of husband and wife at the time of their marriage have any considerable effect on the fertility, the data have been analysed taking two groups of females, one where the difference was up to 5 years and the other where the difference was more than 5 years. It is evident from the Table 2 that the average number of children born to a female with husband having age difference of more than 5 years is higher (3.36) than the other group of females. This difference is statistically significant. ($Z = 2.00$, $P < 0.05$).

Conclusions

The fertility of Khairwar women is lower than the fertility of women of Madhya Pradesh. The age at marriage of women and the difference in age at marriage of husband and wife was found to be associated with the level of fertility. Literacy of husband and nuclear household has positive correlation with fertility of the Khiarwar women. However the occupation of husband and the annual household income were not found to be associated factors.Thus the study reveals that age at marriage of women and literacy of husband plays significant role in determining the fertility of the Khairwar. Improvement in education level and increase in marriage age may improve the fertility and as a result, mortality status of the tribe.

REFERENCES

Agarwala, S.N. 1961. Raising the Marriage age for women, a means to lower the Birth Rate. Economic and Political Weekly, 1: 797-98.

Bhargava, P.T. 1984. Change in Age at Marriage and its effects on fertility: A study of slum dwellers of Greater Bombay. *Journal of Family Welfare*, 31: 32-36.

Bhende, A. and Kanitkar, T. 1985. Principles of Population Studies, Himalaya Publishing House, Bombay.

National Family Health Survey 1998-99, M.P. NFHS 2 International Institute of Population Science, Mumbai.

Pandey, G.D. 1989. A study of couple fertility in a tribal population of Madhya Pradesh. In: Singh, S.N. et al (eds): Population Transition in India, Vol.2. B.R. Publishing Corporation, Delhi, pp. 245-256.

Pandey, G.D. and Tiwari, R.S. 1996. Fertility in Hill-Korwas – A Primitive tribe of M.P. Man in India. 76 : 325-329.

Pandey, G.D. and Tiwari, R.S. 2000. A study of vital rates in the primitive tribes of Madhya Pradesh. In: Choubey, R. and Sharma, K.K.N. (eds): Tribal Health. K.K. Publications, Allahabad.

Roy, J. 2000. Socio-Cultural Determinants of Fertility Behaviour of Khairwars of Madhya Pradesh. Ph.D. Thesis, Rani Durgawati Vishwavidyalaya, Jabalpur.

Russel, R.B. and Hiralal, 1916. The tribes and castes of the Central Provinces of India. Vol. III, Low Price Publication, Delhi, pp. 427-438.

Shukla, H.L. 1986. Tribal Heritage of Madhya Pradesh. B.R. Publishing Corporation, Delhi. pp. 32.

Sinha, U.P. 1981. Growth and distribution of tribal population in India, 1961-71. In: Srinivasan, K. and Mukherjee, S. (eds): Dynamics of Population and Family Welfare in India. Popular Prakashan, Bombay.

Tribal Research Institute, Bhopal, KAIRWAR JANJATI MAIN JANASANKHYA KI KAMI – Ek Adhyan.

Table 1: Socio-demographic Characteristics of the Khairwar

Sl. No.	*Characteristics*		*Percentage (N = 549)*
1	Type of Household (%)		
	Nuclear		66.30
	Joint		33.70
2	Literacy (7^+) (%)		
	Male	28.80	15.90
	Female	5.62	
3.	Occupation (%)		
	Own Agriculture		62.10
	Agriculture Labour + Labour		34.30
	Service, business & Industry		3.60

(Contd...)

4. Vital Statistics (Per 1000)

Crude Birth Rate	43.50
Crude Death Rate	12.40
Infant Mortality Rate	141.70
Sex Ratio	949.00

5. Annual Income per Household (Rs.) 9628.00

6. Age Composition (Year) (%)

00 – 14	42.00
15 – 59	50.00
60 +	8.00

Table 2: Fertility Differentials in Khairwar

Sl. No.	*Variables*	*Number of children born per eligible women*	*Z Statistics*
1	Literacy of Husband		
	Literate	2.28 (150)	2.99*
	Illiterate	2.91 (408)	
2	Occupation of husband		
	Agriculture	2.85 (389)	1.79
	Non-Agriculture	2.46 (169)	
3	Type of Household		
	Nuclear	3.12 (339)	4.76*
	Joint	2.14 (219)	
4	Annual Income (Rs.)		
	< 11000	2.58 (396)	1.42
	11000	2.91 (162)	
5	Land Holding (Acres)		
	Owning Land	3.11 (366)	7.04*
	Having No Land	1.77 (192)	
6	Age Difference of Couples (Years)		
	< 5	2.74 (402)	2.00*
	5+	3.36 (89)	
7	Age at Marriage (years)		
	< 12	3.40 (a) (131)	a & b = 1.81
	13 –14	2.85 (b) (155)	a & c = 2.44*
	15 – 16	2.65 (c) (150)	a & d = 4.78*
	17+	1.93 (d) (122)	b & c = 0.74
			b & d = 3.42*
			c & d = 2.64*

*Statistically significant, P<0.05.

Figures in parenthesis denote number of eligible females studied.

Chapter 17

Fertility and Mortality Profile of the Khairwar of Madhya Pradesh

K.K.N. Sharma and D.K. Adak

The three major demographic events, which affect the population size of an area, are births, deaths and migration. Births and deaths are technically referred to as fertility and mortality in demography (Srinivasan, 1998). This article presents the estimates of fertility and mortality among the Khairwar of Surguja district in Chhattisgarh

Materials and Methods

In order to collect necessary information on fertility and mortality 109 Khairwar mothers were interviewed. For detailed information on study area and methods we refer to earlier article of Sharma published in this volume.

Results and Discussion

Fertility record of the Khairwar mothers according to different age groups is shown in Table 1. It reveals that average number of live births increases with the increase in mother's age, but mothers aged 40-44 years show considerably lower average of live births (7.0), which is lower than the earlier (10.29) and preceding (10.5) age groups. However, the mean live birth is found to be 5.38.

Table 2 describes different mortalities among the Khairwar. Rate of infant mortality (deaths before 1st year of age) is found to be 145 per 1000 live births among them, which is much higher than National level data (72 per 1000 live births; Jain: 2000). It could be seen from Table 2 that like fertility the per cent of infant mortality also increases with the increase in mother's age. An opposite trend is noticed in 35-39 and 40-44 year age groups. In case of child mortality (deaths within 1-4 years of age) by and large a similar trend is perceptible. However, in case of juvenile mortality (deaths within 5-14 years of age) no definite trend is noticed. Child and juvenile mortality are found to be 3.92 and 1.7 respectively, while pre-reproductive mortality (deaths within 15 years of age) is 20.1. Like infant mortality, pre-reproductive mortality also increases with increase of mother's age. The only exception is noticed among the mothers aged 40-44 years.

The per cent of abortions and stillbirths among Khairwar are found to be 1.95 and 2.60 respectively and the percentage of total wastage was 4.55, which indicates a high level of reproductive wastage (Table 3).

REFERENCES

Jain, K. 2000. Infant mortality rate rising in most States. Times of India (05.03.2000), Delhi.

Srinivasan, K. 1998. Basic demographic techniques and applications. Sage publications, New Delhi.

Table 1: Fertility Record of the Khairwar Mothers

Age group of mothers (in years)	*Number of mothers*	*Number of live births*	*Mean live birth*
20-24	15	46	3.07
25-29	32	112	3.50
30-34	33	156	4.73
35-39	17	175	10.29
40-44	8	56	7.00
45-49	4	42	10.50
Total	109	587	5.38

Table 2: Different Mortalities Observed in Khairwar

Age group of mothers	*No. of live births*	*Infant mortality*	*Child mortality*	*Juvenile mortality*	*Total pre-reproductive mortality*
20-24	046	04(08.69)	-	01(2.17)	05(10.87)
25-29	112	16(14.28)	01(0.89)	-	17(15.18)
30-34	156	26(16.67)	06(3.85)	05(3.20)	37(23.72)
35-39	175	24(13.71)	11(6.28)	04(2.28)	39(22.28)
40-44	056	07(12.50)	01(1.78)	-	08(14.28)
45-49	042	08(19.05)	04(9.52)	-	12(28.57)
Total	587	85(14.48)	23(3.92)	10(1.70)	118(20.10)

Figures in parenthesis indicate percentage values.

Table 3: Percentage of Reproductive Wastage Observed in Khairwar

Number of mothers	*Total number of pregnancies*	*Number of abortions*	*Number of still births*	*Total wastage*
109	615	12(1.95)	16(2.60)	28(4.55)

Figures in parenthesis indicate percentage values.

Chapter 18

Some Aspects of Fertility among the Hill Korwa of Bagicha Block in Chhatisgarh

R.A. Kerketta

The three major demographic events which affect the population size of an area are births, death and migration. Births and deaths are technically referred to as fertility and mortality in demography. Measures of fertility are important in demographic study as births are crucial for biological replacement of population and for the survival of the human society as a whole. Any increase or decrease in the population of a country is largely the result of a surplus or deficit of births over death (Srinivasan, 1998).

Fertility and population problems are of central importance to the policy makers both in the government and non-government sectors. There is no aspect of human life, which is not influenced by fertility today. According to Thompson and Lewis, "the fertility of women has always been a matter of vital concern to all the peoples."; for this reason many studies have been conducted on this topic by Sengupta & Chakravarty(1995), Pandey(1991), Pandey and Tiwari(1996), Bhuyan and Bhuyan(1984) etc.

It is a generally acknowledged fact that demographic study at microlevel is limited among the tribal groups of central India. In the present study an effort has been made to trace out the fertility aspect, its rate and factors affecting it, among a primitive tribal group (PTG), the Hill Korwa of Bagicha Block of Jashpur District, Chhatisgarh.

Material and Method

The data for the present study were collected from the two village of Bagicha Block, namely Sardapath (plateau area on top of hill) and Rajpur (plain area close to the main stream of the city), which are located in Jashpur District of Chhattisgarh. The district lies between 22.17 ^{0}and 23.15^0 North latitude and 83.30^0 and 84.24^0-east longitude.

The Hill Korwa is a classic example of isolated population and considered as primitive tribal group (PTG) as this tribe is at a very low stage of acculturation. Their concentration is more in the mountain tracts between the borders of Chhattisgarh and Jharkhand, which is known as Chota Nagpur region. The present study concerns the Hill Korwas, who are considered as a sub-tribe of the larger Korwa tribe.

The samples were collected by the method of random sampling which consist of 102 married women (47 women of sardapath and 55 women of Rajpur village) of all age-group (15-69).

Women were interviewed and the information were gathered through interview-schedule. The schedule included structure, semi-structured, open-ended & close -ended questions. Interview was made possible by using several rapport building techniques.

Results and Discussions

The results of the study are presented in the following tables.

1. Age Structure

Age being an important factor for studying fertility, the sample of women was classified into various age groups, details of which is given in the Table-1.

The table reveals that maximum number of women (26.47%) belong to the age-group of 30-34 years and the least (i.e.0.98%) come from the age-group of 60-64 years. Mean age of the Hill-Korwa in study area was calculated to be 37 years.

Table1: Percentage Distribution of Women in Different Age-groups

Age-Group (in years)	*Frequency*	*Percentage*
15-19	04	03.92
20-24	10	09.80
25-29	13	12.74
30-34	27	26.47
35-39	12	11.76
40-44	08	07.84
45-49	07	06.86
50-54	11	10.78
55-59	07	06.86
60-64	01	00.98
65-69	02	01.96
Total	102	99.97
Mean	37 Years.	

2. Age at Menarche

Age at menarche is the most crucial factor in deciding the age of marriage for females. It is evident from Table2 that half of the females (47%) attained menarche by 14 years of age. The mean age at menarche is 13.59 years among them.

Table 2: Percentage Distribution of Age at Menarche

Age At Menarche (in years)	*Frequency*	*Percentage*
12	09	08.82
13	34	33.30
14	48	47.00
15	11	10.78
Total	102	99.90
Mean	13.59 Years	

3. *Age at Marriage*

Table 3 shows that 27.45 per cent of the females were married by the age of 16 years. The percentage of females marrying below that government prescribed marriage age of 18 years is about 84.29 per cent. 11.76 per cent of females married at the age of 18 years and only 3.92 per cent of females are married after 18 years of age. The mean age at marriage in the females is 15.75 years.

Table 3: Percentage Distribution of Age at Marriage

Age At Marriage (in years)	*Frequency*	*Percentage*
10	01	00.98
11	02	01.96
12	08	07.84
13	04	03.92
14	09	08.82
15	11	10.78
16	28	27.45
17	23	22.54
18	12	11.76
19	01	00.98
20	02	01.96
21	00	00.00
22	01	00.98
Total	102	99.97
Mean	15.75 Years	

4. *Age at First Conception*

It is evident from table 4 that more than half of the females under study became pregnant before the age of 18 years (82.47%) and almost all by the age of 22 years. However, the mean age at first conception is calculated to be 16 years among them.

Table 4: Percentage Distribution of Age at First Conception and Number of Pregnancies

Age at first conception (in years)	*Frequency*	*Percentage*	*Number of Pregnancy*
12	02	02.06	07
13	06	06.18	30
14	12	12.37	69
15	10	10.30	49
16	28	28.86	112
17	22	22.68	99
18	12	12.37	58
19	01	01.03	03
20	02	02.06	09
21	00	00.00	00
22	02	02.06	06
Total	97	99.97	442
Mean		16 years	

5. Disease

Women suffering from severe disease also affect the fertility among them. Table 5 shows the percentage of women suffering from disease among the Hill Korwa.

Table 5: Percentage of Women Suffering from Diseases

Diseases	*Suffering*	*Percentage*	*Number of Pregnancy*	*Average Number of Pregnancy*
Tuberculosis	05	5.15	13	2.6
Syphilis	06	6.18	17	2.8
Nothing	86	88.65	412	4.7
Total	97	99.90	442	10.1

It appears that, 11.33% of women are suffering from disease like tuberculosis(5.15%) and syphilis (6.18%), with 2.6 and 2.8 average number of pregnancies respectively. About 88.65% of women are not at all suffering from any type of disease. Thus, it reveals that diseases do cause negative affect over fertility but since the percentage of women suffering form disease is very small compared to those who are not suffering from any type of severe disease, such a negative affect on fertility among Hill Korwa is not very significant.

6. Duration of Breast-feeding

Longer duration of breast-feeding affects the fertility in a negative way. Table 6 shows the duration of breast-feeding among the Hill Korwa.

Table 6: Percentage Distribution of Duration of Breast Feeding

Duration (in years)	*Number of Women*	*Number of Pregnancy*	*Average Number of Pregnancy*
2-2.5	02	13	6.5
2.5	01	05	5.0
2-3	01	03	3.0
2.5-3	06	16	2.6
3	20	86	4.3
2-2.5-3	01	02	2.0
2.5-3-4	04	17	4.25
3-4	45	219	4.8
4	17	81	4.7
Total	97	442	37.15
Mean	-	3.36 Years	

It reveals that, shorter duration of 2 to 2.5 years of breast feeding have average number of pregnancies (6.5) and longer duration of breast feeding (4 years) have average number of 4.7 pregnancies. The mean year of breast-feeding is 3.36 years. It is also found that about 45(46.3%) women have 3-4 year of duration of breast-feeding while

17 (17.5%) women breast fed for 4 years. This indicates that due to practice of longer duration of breast feeding among the Hill Korwa, a negative affect is seen on the fertility. The sample being small for most of the age groups, a clear trend is not reflected.

Practice of Abstinence

Though Hill Korwa do not practice postpartum abstinence they practice abstinence at the time of lent days. The frequency is shown in Table 7.

Table7: Frequency of Practice of Abstinence

Subject Preferences	*Frequency*	*Percentage*
Lent Days	45	44.1
No Abstinence	57	55.8
Total	102	99.9

It is evident from the table that only 45 (44.1%) females practice abstinence during lent days, which is observed once in year and lasts for three days. Whereas, more than 55% women do not practice any type of abstinence.

8. *Practice of Celibacy*

Celibacy means the social and self-imposed controls on marriage affecting the fertility. The Hill Korwa do not practice celibacy but on the other hand as is evidenced from the table-3, earlier that, 3.96% of the marriages take place before they reach 19 years and only 3.92% of the marriages took place after 19 years.

9. Age at Menopause

Menopause is the end of reproductive period, for this reason age of menopause also affects the fertility.

Maximum women attained their menopause at 44 years (43.3%) and minimum at 47 years (3.3%). The mean age at menopause among the Hill Korwa is 43.7 years. Apart from the above, several bio-social factors also affect fertility.

Table 8: Percentage Distribution of Age at Menopause

Age At Menopause (in years)	*Frequency*	*Percentage*
40	02	13.3
41	00	00.0
42	00	00.0
43	07	23.3
44	13	43.3
45	04	06.6
46	03	10.0
47	01	03.3
Total	30	99.8
Mean	43.7 Years	

10. Type of Marriage

Marriages are mainly of two forms, monogamy and polygamy. If polygamy is compared with a system where monogamy is practiced then there is possibility that fertility per women may be less. Distribution of type of marriage among the Hill Korwa is presented in Table 9.

Table 9: Percentage Distribution of Type of Marriage and Number of Pregnancy

Type of Marriage	*Frequency*	*Percentage*	*Number of Pregnancy*	*No. of Pregnancies per marriage*
Monogamy	76	74.5	346	4.6
Polygamy	26	25.4	96	3.7
Total	102	99.9	442	8.3

It is evident from the table that 74.5% of marriages is monogamy with total number of 346 pregnancy, which is much more than the 25.4% polygamous marriages with total number of 96 pregnancies.

Table 10: Present Age Group against Number of Pregnancy of First and Second Wives in Polygamy

Age-Group (In years)	*Frequency*	*Number of Pregnancy*	
		I-wife	*II-wife*
25-29	05	03	09
30-34	09	22	15
35-39	22	04	06
40-44	02	05	02
45-49	03	06	05
50-54	02	13	-
55-59	02	03	03
Total	25	56	40

It reveals that in case of polygamous marriage total number of pregnancy of first wife is 56 and that of second wife is 40. This indicates that polygamous marriage shows a negative affect over fertility as it results in reproduction of number of pregnancy of second wife and thus affect the fertility. Age-group 25-29 and 35-39 years are exceptional cases probably because of small sample size.

11. Marital Status

Marital status tells about the per cent of women divorced, widowed, separated & living with husband in any group or community. Larger the number of women divorced, widowed, separated and without remarriage show a negative affect over fertility of any community. Marital status distribution among Hill Korwa is shown in Table 11.

It is evident from the table that among Hill Korwa 87 (89.6%) women were living with husband with total number of 404 pregnancy. Only 7 (7.2%) women are either divorced, separated or widowed with only 28 pregnancies. They haven't completed their reproductive period and 3(3.09%) women are those who remarried after separation or divorce, having total number of 10 pregnancy. Thus it shows that about 90 women used their reproductive period fully against 7 women who do not completely had their reproductive period. Since the latter figure is negligible compared to number of women having positive affect on fertility, we can say that among Hill Korwas marital status of women who are living with husband and who remarried after being widowed and separated contribute for high fertility among them.

Table 11: Percentage Distribution of Women's Marital Status against their Number of Pregnancy

Marital Status	*Number of women*	*Percentage*	*Number of Pregnancy*	*Average number of Pregnancy*
With Husband	87	89.60	404	4.6
Divorced	4	4.12	14	3.5
Separated	1	1.03	5	5.0
Separated + Remarried	2	2.06	7	3.5
Widowed	2	2.06	9	4.5
Widow + Remarried	1	1.03	3	3.0
Total	97	99.90	442	21.4

12. Preferences Regarding Number of Children

From the table 12, it is evident that about 24 (23.52%) women have five children and the mean number of children possessed by the women is 4.23 which indicates that Hill Korwas prefer to have 4-5 children, which automatically contribute in an increase in fertility.

Table12: Percentage Distribution of Women in having Number of Children

Possess Number of children	*Frequency*	*Percentage*
0	6	5.88
1	6	5.88
2	9	8.82
3	16	15.68

(*Contd...*)

4	10	9.80
5	24	23.52
6	16	15.68
7	9	8.82
8	4	3.92
9	2	1.96
Total	102	99.9

13. Education of Women

Table 13 shows the percentage of literate and illiterate women among the Hill Korwa. Among the literate women the mean number of children is 3.16 and that of illetrate women is 4.67. This shows that education of women do affect family size. But as the sample size for literate women is too small i.e. only 6, compared to 91 illiterate women, no comparison can be made between the two.

Table 13: Percentage Distribution of Literate and Illiterate Women and Number of Children they Posses

Number of children Possess	*Literate*	*Illiterate*
1	2	4
2	0	9
3	2	15
4	1	9
5	0	24
6	0	16
7	1	8
8	0	4
9	0	2
Total Number of Women	6	91
Mean Number of Children	3.16	4.67

14. Occupation

Occupational pattern of the Hill Korwa couples is shown in table 16.

Table14: Percentage Distribution of Occupation

Type of Occupation	*Husband*		*Wife*	
	Frequency	*Percentage*	*Frequency*	*Precentage*
Agriculture	21	20.5	21	20.5
Agriculture+Labour	74	72.5	77	75.49
Labour	4	3.92	4	3.92
Government servant	3	2.9	0	0
Total	102	99.9	102	99.9

It reveals for table 14 that majority of (75.49%) couples are engaged in agriculture and labour. About 20.5% in agriculture and 3.92% labour work separately. Only 2.9% of males were engaged in government job. This shows that, Hill Korwa do labour work along with their agricultural occupation, which is their actual occupation. It also shows that women also participate in economic activities of family and do labour work along with agricultural work.

15. Income Status

It is evident from the table that one case of lowest income level with income below 500 have 7 pregnancy, which support the view that at lowest income group restrictions are minimum over the family size. As we move further down in the table we find increase in pregnancy with increase in monthly income but as soon as we cross the 1001-1500 income group, we find a decrease in pregnancy with increase in income level. The mean monthly income among Hill Korwa is Rs. 1141.7 and it is evident from the table that this income group shows the maximum number of pregnancy as it come under the income group Rs. 1001-1500. Thus it may be considered the middle income group among Hill Korwas, with no restriction on control over family size, it contribute for high fertility. Income group

501-750 Rs. & 2001-2500 Rs. can be considered as exceptions. This may be because of small size of data.

Table15: Percentage Distribution of Monthly Income against Number of Pregnancy

Monthly-Income (In Rs.)	*Number of Family*	*Percentage*	*Number of Pregnancy*	*Average Number of Pregnancy*
Below 500	1	0.98	7	7
0501-0750	25	24.5	90	3.6
0751-1000	19	18.6	105	5.5
1001-1500	26	25.4	136	5.2
1501-2000	16	15.6	79	4.9
2001-2500	4	3.92	24	6
2501-3000	1	0.98	1	1
Total	92	99.9	442	33.2
Mean		Rs. 1141.7 Monthly Income		

16. Measurement of Fertility

For the various measurements of fertility rates among the Hill Korwas, following formulas have been used:

1. Age-Specific Fertility Rate (ASFR)

The age specific rates of the women in various age-group are very essential. But since, Age specific marital fertility rate (ASMFR) is more refined than the ASFR because, in general it is only the married women who are exposed to the risk of child-bearing. so, both Age-Specific fertility rate(ASFR) and Age Specific marital fertility rate(ASMFR) is presented in the Table 16.

The table shows that the Age-specific fertility rate of total women and also of total married women among the Hill Korwas. The total number of live births are 24 and maximum children, are produced by women in the age-group 30-34 years, during the collection of sample.

Table16: Number of Live Birth and Number of Married Women and Total Female Population in Different Age-groups

Age-Group (In Years)	*Live Births*	*Number of Women*	*ASFR*	*Number of Married women*	*ASMFR*
15-19	2	19	105.2	3	666.6
20-24	6	20	300.0	9	666.6
25-29	5	20	250.0	12	416.6
30-34	9	41	219.5	26	346.1
35-39	2	15	133.3	12	166.6
*40-44	0	10	0	8	0
TOTAL	24	125	1008.0	70	2264.1

*Age-group 40-44 is included in this table for the purpose of calculations of general fertility Rate (GFR).

2. General Fertility Rate (GFR)

It calculates the number of live briths in a year per thousand women of normal reproductive age (15-44). General fertility rate is calculated with the help of table-16, given above.

General Fertility Rate (GFR) = 24×1000/175 = 192

Thus, the General fertility rate(GFR) among the Hill Korwa is 192 per thousand population.

1. Total Fertility Rate(TFR) and Total Marital Fertility Rate (TMFR)

Total fertility rate(TFR) is obtained by summing up the age-specific birth rates and multiplying it by number of years in the age-interval for total female population and when the same is calculated for total married women population, it is the total marital fertility rate (TMFR). Total fertility rate(TFR) and Total marital fertility Rate (TMFR) are calculated with the help of table-18.

Total fertility Rate (TFR) = 1008×5/1000 = 5.04.

Total marital fertility Rate (TMFR) = 2264.1×5/1000 = 11.32.

Thus, the total fertility rate(TFR) is 5.04 and total marital fertility rate (TMFR) is 11.32, per thousand females and married women population respectively.

Thus, in fine, it can be said that the maximum number of children are produced by women in the age-group 30-34 years with total fertility rate (TFR) 5.04, total marital fertility rate (TMFR) 11.32 and general fertility rate (GFR) 192 per thousand population.

Positive factors resulting in high fertility among Hill Korwas are their low age at marriage, as the mean age is 16 years & mean age of menarche is 14 years. The age at first conception is 16 years. Thus, an early age at marriage cause an early age at first conception among them. There is less loss of reproductive period among the women as 89.6 per cent of women were living with husband and 3.09 per cent who did not remarry after divorce, separation or widowhood. About 80.3 per cent of women do not wish to control their family size because of the preference of having at least 2-3 male children in family. Majority of women with 93.8 per cent was illiterate with mean number of 4.67 children and only 6.18 per cent of women were literate with mean number of 3.16 children. Mean number of children, the couples have is 4.23, indicating a moderately large family size. Presence of privacy in nuclear and polygamous families are with average number of 5.2 pregnancies contributes for high fertility compared to only the average pregnancy of 4.1 in joint family. Mean monthly income is Rs. 1141.70, which could be considered as middle income group among Hill Korwa, which results in no restriction in control over family size. Their mean age of menopause is 43.7 years. And with more deaths of children, the couple prefers to have more children and this raises the rate of fertility high among the tribe.

Among the factors which shows a very negligible effect on fertility are that about 11.33 per cent of women were suffering from diseases like tuberculosis and syphilis with 2.6 and 2.8 average number of pregnancy respectively. Practice of abstinence during lent days by about 44.1 per cent women, but it lasts only for three days and once in year. Though as they do not practice such celibacy, it was found that about 3.92 per cent of marriages took place after 19 years of age. Mean period of breast feeding is 3.34 years. Practice of polygamy marriage by women results in reduction in number of pregnancy of second wife. But their percentage is 25.4 per cent and that of monogamy is 74.5 per cent.

At last it could be concluded that with few negative factors, the effect of positive factor is more significant, which results in high fertility among the Hill Korwa tribe. This high rate of fertility may in future cause hindrance in their development. Therefore, the necessity of education and awareness is must among them because only with these two weapons the fertility among Hill-Korwa would be controlled and they would be able to uplift their standard of living and develop them selves.

REFERENCES

Bhuyan, S.B. and Bhuyan, K.C. 1984. Nupticality, fertility and family planning practices in rural Bangladesh- A case study. *Journal of Family Welfare*, 31: 62-75.

Maharanta, A. 1996. Fertility, Mortality and Gender Bias among Indian tribes-what do we really know? In: Samal, P.K. (ed.): Tribal Development Options, Gyanodiya Prakashan, Nanital.

Narayan, A. 1990 The Korwa Tribe-Their sociey and economies. Amar Prakashan, Delhi.

Pandey, G.D. and Tiwari, R.S. 1996. Fertility in Hill Korwas A primitive tribe of Madhya Pradesh. Man in India, 76: 325-329.

Pandey, G.D. 1991. Fertility in the Kol tribe of Madhya Pradesh. *Journal of Family Welfare*, 37:59-54.

Sengupta, S. and Chakravarty, K. 1995. Family type, fertility and mortality-A study among the Ahoms of Assam. Journal of Human Ecology, 6: 197-200.

Sharma, K. 1978. Fertility and mortality in Khonds- A tribal communities of Orissa. Man in India , 58. 77-84.

Srinivasan, K. 1998. Basic demographic techniques and applications. Sage Publications, New Delhi.

Chapter 19

The Raj Gond of Sagar District, Madhya Pradesh: A Demographic Study

M.K. Tiwari, R. Chakraborty, A. Gupta and D.K. Adak

The present study deals with some aspects of demography among the Raj Gond of Kadta village in Sagar district, Madhya Pradesh. Of the total 553 populations there are 285 males and 268 females, which gives the sex ratio 94 temales per 100 males. A relatively low index of aging (5.67) is recorded among them. Side by side, the value of young dependency ratio (84.59) is found to be quite high among the study population, whereas the value of old dependency ratio (4.79) is quite low in the same population. Average number of live births is 3.66 and average number of surviving children is 3.08 in the Raj Gond. Side by side, the rate of infant mortality is found to be 94.4 per 1000 live births in the study population, which is much higher than the national level. However, the index of total opportunity for selection (I: 0.3623) in the Raj Gond is found to be more towards the higher level of Indian populations.

The scope of demography covers the aspects such as (i) study of size, structure, composition and distribution of population, (ii) analysis of changes in these aspects of population and of the components of population change including mortality, nuptiality, fertility, migration and social mobility, and (iii) investigation of social, economic and biological determinants and consequences of population change. Contemporary physical anthropological research emphasized on many demographic aspects such as fertility, mortality, mating, migration, and population numbers etc. These data had been taken into consideration for the study of both long-term human evolution and ongoing biological differentiation of local population in terms of change in gene frequency (Srivastava et al., 1995). It may be a generally acknowledged fact that demographic study at micro level is limited among the tribal groups of Central India. In the present paper an attempt has been made to deal with general demographic trends among the Raj Gond of Sagar district, Madhya Pradesh.

Materials and Methods

The present investigation was carried out among the Raj Gond residing in Kadta village of Sagar district, Madhya Pradesh. Information was collected from 107 mothers residing in this village. Data on demographic variables were collected using structured schedules.

The Raj Gond speaks the dialect, which belong to the Dravidian family of Languages. They mainly depend on agro-forest economy. The commonest form of marriage among the Raj Gond is monogamy. Their religion is entirely of animistic character. They have also accepted many Hindu gods and goddesses with the passage of time.

Results and Discussion

The age and sex composition of the Raj Gond is given in Table 1. Of the total 553 populations there are 285 males and 268 females, which gives the sex ratio 94 females per 100 males. About 45 per cent of the total population is in the pre-reproductive age group (0-14 years), whereas in reproductive (15-49 years) and post- reproductive age groups (50 years and above) show 50 per cent and 5 per cent of the total population. It appears that the number of individuals gradually decreases as age advances in this population. There is a preponderance of male individuals to female individuals in most of the age groups. The exemption in this respect is noticed in 15-19, 20-24 and 30-34 years age groups. The age-sex structure of the Raj Gond population has been presented graphically as population pyramid in figure 1.

In Table 2 some population characteristics of the Raj Gond are presented. A relatively low index of aging (5.67) is recorded among them. This indicates that longevity and aged individuals are less among them. Index of aging is however, found to be much lesser than those of the Ladiya of Madhya Pradesh (Adak and Gharami, 2001) and Brahmin of Uttar Pradesh (Srivastava et al., 1995). The economic implications of age structure of a population can be viewed in terms of dependency ratio, which measures the ratio of the population in ages too young or too old to work to the population of working age (Srivastava et al., 1995). The value of young dependency ratio (84.59) is quite high among the study population, whereas the value of old dependency ratio (4.79) is considerably low among them. This might be due to the large number of individuals falling in the age category of 0-14 years and very low number of individuals falling in the age category of 50 years and above. Child women ratio (i.e. the number of children under 5 years of age per 100 women aged 15 and 49 years: Ghosh, 1976) is found to be 73.91, which is comparatively lower than the Jaintia of Meghalaya (Khongsdier, 1992) and Namasudra of West Bengal (Mukhopadhyay, 1981) but it is higher than that found in the Kota of Nilgiri Hills (Ghosh, 1976), Mahishya of West Bengal (Mukhopadhyay, 1981) and Khampti of Arunachal Pradesh (Chowdury et al., 1994).

Record on conception, fertility, mortality and pregnancy wastage is shown in Table 3. A total of 407 pregnancies with an average number of 3.80 is reported among the 107 Raj Gond mothers. Mean age at marriage among them is found to be 14.41 that is considerably lower than other Indian populations (like those studied by Saini, 1989; Adak and Gharami, 2001 and many others). Average number of live births is 3.66 among them. Side by side, average number of surviving children is found to be 3.08 in this population. Mean number of live births among the study population is more or less the same with that found in the Khampti of Arunachal Pradesh (Chowdhury et al., 1994), Kota of Nilgiri Hills (Ghosh, 1976) and the Ladiya of Madhya Pradesh (Adak and Gharami, 2001), but it is comparatively lower than that of the Jaintia (Deka, 1989) and Khasi (Nag, 1965) of Meghalaya. Mean number of surviving children is found to be slightly higher in the Jaintia of Meghalaya (Khongsdier, 1992) than that of the study population, whereas it is more of less the same with that found in the

Hajong of Meghalaya (Barua, 1983) and Namasudra and Mahishya of West Bengal (Mukhopadhya, 1981).

Rates of infant mortality (up to 1 year) and childhood mortality (1-5 years) are 9.44 and 4.08 respectively. Compared with the tribal populations of Central India (Basu, 1989) infant and childhood mortality among the Raj Gond are reported to be moderate. Turning to the other populations of India, the rate for infant mortality among the study population is much higher than those found in the Christian and non-Christian Khasi of Meghalaya (Khongsdier, 1995), but it is lower than those reported among the Jaintia (Khongsdier, 1992) and Hajong (Adak et al., 1999) of Meghalaya, and Khamti of Arunachal Pradesh (Chowdhury et al., 1994). The juvenile mortality rate (those who died before 15 years of age) is, however, found to be higher among the Raj Gond than many other Indian populations (like those studied by Khongsdier, 1992 and 1995; Adak et al., 1999; Chowdhury et al., 1994 etc.). The frequency of reproductive wastage (i.e. spontaneous abortions and still births) in turn, is reported to be 3.68 per cent among the study population, which is more less the same with those found among the Hajong (Adak et al., 1999) and Jaintia (khongsdier, 1992) of Meghalaya, but it is lower than those reported among the Christian and non-Christian Khasi of Meghalaya (Khongsdier, 1995).

In order to estimate the total selection intensity among the Raj Gond we have applied the formulae of Crow (1958) and Johnston and Kensinger (1971). Variables used in calculating this index are as follows:

Total number of mothers aged 40 years and above = 23

Number of reported pregnancies = 101

Number of live births = 99

Proportion of premature deaths (Pd) = 0.1111

Proportion of embryonic deaths (Ped) = 0.0297

Proportion of survivors up to birth (Pb) = 0.9703

Mean number of live births per woman aged 40 years and above = 4.30

Variance in the number of live births (Vf) = 3.90

The indices of selection intensity calculated according to Crow (1958) and Johnston and Kensinger (1971) are shown in Table 4. It reveals that the fertility component (If: 0.2109) is higher than the mortality component (Im : 0.1250). Fertility component is also found to be higher than the embryonic mortality component (Ime: 0.0306). However, both the calculations indicate that the differential fertility contribute more towards the total opportunity for selection. The index of total selection (I) calculated according to Johnston and Kensinger (1971) is, however, found to be higher than that calculated according to Crow (1958). This is probably because of the inclusion of embryonic deaths is earlier calculation. It reveals that the index of total opportunity for selection among the Raj Gond is more towards the higher level of the Indian populations (like those reported by Murthy and Ramesh, 1978; Reddy and Lakshmanudu, 1979; Saha, 1981; Roy and Bharati, 1982; Gandhi, 1989 and many others).

REFERENCES

Adak, D.K., Chaudhuri, S.S. and Chaudhuri, S. 1999. The Hajong of Meghalaya: A Study on some demographic Aspects. Arunachal University Research Journal, 2: 35-45.

Adak, D.K. and Gharami, A.K. 2001. A Study on the population Composition of the Ladiya of Sagar district, Madhya Pradesh. South Asian Anthropologist, 1: 83-89.

Barua, S. 1983. The Hajongs of Meghalaya : A Biodemographic Study. Human Science, 32 : 190-200.

Basu, S. 1989. Factors affecting Fertility and Mortality Behaviour among Tribal Population groups of Bastar District (Madhya Pradesh). In: Jena, B. and Pati, R.N. (eds.): Health and Family Welfare Services in India. Ashish Publishing House, New Delhi, pp. 353-361.

Chowdhury, D., Behera, M.C. and Adak, D.K. 1994. Some bio-demographic aspects of the Khamti and its demographic transition. In: Mukherjee, S., Hussain, F.I., Chakravorty, P. and Das, G. (eds.): Demographic Profile of North-East India. Omsons Publications, New Delhi, pp. 103-115.

Crow, J.F. 1958. Some possibilities for measuring selection intensities in man. Human Biology, 30:1-13.

Deka, A. 1989. Reproductive performance and selection among the Jaintias of village Saphai. In : Genetical demography of Indian Population. Calcutta : Anthropological Survey of India (ed.), pp 6-11.

Gandhi, L.P. 1989. Fertility and opportunity of natural selection among the Maheswari's. In: Genetical demography of Indian population. Calcutta: Anthropological Survey of India (ed.), pp. 72-81.

Ghosh, A.K. 1976. The Kota of Nilgiri Hills : A demographic study. *Journal of BioSocial Science*, 8 : 17-26.

Johnston, F.F. and Kensinger, K.M. 1971. Fertility and mortality differentials and their implications for micro-evolutionary change among the Cashinahua. Humam Biology, 43: 356-364.

Khongsdier, R. 1992. Some demographic traits among the Pnar of Sutnga and Moopala in Jaintia Hills district of Meghalaya. Man in India, 72 : 491-495.

Khongsdier, R.1995. Prenatal and Postnatal Mortality in the War Khasi of Meghalaya. *Journal of Human Ecology*, 6 : 201-204.

Mukhopadhyay, B. 1981. A comparative microdemographic study of two communities in Coastal Midnapore district, West Bengal. *Journal of BioSocial Science*, 13 : 476-489.

Murthy, J.S. and Ramesh, A. 1978. Selection intensities among the tribal populations of Adilabad district, Andhra Pradesh, India. Social Biology, 25 : 302-305.

Nag, M. 1965. Effect of Christianity on a few aspects of Khasi culture. Bulletin of Anthropological Survey of India, 3 : 95-116.

Reddy, P.C. and Lakshmanudu, M. 1979. Indices of opportunity of selection in Mala, Madiga and other Indian Populations. Journal of Indian Anthropological Society, 14 : 245-252.

Roy, S.K. and Bharati, P. 1982. Selection intensity: Inter and intra-group variation. *Journal of Indian Anthropological Society*, 17 :283-286.

Saha, S.S. 1981. Opportunity of selection in the Muria population of Narayanpur. *Journal of Indian Anthropological Society*, 16 : 185-187.

Saini, K.K. 1989. Reproductive performance among the Muslim women of East Nimar district. In: Genetical Demography of Indian Population. Calcutta: Anthropological Survey of India (ed.), pp. 101-113.

Srivastava, A.C., Chowdhury, A.K., Sankhyan, A.R. and Sahay, B.N. 1995. Genetic Demography of the Jaunsaris: A polyandrous tribe. *Journal of Anthropological Survey of India*, 44 : 1-57.

Table 1: Age-sex wise Distribution of the Raj Gond

Age cohort	*Male*		*Female*		*Total*		*Sex ratio*
	No.	*per cent*	*No.*	*per cent*	*No.*	*per cent*	
0-4	57	10.31	45	8.14	102	18.44	78.95
5-9	47	8.50	36	6.51	83	15.01	76.60
10-14	30	5.42	32	5.79	62	11.21	106.67
						44.66	
15-19	26	4.70	35	6.33	61	11.03	134.61
20-24	19	3.43	38	6.87	57	10.31	200.00
25-29	34	6.15	24	4.34	58	10.49	70.59
30-34	16	2.89	18	3.25	34	6.15	112.50
35-39	15	2.71	14	2.53	29	5.24	93.33
40-44	14	2.53	9	1.63	23	4.16	64.28
45-49	10	1.81	7	1.26	17	3.07	70.00
						50.45	
50-54	6	1.08	2	0.36	8	1.45	33.33
55-59	3	0.54	2	0.36	5	0.90	66.67
60-64	2	0.36	3	0.54	5	0.90	150.00
65-69	1	0.18	1	0.18	2	0.36	100.00
70+	5	0.90	2	0.36	7	1.27	40.00
						4.88	
Total	285	51.51	268	48.45	553	99.99	94.03

Table 2: Population Characteristics of the Raj Gond

Index of aging	5.67
Young dependency ratio	84.59
Old dependency ratio	4.79
Total dependency ratio	89.38
Child women ratio	73.91

Table 3: Record on Conception, Fertility, Mortality and Pregnancy Wastage

Total number of mothers	107
Mean age at marriage	14.41
Mean age at first child birth	16.51
Total number of pregnancies	407
Mean number of pregnancies per ever married woman	3.80
Total number of live births	392
Mean number of live births per married women	3.66
Mean number of surviving children per ever married women	3.08
Infant mortality (in per cent)	9.44
Childhood mortality (in per cent)	4.08
Juvenile mortality (in per cent)	14.80
Reproductive wastage (in per cent)	3.68

Table 4: Indices of Selection Intensity

Calculated according to Crow's formula(1958)			*Calculated according to Johnston & Kensinger's formula (1971)*			
Im	If	I	Ime	Im	If	I
0.1250	0.2109	0.3623	0.0306	0.1250	0.2109	0.4039

Fig. 1 Population Pyramid of the Raj Gond

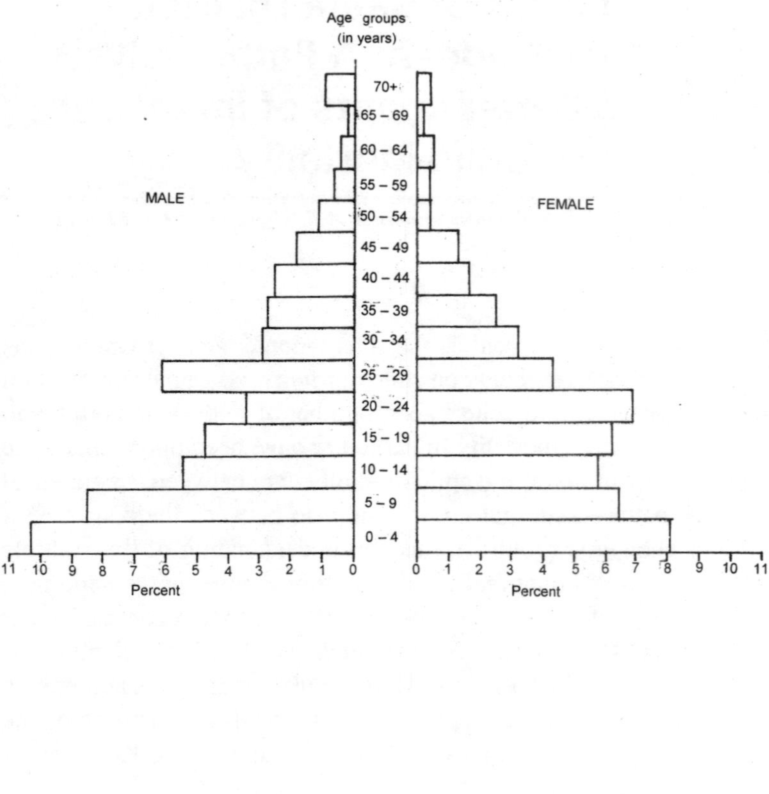

Chapter 20

The Kol of Satna District, Madhya Pradesh: A Path-analysis on the Determinants of Infant and Child Mortality

D.K. Adak, P.B.S.V. Padmanabham, A.K.Gharami and P. Bharati

United Nations celebrated as the International Year of Child in the year 1979. Since then study on child mortality did gain its momentum all over the world and quite a good number of studies on mortality in general and infant mortality in particular have been undertaken. The determinants of infant and child mortality vary between geographical regions, between cultural groups and also between the countries of various economic groups. Hence, an understanding of the multiple determinants of infant and child mortality is immensely important. Though only a few studies on this aspect have so far been carried out in some populations of this country, such investigation in Central part of India is limited (Koshy and Guru, 1999). In the present study an attempt has been made to deal with path analysis on some of the determinants of infant and child mortality among the Kol tribe of Satna district, Madhya Pradesh.

Material and Methods

For the present study data were collected from Nagod, Suhawal, Majhawan and Uchehara Development blocks of Satna district, Madhya Pradesh, during the period between March and May 2001 by AKG. Information on general demographic and socioeconomic variables was collected by visiting the families. Households were selected from different villages of these blocks without following any specific sampling techniques, but care was taken that each of the family contained at least one ever-married individual.

To examine the effects of mother's education, mother's age at marriage and economic status of the family on infant (0-1 year) and child (1-4 years) mortality an exhaustive schedule was prepared. This was filled in case of 47 Kol mothers, who have completed fertility. In this connection a sub-sample was drawn from a total of 444 Kol mothers.

The Kol tribe belongs to the Munda group. Their total population was estimated 14,65,384 in the Satna district in 1991 census. They counted more than 70 per cent of the districts total tribal population. Agriculture is their main occupation. They believe in animatism.

Results and Discussion

Non-literate mothers have higher percentage (14.98) of infant deaths (0-1 year) than the literate mothers (Table 1). Side by side, among the just literate mothers slightly higher percentage (13.79) of infant deaths is recorded than that of the primary and above educated mothers (13.33). Occurrence of infant deaths is found to be more when the Kol women marry at a younger age, particularly below 15 years (15.15%), which decreases as the age at marriage increases (Table 2). Infant deaths are lower among the mothers of high economic group than the mothers belonging to the lower group (table 3). However, when the relationship of these factors with infant deaths was examined infant mortality was found to be positively related with mother's education and economic status of the family but negative with mother's age at marriage (Table 4).

Occurrence of child mortality (1-4 years) is quite high (17.98 %) among the Kol non-literate women (Table 5). Side by side, high child mortality occurred among the mothers who married at an early age, particularly below 15 years (16.02 %), and decreases among the mothers who married comparatively at higher age (Table 6). Child deaths increase as the economic status of the family decreases. Child mortality is recorded in highest frequency (20.00%) among the mothers belonging to the low-income family, whereas the mothers of high-income family show lowest frequency (12.12%) of child deaths (table 7). However, when the relationship of these factors with child mortality is examined it is found that child mortality is positively related with mother's age at marriage but the relationship with mother's education and economic status of family is negative.

Path Analysis

In order to find out the causal model to depict the relationships among the socio-economic factors and infant mortality as well as child mortality the path analysis is performed following the multiple regression equations as given by Wonnacott and Wonnacott (1990). For this purpose each factor was assigned independent scores. Which is as follows:

SCORE ASSIGINED

Variables	SCORE			
	1	2	3	4
Dependent variables				
Infant mortality (Y)	Nil	1	2	3+
Child mortality (Y)	Nil	1	2	3+
Independent variables				
Mother's education (X1)	non-literate	Just literate	Primary and above	-
Mother's age at marriage (X2)	Up to 14 years	15-17 years	18 and years above	-
Economic status of the family (X3)	Low	Medium	High	-

The direction of causal relationship between three independent variables (i.e. mother's education, mother's age at marriage and economic status of the family) and two dependent variables (i.e. infant and child mortality) have been conceptualized and presented in path diagram 1 and 2 respectively. Based on these paths the following structural equations were evolved.

For infant mortality:

$$Y = .9420X1 - .3584X2 + .0202X3$$

$$X3 = .2714X1 + .3951X2$$

$$X2 = .9121X1$$

For child mortality

$$Y = -.3800X1 + .4781X2 - .6129X3$$

$$X3 = .2714X1 + .3951X2$$

$$X2 = .9121X1$$

The total effect of these variables on infant and child mortality is as follows :

For infant mortality

Direct effect of X1 on Y		= 0.9420
Indirect effect via X3	(0.2714) × (0.0202)	= 0.0055
Indirect effect via X2 alone	(0.9121) × (- 0.3584)	= -0.3269
Via X2 and X3	(0.9121) × (0.3951) × (0.0202)	= 0.0073
	Total effect	= 0.6279

For child mortality

Direct effect of X1 on Y		= -0.3800
Indirect effect via X3	(0 .2714) × (-0.6129)	= -0.1663
Indirect effect via X2 alone	(0.9121) × (0.4781)	= 0.4361
Via X2 and X3	(0.9121) × (0.3951) × (-0.6129)	= -0.2209
	Total effect	= -0.3311

Thus it appears that the total effect of mother's education, mother's age at marriage and economic status of family on infant mortality is positive (.6279) but it is negative (-.3311) in case of child mortality. However, all these differences deserve further intensive investigation to find out the root causes.

REFERENCES

Koshy, A.K. and Guru, S.S. 1999. A Path-Analysis on the Multiple Determinants of Infant mortality Among the Oraons. *J. Hum. Ecol.*, 10(2):93-98.

Wonnacott, T.H. and Wonnacott, R.J. 1990. *Introductory Statistics*. John Wiley and Sons, New York.

Table 1: Mother's Education and Infant Mortality

Educational status	*No. of mothers*	*Total live births*	*Infant mortality*	
			No.	*%*
Non-literate	37	267	40	14.98
Just literate	7	29	4	13.79
Primary and above	3	15	2	13.33

Table 2: Mother's Age at Marriage and Infant Mortality

Age at marriage	*No. of mothers*	*Total live births*	*Infant mortality*	
			No.	*%*
Up to 14 years	33	231	35	15.15
15 to 17 years	12	72	10	13.89
18 years and above	2	8	01	12.50

Table 3: Economic Status of the Family and Infant Mortality

Economic status of the family	*No. of mothers*	*Total live births*	*Infant mortality*	
			No.	*%*
Low (<Rs.1000)	12	75	14	18.67
Medium (Rs. 1001-1499)	23	170	24	14.12
High	12	66	8	12.12

Table 4: Relationship of Socio Economic Factors with Infant Mortality

Socio economic factors	*Coefficient of correlation*
Mother's education	0.2950
Mother's age at marriage	-0.1509
Economic status of the family	0.0565

Table 5: Mother's Education and Child Mortality

Educational status	*No. of mothers*	*Total live births*	*Child mortality*	
			No.	*%*
Non-literate	37	267	48	17.98
Just literate	7	29	-	-
Primary and above	3	15	-	-

Table 6: Mother's Age at Marriage and Child Mortality

Age at marriage	*No. of mothers*	*Total live births*	*Child mortality*	
			No.	*%*
Up to 14 years	33	231	37	16.02
15-17 years	12	72	11	15.28
18 years and above	2	8	-	-

Table 7: Mother's Status of the Family and Child Mortality

Economic status of the family	*No. of mothers*	*Total live births*	*Child mortality*	
			No.	*%*
Low (<Rs.1000)	12	75	15	20.00
Medium (Rs.1001-1499)	23	170	25	14.71
High	12	66	8	12.12

Table8: Association of Some-economic Factors with Child Mortality

Socio-economic factors	*Correlation Coeficient*
Mother's education	-0.1833
Mother's age at marriage	0.2393
Economic status of the family	-0.3093

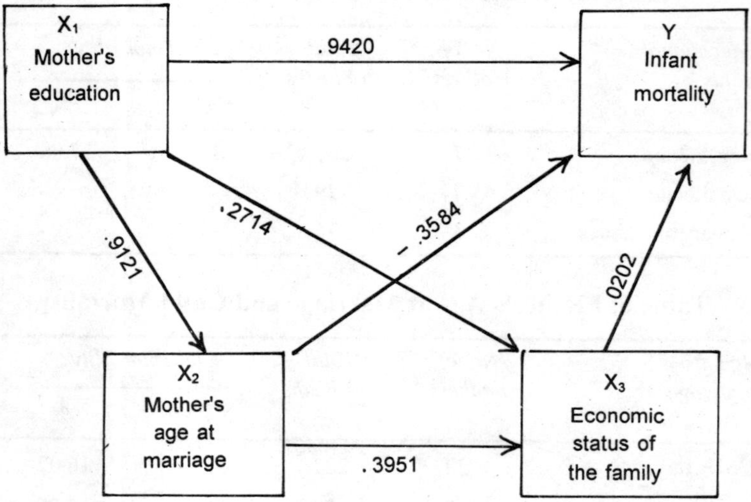

Path diagram 1 : For Infant mortality

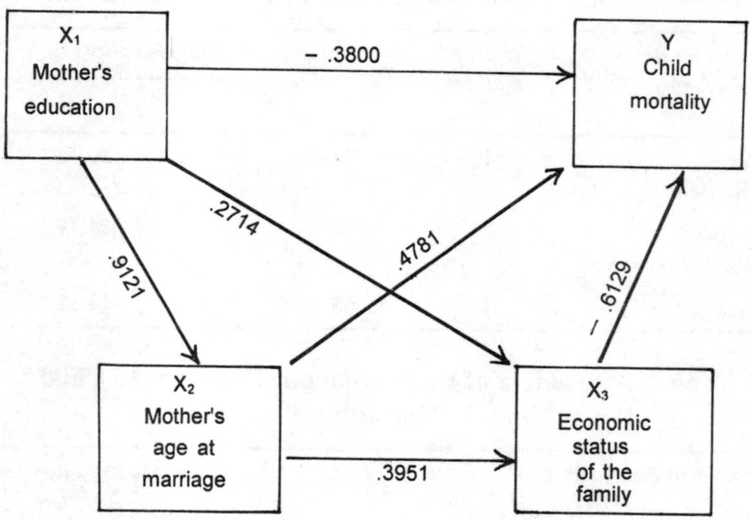

Path diagram 2 : For child mortality

Chapter 21

Impact of ABO Incompatibility on Reproductive Performance: A Study among the Khairwar of Madhya Pradesh

K.K.N. Sharma

Introduction

It is an established fact that maternal-fetal incompatibility for the ABO blood groups lead to early fetal deaths and abortion in human populations. Mc Kusick (1978) opined that as many as 5 per cent of conceptions are lost through ABO incompatibility. In which antibody, originating in the maternal circulation, enters the fetal circulation through the placenta, attaches to the blood group antigens on the infants red cells. This results into the destruction of those cells and threatens the survival of the new born.

It is an acknowledged fact that in the state of Madhya Pradesh hardly any such micro level study has been carried out concerning the impact of ABO incompatibility on reproductive performance. The present study is an endeavours to deal with the same among the Khairwar tribal population of Madhya Pradesh.

Material and Methods

For the sake of present investigation 89 Khairwar women who

had completed 49 years of age were randomly selected from Harra, Pandri, Anjni and Chapra villages of Surguja district, Madhya Pradesh. Out of these 89 women, 40 women belonged to the compatible mating type, while the rest i.e., 49 women were from incompatible mating types.

Data with respect to fertility and mortality profiles were collected by a structured questionnaire, drawing extended genealogies and cross checking the information from the elderly ladies of the households. Blood samples of both husband and wives were collected in tubes containing EDTA and analysed for ABO group in the field on the same day using standard technique.

Results and Discussion

Data on compatible and incompatible matings together with reproductive wastage are presented in Table 1. The incompatible mothers show higher percentage of abortion (3.11) and stillbirth (4.44) than the compatible mothers (abortion; 1.12, still birth: 1.68). Thus, the incompatible mothers show higher percentage of reproductive wastage (7.55) than that of the compatible mothers (2.81). However, when the chi-square test is performed it is seen that there exists significant difference between the incompatible and compatible mothers ($X_1^2 = 3.90$, $p < 0.05$) in this respect. Incompatible mothers suffered higher neo-natal deaths (8.17%) compared to the compatible mothers (3.47%). The incompatible mothers show 92.45 per cent live births in comparison with the compatible mothers, who delivered 97.19% live births.

Thus the present study is in conformity with the earlier views, which suggest that higher rates of abortion, stillbirth and neo-natal deaths occur among the incompatible offspring due to the destruction of red cells caused by the ABO blood group incompatibility.

REFERENCE

Mac Kusick, V.A. (1978). *Human Genetics*. Prentice Hall of India, New Delhi.

Table 1. ABO Incompatibility and Reproductive Wastage

Mating type	*No. of Mothers*	*Total Pregnancies*	*Total Live births*	*Reproductive wastage*			*Neonatal deaths*
				Abortions	*Still births*	*Total wastage*	
Compatible	40	178	173 (97.19)	2 (1.12)	3 (1.68)	5 (2.81)	6 (3.47)
Incompatible	49	225	208 (92.45)	7 (3.11)	10 (4.44)	17 (7.55)	17 (7.55)

Figures in parenthesis are percentage values.

Contributors

Adak, D.K. Anthropological Survey of India, Field Station, Sagar- 470003, Madhya Pradesh.

Ali, A. Consultant (Population Policy Advocacy) UNFPA and Department of Family Welfare, Ministry of Health and Family Welfare, Government of India and Honorary Consultant (RCH), NIHFW.

Bharati, P. Anthropology and Human Genetics Unit, Indian Statistical Institute, 203 B. T. Road, Kolkata -700108.

Bhattacharya, B.N. Population Studies Unit, Indian Statistical Institute, 203 B. T. Road, Kolkata- 700108.

Chakraborty, R. Anthropological Survey of India, 27, Jawaharlal Nehru Road, Kolkata -700016.

Dey , D. Population Research Center, M. S. University of Baroda, Baroda.

Dey, A.S. Population Research Center, Dr. H. S. Gour University, Sagar- 470 003, Madhya Pradesh.

Dey, D.K. Office of the Registrar General of India, New Delhi.

Dwivedi, S.N. Department of Biostatistics, All India Institute of Medical Sciences, Ansari Nagar, New Delhi-110029.

Gharami,A.K. Department of Anthropology, Dr.H.S.Gour University, Sagar- 470003, Madhya Pradesh.

Gautam, H.N. Department of Statistics, Science Model College, Rewa University, Rewa, Madhya Pradesh.

Ghosh, R. Anthropology and Human Genetics Unit, Indian Statistical Institute, 203 B. T. Road, Kolkata- 700108.

Govil, D. International Institute for Population Sciences (IIPS), Govandi Station Road, Deonar, Mumbai - 400088.

Gupta, A. Department of Anthropology, Dr.H.S.Gour University, Sagar- 470003, Madhya Pradesh.

Kumar, A. Medical college and Hospital, Azamgarh, Uttar Pradesh.

Mathur, Y.N. National Institute of Nutrition, Indian Council of Medical Research, Jamai-Osmania P.O., Hyderabad - 500 007.

Meera, A. International Institute for Population Sciences (IIPS), Govandi Station Road, Deonar, Mumbai - 400088.

Mitra, M. School of Studies in Anthropology, Pt. Ravishankar Shukla University, Raipur.

Nanda, J. School of Studies in Anthropology, Pt. Ravishankar Shukla University, Raipur.

Nanda, S. Consultant (Health and Dev. Research), UNICEF, Home: Radhagovind lane-I, Puri-752001, Orissa.

Nangia, P. International Institute for Population Sciences (IIPS), Govandi Station Road, Deonar, Mumbai - 400088.

Nath, D.C. Department of Statistics, Gauhati University, Gauhati-781014, Assam.

Padmanabham,P.B.S.V. Anthropological Survey of India, Central Regional Centre, Nagpur- 440006.

Pal, M. Economic Research Unit, Indian Statistical Institute, 203 B. T. Road, Kolkata- 700108.

Pandey, G.D. Regional Medical Research Centre for Tribals, (I.C.M.R.), Nagpur Road, Jabalpur - 482 003, Madhya Pradesh.

Radhaiah, G. National Institute of Nutrition, Indian Council of Medical Research, Jamai-Osmania P.O., Hyderabad -500 007.

Ram, F. International Institute of Population Sciences (IIPS), Govandi Station Road, Deonar, Mumbai - 400088.

Ram, U. Gokhale Institute of Politics and Economics, Pune-411004.

Ranjan, A. Shyam Institute, Mudian Ka Kuan, Datia, Madhya Pradesh-475 661.

Rao, D.H. National Institute of Nutrition, Indian Council of Medical Research, Jamai-Osmania P.O., Hyderabad-500 007.

Rao, K.M. National Institute of Nutrition, Indian Council of Medical Research, Jamai Osmania P.O., Hyderabad-500 007.

Rao, N.P. National Institute of Nutrition, Indian Council of Medical Research, Jamai-Osmania P.O., Hyderabad-500 007.

Roy, T.K. International Institute for Population Sciences (IIPS), Govandi Station Road, Deonar, Mumbai - 400088.

Roy, J. Regional Medical Research Centre for Tribals, (I.C.M.R.), Nagpur Road, Jabalpur - 482 003, Madhya Pradesh.

Sharma, A.N. Department of Anthropology, Dr. H.S. Gour University, Sagar- 470003, Madhya Pradesh.

Sharma, K.K.N. Dept. of Anthropology, Dr. H.S. Gour University, Sagar -470003, Madhya Pradesh.

Som, R. K. Dakshinayan, Flat 9/A, 95 Southern Avenue, Kolkata -700 029.

Tiwari, M.K. Department of Anthropology, Dr.H.S. Gour University, Sagar- 470003, Madhya Pradesh.

Tiwary, R.S. Regional Medical Research Centre for Tribals,

(I.C.M.R.), Nagpur Road, Jabalpur - 482 003, Madhya Pradesh.

Vasulu, T.S. Anthropology and Human Genetics Unit, Indian Statistical Institute, 203 B. T. Road, Kolkata -700108.

Yadava, K.N.S. Department of Statistics, Banaras Hindu University, Varanasi-221005, Uttar Pradesh.

Index